HYDROPONIC CROP PRODUCTION

HYDROPONIC CROP PRODUCTION

Joe Romer

Kangaroo Press

Reprinted in paperback 1997 and 2000

First published in Australia in 1993 by Kangaroo Press
an imprint of Simon & Schuster (Australia) Pty Limited
20 Barcoo Street, East Roseville NSW 2069

A Viacom Company
Sydney New York London Toronto Tokyo Singapore

ISBN 0 86417 833 6

Printed by Australian Print Group, Maryborough

Contents

1 Introduction

Many people think of hydroponics as being relatively new. In one of its most basic forms—growing plants on rafts in rivers—a number of cultures have used it for countless generations. Probably one of the earliest recorded applications of hydroponics was in the Hanging Gardens of Babylon, in which the plants were grown in a steady trickle of water. Very simply, hydroponics is growing plants in an aerated solution of water containing dissolved natural mineral salts. The plants may be supported by an inert growing medium or the plants may be held in place by other techniques.

During the past 60 years or so, our knowledge and understanding of plants and their physiology has expanded rapidly. We are becoming ever more aware of their needs and the conditions required for efficient growth, flowering, and fruiting, and this has encouraged the development of hydroponics. Other factors contributing to the development of hydroponics include the impact on commercial soil-grown crops of soil-borne diseases and parasites, the desire of growers to reduce the heavy physical labour involved in soil growing, the world-wide degradation of fertile soils, and the desire to increase yields at a competitive price.

What makes hydroponics so exciting is that it removes plant growing from the vagaries and unpredictability of soils, climate, and seasons into the areas of skill, expertise and control. Many experts and qualified people in the area of plant agriculture feel that hydroponics is not their field. However, growing plants in hydroponics follows much the same rules as growing in soil, and the physical growing conditions, nutrients, aeration, water, and light requirements are virtually the same. Hydroponics attempts to provide these in a balanced way in a more controlled environment.

Soil is unpredictable

Soil is a growing medium with its own special problems of unpredictability in temperature, moisture-holding capacity, available nutrient supply, root aeration, and its capacity to harbour pests and diseases. As an alternative to soil growing, hydroponics aims to provide conditions which are more favourable to the roots and consequently the growth of the plant, maximising the production of the parts of the plant which provide the economic return. Hydroponics allows the grower to exercise precise control over what happens to the plant, so that tomatoes provide a heavy crop of fruit rather than leaves, and lettuces provide a solid leaf mass rather than going to seed.

Types of systems

Hydroponic systems are broadly divided into systems which utilise an inert growing medium to support and feed the plant, and systems in which no medium is used to support and feed the plant. These are then further classified into systems in which the nutrient solution is recirculated ('nutrient flow') or not recirculated ('static systems'). Recirculating systems may or may not involve a support medium.

Those systems in which there is no support medium are Water Culture, Nutrient Film Technique (NFT) and Aeroponics. In Water Culture, the plants are floated on top of an aerated nutrient solution, with their roots hanging in the solution. In an NFT system, the nutrient solution flows down a channel or gully as a very thin film of solution, bathing the roots of the plants. In Aeroponics, the roots hang in an enclosed air space and are kept misted with nutrient solution. Of the above, the most common commercial system is NFT.

Systems which utilise a support medium feed the plants by providing the nutrient solution to the roots, which spread through the medium as they do in soil. The nutrient solution may be provided to the roots in a number of ways. It may be dripped through the medium from the top; provided in a pool at the base of the medium so that the roots feed by capillary action and by reaching down into the solution; or pumped up at regular intervals from beneath the medium thereby bathing the roots in a nutrient solution.

Regardless of the type of growing system in use, the nutrient requirement for a particular crop is the same, and the foundation stone of any hydroponic system is the aerated nutrient solution that the plants feed on.

Recirculation—Nutrient Flow Systems

NFT systems use no support medium, and the roots remain bare in the growing channel, bathed in a thin film of nutrient solution. To prevent the roots drying out, the nutrient solution must be recirculated continuously. While the lack of medium reduces the amount of labour involved in maintaining the system, particularly with regard to cleaning up and replanting, it does require increased monitoring of the system and backup in cases of power failures which would quickly cause the roots to dry out. While many NFT systems do use some medium in the growing cups, this is simply to initially establish the plant, and provides little or no ongoing support or feed.

Recirculating systems using a support medium require a medium that is inert, sterile, and has good drainage properties. A typical medium with

these properties is coarse gravel. Growing media such as perlite are not recommended for recirculating systems because they hold too much nutrient solution and give poor root aeration or poor drainage under these conditions.

Media-based recirculating systems usually have an intermittent nutrient flow cycle. Depending on the choice of medium and other factors, the flow cycle is adjusted to maintain the medium in a moist condition.

Non-Recirculation—Static Systems

Static systems or non-recirculating systems generally involve the use of an inert medium such as perlite, rockwool or fine sand because they rely on the medium to have good nutrient holding capacity. Nutrient solution is supplied from as often as a few times each day to once every few days. The medium dries out slowly, and this drying out process helps aerate the roots of the plants. Such systems are very good for plants such as cucumbers or tomatoes that transpire large quantities of water.

Root aeration is critical

A major emphasis of hydroponics is supplying the root system with adequate aeration. Root aeration is a fundamental need of the plant. According to one old-time grower, the three most important things required when using hydroponics are drainage, drainage, and drainage. This was his way of saying that root aeration or available dissolved oxygen is critical for good plant growth. This aeration may take the form of pockets of air between the particles of the growing medium, or it may be in the form of dissolved oxygen in the nutrient solution, particularly with nutrient flow techniques.

Regardless of how good the nutrient balance is, plants will die without sufficient oxygen in the nutrient solution. One could almost go so far as to say that ninety percent of most problems encountered in hydroponics are caused by poor root aeration. Roots obtain their energy from respiration by combining sugars with oxygen to release the stored energy in the sugars. A lack of oxygen necessarily results in a lack of energy. In hydroponics, most nutrient deficiencies occur not because the mineral element is not present in the nutrient, but because the roots are incapable of absorbing or utilising it because of a lack of energy.

If a medium retains too much water or nutrient solution, poor drainage will occur, and consequently the plants will suffer from poor root aeration. A good way to increase aeration in the root zone is to supply the nutrients on an intermittent basis, or to maximise the dissolved oxygen in the nutrient solution by aerating it. Aeration can be achieved by pumping air into the nutrient solution; spraying the nutrient solution through a watering rose; or in recirculating systems, a venturi system may be used to inject air into the nutrient solution. The venturi system involves the nutrient solution being forced under pressure past a small hole, creating a vacuum which draws in air from an air pipe.

2 Plant Nutrients

A Look at Plant Foods

While you and I may dream of a pepper steak with trimmings, the plants we grow have a different perspective on their exotic meals. They look forward to a well-balanced feed of mineral salts, including nitrates, sulphates, phosphates, potassium, phosphorus, calcium, iron and magnesium, garnished with traces of boron, manganese, copper and zinc with a touch of molybdenum, all served at the right pH (acidity or alkalinity). Add a gentle slurp of water and plenty of fresh air rich in carbon dioxide absorbed through the leaves, and you have plant heaven.

There are very few methods that can feed plants as effectively as hydroponics. When plants are grown using this technique, on demand they receive a balanced mix of all the essential salts they require dissolved in aerated water. Hydroponics is not very different to soil growing or organic growing except that with hydroponics, the salts are balanced and in the form that the plants can use directly.

Macro and micro nutrients

Both the roots and the leaves of plants search for sustenance. The roots seek mineral salts, water and oxygen, while the leaves seek carbon dioxide and oxygen. If 2 kilograms of typical green plant material is dried out, it would weigh only about 150 grams. If we burn this dry matter it will be reduced to about 12 grams of ash or a mere 0.6% of the original mass. That 12 grams represents the mineral salts in the plant.

Some of these salts are required in relatively large quantities while others are only required in very small quantities. Plant growth is restricted if any of these salts is in short supply, even though there may be ample supplies of all of the others.

Hence there is a need for a complete and balanced soluble nutrient supply.

Plants use dissolved salts

All of the required salts enter the roots dissolved in water. Many people are unaware that plants cannot directly utilise organic matter for growth until it has undergone decomposition by micro-organisms such as bacteria and fungi to release the available inorganic salts. In soil or organic growing, the essential mineral elements may be present but not immediately available for use by the plants, as they need to be broken down to their constituent elements. This is partly because the physical size of organic molecules makes them generally too large for plants to absorb, although some may act as nutrient carriers. The decomposition process may be a slow or rapid process, depending on temperature, the type of organic residue, and the types of soil organisms present, and is very unpredictable. Any substantial delay may lead to deficiencies or uncontrolled growth, and the plants may well be in a situation or cycle of feast or famine. Hydroponics aims to overcome that problem.

NPK—What does it mean?

The lack of formal knowledge of chemistry by the untrained makes it particularly difficult for such people to understand some of the complex nutrient formulae. Even with formal training I am frequently confused by what is presented. The N:P:K (Nitrogen:Phosphorus:Potassium) ratio on a nutrient label generally means very little, and it means even less to growers who can't interpret it. The N:P:K ratio at best simply gives a indication of how the nutrient may affect the crop and that is all.

Frequently it is assumed that a high level of nitrogen will produce foliage growth, but if the calcium level is very high then growth is in fact retarded. The form of nitrogen present is also important. Plants take up the ammonium form of nitrogen faster than if it is present as nitrates. However, if the level of ammonium ions is too high, the plant will suffer from ammonium toxicity.

What is really important is the total nutrient combination, including the trace elements. Excellent growth is achieved not only by avoiding deficiencies, but more importantly by having the correct ratio for optimum plant growth.

A well-balanced nutrient has all of the essential elements in the correct proportions to optimise growth for the particular plant. What is more confusing is that these ratios are often expressed differently depending on the country of origin of the nutrient. It is therefore very difficult to directly compare NPK ratios of nutrient formulae from different parts of the world. For example, phosphorus is frequently expressed in the USA as phosphoric acid (P_2O_5), whereas in Australia it is expressed as P. The result is that the phosphorus levels of typical American formulae seem to be considerably higher than the Australian formula, whereas in fact they may well be the same.

What are you growing?

Linked with the nutrient combination is the grower's idea of what type of growth is desirable. It is often very difficult to convince a grower that lush foliage growth on strawberry plants is undesirable and will limit the plants' ability to produce strawberries. A good nutrient formulation is a delicate blend of basic salts and trace elements which interact to produce optimum foliage, or flowering and fruiting, depending on the crop. A well-balanced lettuce or tomato or strawberry nutrient will perform equally well, irrespective of climate or season. What may change is the nutrient concentration that is advisable.

What to Feed When

Most suppliers of nutrients emphasise foliage growth because the grower understands foliage growth. It is often difficult for growers to appreciate that flower development starts at a very early stage and that the buds are formed one or more months before the plant starts flowering. In fact, with strawberries, the bud development usually starts back in autumn for the spring crop and unless the conditions were suitable at the time for bud development, the yields will suffer.

Using a similar example, a commercial orchid grower could not understand why another professional orchid grower who was producing excellent blooms used a very high nitrogen-based nutrient while the flowers were still on the plant. This grower was starting his foliage push early because he was looking for well developed healthy tubers and foliage before the cooler temperatures had set in. He realised that he needed to initiate his foliage buds long before they started to appear.

While good foliage is required to supply the fruit with sugars, it is very important to push along flower and fruit development right from the start. Like strawberries, tomatoes need to begin flower bud development almost from the start, and if pushed with a foliage nutrient early in the development of the plant they will stay vegetative. A good nutrient maintains a fine balance between foliage development and flower and fruit development. But the grower also needs to anticipate the plants' needs long before the buds appear.

The fine tuning of the nutrient or its composition takes time and perseverance. Most nutrient research carried out by various establishments does not cover the full growing period of the crop, nor does it monitor or keep records of day to day variations in temperature and humidity. More importantly, the researchers very seldom, if ever, are involved in the physical growing. Instead they concentrate on the end result, and the number of plants in the studies is generally much smaller than typical commercial operations. Good nutrient research requires a hands-on approach as well as evaluation of the formulae in working commercial installations.

3 The Nutrient Solution

Nutrient Developments

The upsurge in the popularity of hydroponics has led to some very good quality balanced nutrients becoming available in liquid or powder form to both commercial growers and hobbyists. Some formulations are described as 'general purpose', meaning that they contain a blend of nutrient salts designed to produce good foliage growth as well as good flower and fruit development. Because of the problems of 'lock-up', especially of calcium, most are sold as a two-part mix, but more technically advanced formulations are available that combine all the salts together into a single part concentrate.

Nowadays, most formulations are dosed to the plants in liquid form. This is because with powder nutrients it is very difficult to ensure that the microelements are evenly distributed throughout the mix, especially when using only small amounts of the powder, for example, 5 grams. It is something like trying to evenly mix a kilogram of common salt into a truckload of sand and expecting each teaspoonful of the mix to contain the same amount of salt. With the commercial grower this does not present such a serious problem because of the quantity that is used. Nevertheless, the most effective way to ensure accurate dosing is to use concentrated 'stock' solutions in which the total amount of powder has been dissolved.

While general purpose nutrients are a careful blend of the essential salts from which the plant will select specific salts at different stages, there are some hydroponic nutrients that are available to promote vegetative growth and others to promote flowering and fruiting. These specific mixes are of particular value to the commercial grower, and allow the maximisation of the crop.

Because of its unique blend of essential salts required for plant growth, hydroponic nutrient is also ideal as a foliar spray to boost the crop. In fact, a bi-weekly liquid foliar feed of a hydroponic nutrient ensures that the plants receive the minerals that may not be taken up readily by the root system because of such factors as low temperatures or root system problems.

Solubility of Nutrients

Different salts have different solubilities. Some dissolve easily in water and others with difficulty. Most salts require energy to dissolve them. This energy is used to break the bond between the components of the salt and to separate the components into their ionic parts. The energy may come from the water itself as heat energy is taken out of the water, but this causes the temperature of the water to drop dramatically, lowering the overall solubility. The energy may also come from mixing equipment such as an agitator or propeller blades, or from stirring for long periods. Energy must be expended to get the salts into solution, so letting the mix stand overnight is generally insufficient.

As the nutrient is a mixture of salts, when combined the components of the salts will rearrange themselves to form new salts, some of which are lower in solubility. Take for example calcium nitrate and epsom salts. Both are easy to dissolve on their own. When combined in concentrated form, they react to form calcium sulphate or gypsum, which is relatively insoluble and dissolves only with great difficulty, locking up the calcium and preventing it from being available to the plants. This can occur if the contents of a two-part commercial pack are mixed in concentrated form, or if a one-part commercial pack is added to too little water.

Many growers use a two-part nutrient, usually labelled Part A and Part B, which are made up separately into two concentrated solutions. They are particularly suitable for growers who use automatic dosing equipment which pumps equal amounts of each of the solutions into the main nutrient tank in response to low conductivity or dissolved salts concentration of the final nutrient solution. Two-part nutrients are also commonly used in systems which are manually dosed.

With single-part powder packs, it is preferable to add the complete mix directly to the water in the tank slowly with agitation or recirculation using a pump, rather than trying to make it into a concentrated solution and then adding it. Some growers even dose the nutrient powder at a point along the return line from their recirculation system.

Automatic Controllers

Automatic dosing equipment is controlled by a sensor which senses the conductivity of the solution or the nutrient concentration. If a grower has automatic dispensing of nutrients with a controller, then it is generally preferred that the nutrients are in two separate parts (A & B) and that they are dissolved into two concentrated solutions.

Many growers make up their liquid nutrient concentrates and keep them for weeks. This can lead to problems of nutrient deficiencies, such as occurs when iron drops out of the solution. It is preferable to make up liquid nutrient concentrates only as needed.

Crop Specific Nutrients

Technology has even gone as far as to provide specific nutrient mixes for specific crops. Typical nutrient formulae designed for foliage or for

flowering and fruiting would be similar to the following examples:

Basic Formulae	Foliage NPK 14.3:2.3:12.6	Flowering NPK 10.4:3.2:16.6
Total Nitrogen (N)	14.3	10.4
Total Phosphorus (P)	2.3	3.2
Total Potassium (K)	12.6	16.6
Calcium (Ca)	12.0	12.0
Magnesium (Mg)	4.0	4.0
Sulphur (S)	10.0	10.0
Iron (Fe)	1.0	1.0
Boron (B)	0.11	0.11
Manganese (Mn)	0.09	0.09
Copper (Cu)	0.01	0.01
Zinc (Zn)	0.01	0.01
Molybdenum (Mo)	0.001	0.001

At some stages in the plants' growth the grower may decide to give the plants a boost to stimulate additional foliage or flowering. A booster is added to the nutrient solution for a short period and then the grower continues with the basic nutrient mix. Booster nutrients may also be used as a foliar feed instead of adding them to the nutrient solution. Foliar feeding generally gives a much faster response by the plant.

Typical examples of boost formulae are:

Boost Formulae	Foliage NPK 20.6:3.6:13.2	Flowering NPK 3.2:3.6:20.6
Total Nitrogen (N)	20.6	13.2
Total Phosphorus (P)	3.6	3.6
Total Potassium (K)	13.2	20.6
Magnesium (Mg)	4.0	4.0
Sulphur (S)	10.0	10.0
Iron (Fe)	1.0	1.0
Boron (B)	0.11	0.11
Manganese (Mn)	0.09	0.09
Copper (Cu)	0.01	0.01
Zinc (Zn)	0.01	0.01
Molybdenum (Mo)	0.001	0.001

These are designed to provide the plant with additional specific mineral elements when added to a standard complete nutrient. The usual rate of application is about 1.5 kilos per 1000 litres of water.

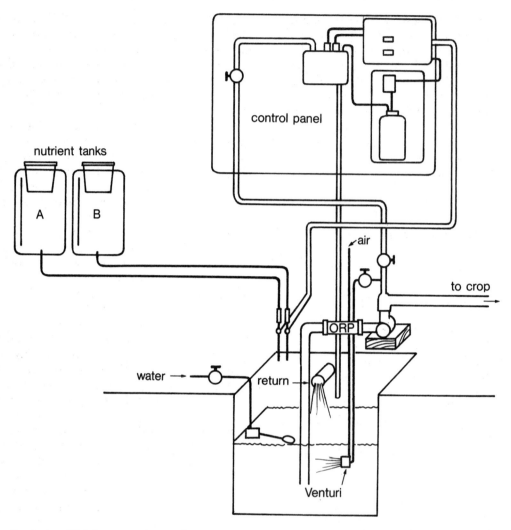

Automatic dosing. This is a typical setup for automatic dosing and controlling nutrient concentration and pH in an NFT system.

What pH?

The pH is a measure of the acidity or alkalinity of the nutrient solution. The scale measures between 0 and 14. The neutral point is pH 7. Just as a metre is a measure of distance, pH is a measure of the acidity or alkalinity.

Acids include lemon juice, orange juice, vinegar, phosphoric acid, nitric acid, hydrochloric or muriatic acid, and sulphuric acid (battery acid). Some acids are stronger than others and change or drop the pH quickly (for example nitric acid). A solution is acid if the pH is less than 7.

Alkalis or bases include lime, ammonia, potassium hydroxide, caustic soda and sodium carbonate (washing soda). Some alkalis are stronger than others and cause the pH to rise more rapidly. A substance is alkaline if the pH is above 7.

Most plants prefer a pH of about 6.2, which is slightly acid. The range of pH used in hydroponics is normally between 5.5 and pH 6.5.

The pH scale is logarithmic rather than linear. For example, if a solution requires 1 litre of acid to adjust the pH from 7 to 6, then it will need 10 litres of acid to adjust the pH from 6 to 5, and 100 litres to adjust the pH from 5 to 4. If the grower tries to maintain the nutrient solution at a pH of about 6.5, then it does not take very much acid or alkali to cause the pH to change rapidly. If the plant suddenly preferentially starts to select a particular element, rapid pH fluctuations will occur, either upwards or downwards. A nutrient solution with a low pH will accommodate the plants' needs more effectively and balance out their needs without these wide fluctuations in pH. Trying to maintain a fixed pH value by constantly adding acids or alkalis generally leads to trouble.

Standardise the meter

The pH is measured at a specific temperature using a sensitive pH electrode and a pH meter. The electrode and the meter should be checked regularly with a buffer solution or standard solution. After each test, the standard solution should be discarded to avoid contamination.

The pH electrode should be kept moist at all times by standing it in distilled water—never allow it to dry out. It is a very sensitive probe which should be kept clean to avoid contamination, and it must not be damaged by rough handling or cleaning.

How critical is pH?

In soil the pH is vital because it affects the type and concentration of the various mineral salts that are available to the plant. The pH of a hydroponic nutrient is less critical, but it should be maintained between 5.5 and 6.5, although some drift is acceptable. The critical pH levels are below 4.5 and above 7.5.

A pH on the acid side, say 5.5, is far preferable to a high pH. If the pH rises above pH 7.0, iron will tend to drop out of solution, resulting in paleness and yellowing of the leaves, particularly the new young leaves. Interveinal whitening caused by iron deficiency will result in reduced photosynthesis and poor growth.

Levels of pH above 7.0 or below 5.0 can cause burning of the old roots as well as the new young roots. Plants which are subjected to rapid changes in pH levels, for example, during adjustments of the solution, are particularly susceptible to root

burning. The damaged roots will turn brown to grey to black in colour, depending on the severity of burning, and since the tips of the new roots are brown, this is frequently mistaken for disease attack. The same symptoms occur when excessive levels of chlorine have been used to sterilise the nutrient solution.

Other than pH and concentration, factors such as low or high nutrient temperatures, oxygen depletion of the nutrient solution, damaged root systems, poorly formulated nutrients, excessively high nutrient concentrations and mineral contaminants in the water supply may all affect the uptake of a particular mineral salt.

During the process of nutrient uptake, roots give off carbon dioxide, which is toxic and acidic. If carbon dioxide or bicarbonate levels build up in the nutrient solution, growth is retarded and the pH of the nutrient solution tends to drift down. One theory is that as plant activity increases, the bicarbonates and carbon dioxide produced by the plant cells are transferred to the roots and excreted there, causing rapid fluctuations in pH. If the pH of the nutrient solution is already low, then carbon dioxide gas is formed and is more easily removed than if the pH is closer to pH 7.

Although these factors are important, over-attention to maintaining strict pH control at the expense of other factors can lead to severe nutrient imbalances and problems. Root aeration, for example, is a much more important factor and is the major cause of problems experienced by the grower.

Plant growth and pH

It is normal for the nutrient pH to fall when the plants are small, and as the plants mature, this reverses, resulting in the pH rising constantly. However, nutrient formulation plays a major part in the pH stability of the nutrient solution, as does the pH of the water supply. In systems in which the plants vary in their maturity, the pH may remain reasonably steady as the younger plants balance the older plants. The time of the year and the vigour of the plants can also affect the pH. In spring the nutrient solution pH tends to want to rise continuously, regardless of the age of the plants.

Many growers become greatly concerned with the pH of the water that they use to top up their nutrient tank. I often wonder whether these growers have ever looked at the pH of their nutrient solution concentrates when using a two-part nutrient solution. If the nutrient solution has a pH which drifts then the addition of small amounts of acid or alkali may be better carried out by adding it to the nutrient concentrates. This is the obvious place to try and make pH adjustments rather than directly into the nutrient tank. The potassium nitrate part of a two-part nutrient is the obvious choice for pH adjustments.

Adjusting pH

Most growers tend to use phosphoric acid for flowering and fruiting crops, or nitric acid for vegetative crops, to adjust the pH downwards. A mix of both is preferred to maintain the nutrient balance. Nitric acid will cause the pH to change rapidly while phosphoric acid tends to buffer the pH more and adjustment is more controlled. If using phosphoric acid it is important to add it slowly over a period, preferably in very dilute form (5% or 10% solution), and once it has been added it should not be sent to the crop immediately—it needs time and thorough mixing to complete certain reactions with other nutrient components.

Since many nutrient formulae are low in sulphur, in many cases it would be preferable to use diluted sulphuric acid to make pH adjustments. Other acids that can be used include acetic acid (vinegar) and hydrochloric acid in diluted form. Hydrochloric acid adds chlorides (not chlorine) to the nutrient solution and is safe for minor adjustments. The quantities that are used will not normally cause problems and in some crops (such as tomatoes) may be of benefit.

In order to raise the pH an alkali is used. The most common is caustic potash or potassium hydroxide, dissolved in water as a 5% solution. However, caustic soda (sodium hydroxide), washing soda (sodium carbonate or soda ash), or sodium bicarbonate may be used. While these will increase the sodium level of the nutrient solution, they are suitable for minor adjustments. Even a solution of lime (calcium hydroxide or calcium oxide) can be used if

nothing else is available.

Large and constant pH changes generally indicate problems, and where this occurs the nutrient solution may need changing. If a fresh nutrient solution does not maintain a reasonably steady pH, the nutrient formula may need to be changed. If the water supply has a very high or low pH, then it may be advisable to adjust it before it is used, and the same applies to the nutrient concentrates if automatic dispensing systems are used.

A number of growers test their pH regularly but very seldom try to adjust it. If the pH of the nutrient solution gradually keeps rising the best technique is to fill up a plastic 200-litre drum with a 1% acid solution and allow it to drip slowly into the nutrient solution throughout the day. If the pH is still a little high at the end of the day, the acid concentration can be increased to 2%. Continue increasing the acid concentration (within reason) until the nutrient solution pH remains steady.

Nutrient Concentrations

Many growers want a chart that will tell them what nutrient concentration to use for a particular crop. There is no such reliable chart. However, in general, the normal or average level of nutrient concentration for all crops is about 1.5 kilograms of nutrient salts per 1000 litres of water, or about 1500 parts per million of dissolved solids. This is equivalent to a conductivity reading of 2100 uS/cm.

The effect of growing conditions

A simple rule of thumb is that the nutrient solution concentration depends on the growing conditions. If, for example, the growing conditions are very stable, such as may occur in an environmentally controlled shed with good air movement, stable temperatures and relative humidity in the range of 70% to 80%, the nutrient concentration can be increased to about 2.5 kilograms per 1000 litres of water (2500 parts per million), but only if it improves the plants' growth or fruiting.

The best level is that nutrient concentration which optimises plant growth and fruit production without stressing the plants. Generally the higher the nutrient concentration used, the better the keeping quality of the produce. If the growing conditions are variable the nutrient concentration should be lowered to reduce stress on the plant. Under conditions of consistent low humidity, the nutrient concentration can be increased to reduce excessive transpiration and plant stress (such as wilting in the heat of the day). Some nutrient formulations can also cause the plant to stress (and wilt) severely under adverse conditions of hot weather and low humidity, and cause severe to moderate tip burn even under conditions of high humidity.

If the nutrient concentration level is to be changed, it should be done slowly over a period of about one week otherwise the plants can suffer severe stress. Watch the plants and see how they are reacting. Experience has shown that many plants will respond very favourably to regular slow changes in nutrient concentration.

Conductivity Meters

A conductivity meter indicates the total amount of dissolved salts in the solution but tells the grower nothing about the concentration of individual nutrients in the solution. Therefore, while some nutrients are being depleted, others will be rising, and the system can become unbalanced very quickly. This situation is more likely to occur in recirculating systems and can be detrimental to the plants' performance. Hence, regular additions of fresh balanced nutrients are important.

Nutrient Fluctuations

The nutrient solution and factors relating to it are very finely balanced. A nutrient solution which is giving good healthy growth may suddenly change. This may occur for a number of reasons including temperature, aeration, pH, carbon dioxide buildup, nutrient concentration changes (such as dilution by rainwater), or a reduction in some available element due to preferential depletion by the plant. Using very low levels of nutrient concentration can often accentuate problems such as preferential nutrient depletion, which may show up as a deficiency in the plant.

Simple factors such as a reduction in nutrient flow caused by the feeder lines blocking up can be a contributing factor in plant stress. Complete blockages are obvious potential disaster situations. Small changes in flow are less obvious, and so is reduced nutrient aeration. Factors such as roots interlocking and reducing aeration are frequently ignored because they occur gradually and only become apparent when the plant shows obvious signs of stress (for example, when day temperatures increase).

What is Measured?

The nutrient concentration is measured with a conductivity meter which measures the flow of charged particles or ions between two electrodes. As the concentration of salts in the nutrient solution increases, so does the conductivity. This may be measured in micromhos, millimhos, microfarads, EC (electrical conductivity), or as total dissolved solids in parts per million (ppm). They are all expressions of the same thing—total dissolved solids or ionisable salts at a specific temperature.

Just as common salt splits into positively charged sodium ions and a negatively charged chloride ion, so do all the common nutrient salts. It is the total of these charges that are being measured, and it is important to note that conductivity does not indicate the concentration of individual salts in the water or the solution.

Theoretically, if we dissolve 1 gram of common salt in a litre of water we should obtain a reading of 1000 parts per million (ppm). If we dissolve 2 grams in a litre of water then the reading should be 2000 ppm. However, because some salts do not ionise completely we frequently do not obtain the theoretical reading. As temperature increases so does the conductivity, and starts to approach the theoretical reading. Conductivity can also be affected by changes in pH.

The conductivity of the nutrient solution is more critical to plant growth than pH, and hence should be controlled more closely.

The conductivity probe, while less fragile than the pH probe, should be cleaned regularly and checked against a standard solution.

Water Supply

Water quality is the subject of the greatest myth in hydroponics. The idea that water must be absolutely pure has probably developed from academics involved in laboratory growing of plants. In fact, most water supplies are suitable unless there is something drastically wrong. Generally, if the water can be used on the normal household garden or lawn without any detrimental effects, then it is suitable for hydroponics.

A conductivity meter will indicate the level of dissolved salts. The pH is less critical because it can normally be adjusted before it is used. Most pool supply companies can carry out the basic tests.

If dam water is used, it is normally beneficial to treat it with some pool chlorine (preferably calcium hypochlorite) at the rate of about 6 grams per 1000 litres of water. The pool chlorine not only sterilises the water but if allowed to stand for a day or so will help clarify the water.

If your water supply has a conductivity or dissolved salts level of say 300 parts per million, then the addition of 1.5 kilograms of nutrient solution will bring it up to about 1500 parts per million, and the initial mineral content is of very little importance. However, even if the dissolved salts level is higher, all this means is that you may have to dump your solution more frequently, say every two to four weeks, or if operating a non-recirculating media-based system, you may have to allow up to 5% go to waste to stop nutrient imbalances.

If your water is very high in dissolved salts, a reverse osmosis unit may be needed. However, while these units take out the salts from the water, producing very pure water, there is also a stream of very salty water to dispose of. Standard units are capable of producing up to 36,000 litres in 24 hours and will handle water containing up to 15,000 mg of salt per litre of water or 15 grams per litre of water. They may be powered by electric, diesel or petrol motors. The water must be prefiltered with a carbon/sand filter to remove any suspended solids greater in size than 10 microns. Performance is temperature dependent, and the feed water should be as cool as possible for maximum performance. The efficiency of recovery is normally between 50% and 80% of the water used. The waste water not recovered will have a higher concentration of dissolved salts and is usually sent to waste.

The reverse osmosis membrane needs flushing at least once a week and is normally replaced after 2 years of operation. An antiscalant injection system may also be required for some bore water applications.

Depending on the particular mineral salts present and their concentration in the water supply, it is possible to use an ion exchange resin to replace some of the more toxic components with more acceptable components. Hence some of the sodium ions may be replaced with ammonium ions or even potassium ions, and chlorides with sulphate ions. However, this requires careful selection of the available resins to choose the most appropriate ones.

4 Recirculating Systems

Systems that recirculate the nutrient solution but do not use a growing medium are generally classified as nutrient flow systems. The conventional nutrient flow system involves the nutrient solution flowing past the roots as a very thin film. There are also a number of systems of the 'flood and drain' type which use intermittent flow, in which the roots are immersed for a short time in the nutrient solution and then the solution is drained away.

It is very important when using a recirculating system to have both a pH meter and a conductivity meter. The pH meter is used to measure the acidity or alkalinity of the nutrient solution, while the conductivity meter measures the amount of total dissolved solids in the nutrient solution.

Every hydroponic system and technique is based on providing the roots with a balanced, oxygenated nutrient solution. Systems in which the roots are suspended, or rest in a flow of nutrients, benefit from intermittent flow where the excess nutrient solution drains away from the roots before restarting the flow.

One of the advantages of using a medium is to keep the roots separated. In NFT systems, the roots tend to mesh together and restrict the flow of aerated nutrient. This is probably why plants in this system are more prone to root diseases than media-based systems.

Aeroponics, a newer technique which involves spraying the root system with a fine mist of nutrient solution, seems to provide better root aeration. However, the root system seems to grow rapidly at the expense of other parts of the plant.

Most growers attempt to incorporate air into their nutrient solution using a number of techniques including air pumps, venturi systems, weiring and cascading the solution as it returns to the tank, agitators and stirrers, but the efficacy of intermittent flow is ignored.

There is no one system that is superior to any other. Some are more suited to certain crops than are others, while some offer advantages in certain circumstances. NFT systems involving the flow of a film of nutrient solution with recirculation and no growing medium are ideal for large scale operations and single cropping, but are less suitable for the home grower. Recirculating systems with a medium are less suitable for short term crops, such as lettuce, because of the heavy physical work involved in cleaning up and replacing the gravel medium between crops, particularly in a large scale operation. However, many growers consider the use of gravel in channels for lettuce growing is preferable to the nutrient film technique because the gravel is more forgiving and offers protection against interruptions to the power supply. Also, the cost of operating the pump intermittently allows the growers to keep their costs down, and the gravel tends to provide more even temperatures throughout the day. By comparison, nutrient film systems tend to have more rapid and wider fluctuations in temperature, pH, and nutrient concentration (or conductivity) over the day.

a) Flood and Drain

Flood and drain systems have been used for many years. This system uses long troughs which may or may not contain a growing medium such as gravel or coarse sand, and the nutrient solution is pumped into the bed until it is just below the level of the media or is sufficient to bathe the roots. The nutrient solution is then drained back to the tank or nutrient reservoir.

Very few growers would consider setting up a flood and drain system because of the complexity of valving and controllers, and because the volume of nutrient solution required is large compared to the size of the troughs or beds. The other disadvantage in flood and drain techniques is the amount of growing medium required and the physical labour involved in handling it. One of the few people using this system is growing a long term crop (roses). A few lettuce growers are also utilising this technique using 90 mm plastic pipes and pots to hold the plants; they also use the same system for strawberries at other times.

b) NFT systems

Nutrient Film Technique (NFT) is a recirculating system in which the roots are bathed in a constantly flowing nutrient solution without the use of a support or growing medium. The theory of the use of a thin film is that it allows better air exchange and oxygen replacement.

NFT is most suitable for short term crops such as lettuce, but some growers are using it for tomatoes, strawberries and cucumbers. This is not a system recommended for new growers, although experienced growers find it has many advantages such as rapid replanting and less physical work involved in cleaning up after each crop.

When most people think of a nutrient film system they tend to think in terms of plastic channels such as rectangular downpipe, round stormwater piping, or similar pipes. The original lettuce systems used 'Super Six' fibro roofing, while tomatoes were grown in strips of black plastic formed up into gullies. One innovative person on one of the Pacific islands even came up with the idea of using channels made from local bamboo. Problems can occur quickly, particularly in nutrient film technique systems without a medium, and unless one knows what to do, an entire crop can be very easily lost.

Beans and peas have been grown very successfully in this system. This system is not recommended for carnations because of the potential disease problems and the problem of supporting the plants. Very few growers have been successful growing parsley in this system unless the grower uses an intermittent flow, protects the root system from diseases, and provides exceptionally good nutrient aeration and short length channels.

NFT systems require good wind protection because movement of the plants can cause the roots to be damaged, resulting in root diseases and plant stress (which shows as leaf tip burn and setback of growth).

Most growers use NFT cups or small pots to hold their seedlings firmly during the early stages of planting out. This reduces transplant shock and protects the young seedlings from wind damage.

It is very important that the pots or containers used when planting into the main system do not restrict the root development and allow the roots to escape easily. A common problem associated with the use of small pots filled with a medium is that the medium tends to have a high water holding capacity, which reduces root aeration and results in plant death. There is also an increase in the incidence of root diseases.

Disposable NFT Cups

Disposable NFT cups are mainly used in lettuce production, but are also used for a number of other crops including parsley, strawberries, celery and silver beet. They are usually supplied in sheets or trays of connected cups which can be easily separated. A major feature of these cups is their low cost and simplicity.

Disposable NFT cups were developed after extensive trials of various standard pots showed that many of the standard pots restricted root development of lettuce seedlings and mature lettuce. If the lettuce seedlings were planted directly into the pipes or channels, the plants fell down into the hole or were easily blown out by wind. The propagation medium also tended to wash off the roots, resulting in contamination of the nutrient solution.

A number of growers use a nursery stage in which seedlings are placed into a 'nursery' system before being planted into the main channels. Disposable NFT cups eliminate the double handling of seedlings from propagation stage into the seedling nursery stage using small pipes, and the subsequent transfer of the seedlings into the main growing channels. When using the disposable NFT cups, the nursery stage can be eliminated and the seedlings transferred directly into the growing channel without any transfer shock.

Nursery System

NFT growers often use large pots or seedling trays with large cavities so that they can grow their plant to a more mature stage before transplanting. This frequently leads to problems. If they remove the seed raising medium from the roots by washing off the medium, the plant can suffer transplant shock. However, if they don't remove the seed raising medium, the medium may become saturated or stagnant when placed in a constant flow of water. The plant roots will be prone to disease, and stem rot or crown rot may occur.

Stem rot or crown rot may not become apparent for a few weeks after transplanting into the system.

Plant spacing

As with any system the size of the channels or troughs and the planting distance is very important. If the trough or channel is too small, the root system becomes compacted, too dense, will block up and restrict the nutrient flow, and will restrict root aeration. This results in stunted growth, reduced yields, and greater potential for diseases.

Some growers use a thin layer of gravel in NFT troughs to help open up the root system and keep the roots separated. The NFT channel or trough should be wide at the bottom to allow the roots to spread out.

The size and shape of the pipes can influence the amount of root mass that develops. If round pipes are used, the depth of the root mass increases rapidly as the plant grows and the bottom roots tend to become starved of oxygen, and will turn brown and die, hence increasing the potential for diseases.

If tomatoes are grown in 90 mm plastic pipes, the root mass will quickly fill up the pipes, the plants will be stunted, and the fruit size will be small. The preferred pipe size is about 150 mm for round plastic pipes, or 150 mm wide by 75 mm deep for rectangular plastic channels. Wider channelling is preferred. To achieve this, some growers use aluminium sheeting to form up channels measuring 200 mm wide and 100 mm deep which they line with Panda film (polythene—black on one side and white on the other) as the channelling material. The polythene film is supported in the form of a triangle by a strand of wire along the top.

c) Recirculation with a medium

Most recirculating systems involving a medium such as gravel use intermittent flow (for example, 30 minutes on and 15 to 30 minutes off). To a large extent, the cycle used will depend on environmental factors.

Some media are not suitable

The problem with gravel, particularly in larger systems, is the weight and volume of gravel that is required. A lightweight medium with minimal water holding capacity or good drainage is preferable. Some examples include scoria (volcanic rock), pumice, expanded clay (Light Expanded Clay Aggregate—LECA), and some diatomaceous earth materials. Media such as perlite, vermiculite and rockwool are not generally satisfactory for these systems because of their high moisture-holding capacity (or poor aeration when saturated).

Depending on your location, alternative media may be available, but in most cases they are expensive and not always inert. Some gravels interact with the nutrients, either binding them up or releasing new salts. Blue metal gravels are a prime example of an apparently inert gravel that can dissolve in the nutrient solution, causing the sodium sulphate level to increase significantly overnight. In areas where limestone is found, many of the river gravels are high in calcium and magnesium, which can cause problems with the nutrient solution. The water supply in these areas is also usually high in calcium and magnesium.

Many growers have been caught by suppliers giving them washed gravel or coarse sand that has been washed with water containing salt. One of the other problems which may be encountered is that the gravel or sand contains high levels of disease-bearing organisms. Hence it is important when receiving deliveries of the medium to place it on a concrete sterilised floor or on plastic sheeting and to treat it with a sterilant such as sodium or calcium hypochlorite.

Suitable containers

The most common recirculating system using a medium is half round stormwater pipes with gravel medium. This is used for lettuce, parsley, silver beet and other crops.

In principle the system consists of a channel or trough made from an inert material along which the nutrient flows. A free draining medium is used to provide support for the plant. The nutrient is collected and repumped through the system at regular intervals.

Rockwool is frequently used for strawberry production. In this case a small block, 75 mm × 75 mm and about 120 mm deep, is used to hold the plant in a round 110 mm stormwater plastic pipe.

Cucumber and tomato growers often use plastic sheeting to line troughs, which contain a small amount of medium such as gravel to hold the plants. This system could also be suitable for rose production. A similar system has been used for tomatoes; in this case the 35 m troughs were formed by clipping plastic sheeting to two wires which were strung between supports. A layer of gravel was placed in the trough to support the plants and the nutrient pumped intermittently.

The Growing Medium and Feeding

When using recirculating systems, the medium must be free draining, and consequently, most growers use a large particle medium. Static systems generally use a finer medium that has good drainage but much higher water and nutrient holding capacity.

Gravel is the most common and readily available material for use as a growing medium. The actual size of gravel used will depend on its application. For example, lettuce in channels are normally fed at intermittent intervals of around 30 minutes on and 30 minutes off. If coarse gravel (about 12 mm diameter) is used, the cycle will need to be shortened so that the nutrient flows for 15 minutes and drains for 15 minutes, particularly in the warmer climates and seasons. If using very fine gravels (5–8 mm), the cycle may be lengthened to 30 minutes on and 45 minutes off.

The change in the cycle is determined by the nutrient-holding capacity of the bed and the degree of root aeration provided during the draining cycle. If a coarse gravel is used, the cycle will not change during the plants' growing cycle. However, if a finer medium is used, it may be necessary to reduce the period of pumping or nutrient flow and to increase the time allowed for drainage as the plant grows and the root system enlarges. Hence, what applies to one person's system may not be correct for someone else's system, because of difference in particle size and moisture-holding capacity of the growing medium.

The colour of the gravel is also important. Black gravel heats up quickly while light coloured gravels reflect heat and tend to stay cooler. Gravel can also act as a heat sink and thereby reduces the rapid temperature changes which occur in nutrient solutions in recirculation systems without a medium. This is especially important in winter when the heat sink effect of the gravel helps to keep the root zone warmer even after the sun has gone down, and thereby promotes better growth.

The grower should also be aware that white gravels are frequently calcareous (contain high levels of calcium), which can interfere with the nutrient balance. Black gravels or blue metal gravels may dissolve in the nutrient solution and may contain high levels of sodium sulphates. Siliceous gravels (gravels formed from silica) are generally white and free from salts which may change the nutrient balance.

While gravels may be classified according to the mean particle size, the particles are generally not consistent and will contain a range of particle sizes. This is referred to as particle size distribution, and it has a significant effects on the water-holding capacity and drainage capacity of gravels. For example, a course gravel with a high percentage of very fine particles will have a high water-holding capacity and poor drainage characteristics, whereas a coarse gravel with a consistent particle size will have better drainage but a lower water-holding capacity.

Very coarse gravel (10 mm) is often placed in a thin layer (1–2 cm) in the channels used to grow tomatoes, cucumber and zucchinis in nutrient film systems. The gravel helps to keep the roots separated and assists in the distribution of the nutrient in the channels when planting out. It also improves root aeration.

Flood and drain systems generally use a gravel with a particle size of about 8 mm diameter and very few fines. This allows free drainage but gives a reasonable moisture and nutrient holding capacity.

The gravel should be washed with fresh water and sterilised with chlorine solution (20 ppm) between crops. Some growers push the old gravel down the channel and top up the top end of the channel with fresh gravel to replace the gravel lost in harvesting.

Expanded clay (LECA) is ideal for recirculating systems because it is porous and retains moisture and nutrients without restricting drainage. It also has a smooth surface to which roots do not bind.

Scoria is also a very good medium because it tends to stay cool in hot weather and retains moisture without interfering with the plants' drainage requirements. However, the roots will bind onto it and loss of media can be a problem. Pumice is another good medium if available in the correct size.

Perlite, vermiculite and rockwool are not recommended because they tend to be too wet and insufficiently well-drained for recirculation systems. Furthermore, a lot of medium is lost when the plants are removed.

5 Non-recirculating Systems (Static Systems)

Static systems are popular with a wide range of growers, including growers of carnations, tomatoes, cucumbers, capsicums and zucchinis. One of the main advantages of these systems is that the plants are less prone to root diseases.

Many people are turned off 'Go-to-Waste' systems because of the name. These are static systems in which the plants are fed on demand and the nutrient solution is not recirculated. This is one of the most versatile systems and there is very little wastage of nutrients if operated correctly.

Non-recirculating systems require a medium with a reasonable moisture-holding capacity, such as rockwool, perlite or potting-type mixes (soilless mixtures).

The nutrient is made up on a regular basis and the plants are supplied with fresh nutrient three, four or more times per day (although in some cases it may be supplied every two to three days). One of the benefits of this system is that the grower knows precisely what is being fed to the plants at each feeding. However, one of the problems is that some nutrient elements can be depleted with time and others may build up.

Many growers incorporate a separate water flush to stop salt buildup. However, this is not advisable because with each feed a small amount of solution is going to waste, hence the medium is being given a regular nutrient flush. Salts only build up on the surface of the medium if there is evaporation from the surface, and these salts can only be removed by spraying the surface of the media regularly with water or keeping the surface moist.

A non-recirculating system which works well uses seed hulls to a depth of about 75 mm, in channels 200 mm wide and 30 m long. The nutrient solution is filtered and pumped from the tank for 5 minutes, 6 times a day, using T tape type drippers which drip about 4 litres per metre per hour. The nutrient solution is adjusted every 2 days, and using a float valve, the nutrient tank is topped up automatically with fresh water. This keeps the dripper line from blocking up as the salts dry out and reduces the wastage of nutrients.

Unlike most systems that feed a fixed nutrient concentration to their plants all the time, this system monitors the nutrient to the plants in a different way—the plants are fed a known amount of nutrient each day. This is because the plants' nutrient uptake is irrespective of the amount of water used per plant. It is most important that the feeding cycle is such that there is very little solution going to waste at any time. In other words, in winter when the plants are not growing or feeding very much, the cycle may need to be modified to 2 or 3 feeds of 5 minutes per day. A feature of this system is that there is very little residue left in the tanks and they do not need cleaning out, even after 6 months. This system can be used to grow tomatoes, cucumbers, capsicums, chillies, and Asian

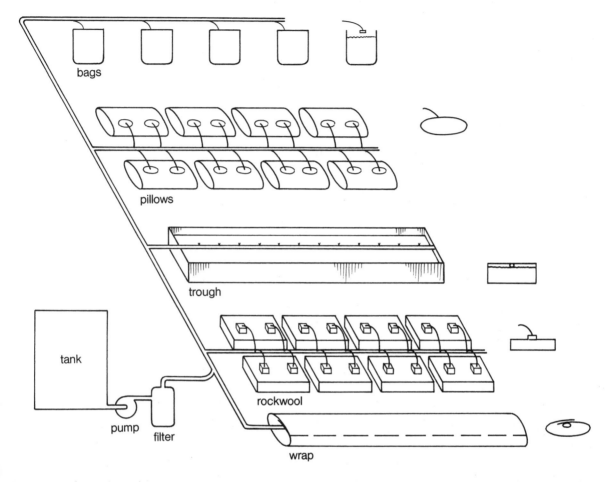

bags

pillows

trough

tank

pump

filter

rockwool

wrap

Non-recirculating (static) systems

vegetables. The quality of the produce is very high and the amount of spraying required for pests and diseases is almost negligible.

Many growers get into trouble by feeding their plants until the nutrient solution pours out of the beds and then let the plants almost go into shock before they feed them again. Regular short feeding, even once a day (depending on the medium and its water-holding capacity), will produce healthier and more productive plants. With simple timers and a few solenoid valves, the feeding system can be automated. There are two important features of this system which every grower should bear in mind:

1. The slower the dripper rate, the greater the control the grower has over the amount of solution going to the crop; and

2. The more often the crop is fed, the more consistent will be the amount of moisture and nutrient available to the plants.

Once a bed has dried out it can be very difficult to re-wet consistently. Plant growth is thus retarded and inconsistent, and yields are adversely affected.

Use of Bags

A number of tomato growers use bags to hold the medium and have one to two drippers per bag. However, the bags they often use are tall and thin, and are often raised off the ground with wire (concrete mesh supports) or other supports to reduce disease cross-contamination.

The medium in tall thin bags tends to be very dry at the top and wet at the bottom. A squat bag with a larger diameter (for example, 600 mm long, 100 mm deep and 300 mm wide) is far superior and ensures more consistent moisture content through the bag. The squat bags use the same amount of growing medium, and are easier to clean up when the crop is finished.

Some strawberry growers use a hanging bag system. The problem of the medium being dry at the top of the bag and saturated at the bottom of the bag is very obvious: the strawberry plants at the top are very small and productivity is low, while those on the bottom of the bag are usually yellowing or dead from too much water and not enough oxygen.

The choice of growing medium, and the rate and timing of feeds is critical to efficient plant growth in the hanging bags. A suggested medium would be small chopped polystyrene pieces and some perlite or peat moss. The feeding cycle for this medium would be 7 short feeds per day (of 5 minutes or 100 ml per plant). The frequency and the amount of feed must be governed by common sense, environmental factors, and the size and stage of development of the plants.

It has taken a number of years to work out why some growers are successful and others have so many problems. The answer lies mainly in the method of nutrient distribution into the hanging bag. An individual dripper in a bag leads to the nutrient solution channelling down through the bag. A spreader at the top of the medium or bag will help overcome this problem.

Close Planting

Non-recirculating systems tend to lend themselves to dense planting as growers try to get more plants into their system. Dense planting tends to create two problems. The more obvious one is the restricted air movement between plants, while the less obvious one is the restriction on the development of the root system as the roots of different plants strangle each other. Both of these problems lead to lower yields and poor quality produce.

Restricted air movement promotes the incidence of plant diseases, and reduces the exchange of air from the leaves, thereby slowing growth. Good air movement ensures good strong healthy plants with high quality fruit and yields.

The problems of close planting become more apparent in those crops grown under greenhouse conditions. Most growers have very little idea of how little air movement occurs in their polyhouses. There are a number of ways of producing good air movement in polyhouses including building the polyhouse so that it has a moderate slope from end to end. Another way is to have top vents so that the hot air can escape and draw fresh cool air across the crop. Also of value are high side curtains that can be opened in hot conditions, and internal air movement fans which force air across the crop (particularly where the polyhouse is on level ground or in winter when the shed is closed up to retain heat). If the leaves of the plants can be kept dry, the incidence of disease is reduced and the amount of spraying required is reduced considerably. Condensation of moisture on the leaves of plants provides an ideal situation for diseases to develop.

Media in Static Systems

While the media required for non-recirculating or static systems must have good drainage, the moisture-holding capacity is also very important. The common media used in these systems include fine gravel, coarse sand, perlite, vermiculite, scoria, rockwool, pumice, seed hulls, sawdust, and even soilless potting mixes.

Feeding

The grower is trying to achieve a constant moisture content throughout the growing media, hence short regular feeds are preferred to irregular long feeds. It is important to keep the medium moist, but not wet and saturated.

If coarse sand or fine gravel is used, the frequency of feeding needs to be increased and the time length of feeding reduced, as this medium does not hold very much water or nutrient solution and requires careful control to obtain the best plant growth.

While these systems are generally referred to as 'go to waste systems', the amount of nutrient sent to waste can be as low as one percent. This will depend on the amount of salts in the water supply. For example, if the water supply has a conductivity of 500 to 800 uS, the amount of nutrient solution going to waste may be as high as 5 to 8%. However, it is preferable to keep it to about 1% and use fresh water to flush the bed at least once or twice a month. (Flushing is simply watering the bed to the point of runoff). Salt buildup can occur with a number of media, including potting mixes, sawdust, rockwool and perlite, and is associated with irregular feeding and the bed drying out between feeding.

Transpiration

Most growers believe that the moisture loss from these systems is due to evaporation from the surface of the medium and constantly talk of salt buildup on the surface. If, for example a tray is filled with sand, gravel, perlite or similar growing media, then water is added to wet out the media, it can take weeks for the tray to dry out. However, when a few plants are planted into the tray, the drying out is speeded up considerably. This occurs because of transpiration (plants' breathing) or loss of water through the leaves. As the plants grow, the tray will dry out much faster.

If the plants are subjected to warm conditions, particularly warm or hot dry winds, the rate of water or moisture loss can be considerable. However, high humidity around the plants will reduce moisture loss. For example, tomato plants subjected to temperatures of 25°C when the air has a relative humidity of 70% will use about 1 litre of water in 4 days. If the temperature rises to 30°C and the humidity of the air is about 50%, the same plants will use about 4 litres of water in 3 days. However, if there is a lot of air movement, such as winds of say 10 km per hour or more, the water loss will increase to 4 litres in 1 to 2 days.

If the nutrient solution is reasonably well balanced, the plant will take up water and nutrients at the same rate. Hence the nutrient solution in the tray will stay relatively constant in concentration, although some nutrient components may be taken in preferentially. If the nutrient solution concentration added to the medium is say 3000 ppm, the transpiration rate will be lower than if the nutrient concentration is 1000 ppm, hence water losses will be reduced.

However, at the higher nutrient concentrations, in conditions of high temperatures and low air humidity the plant may undergo stress, such as wilting; this is especially likely to occur if the plants are subjected to wind or air movement. Similarly, if the nutrient solution concentrations used are low, then wilting or plant stress can occur because the uptake of the water and nutrients by the roots cannot match the rate of water loss through the leaves. Under stable environmental conditions, such as reasonably constant day to day temperatures and humidity, together with some air movement (breezes rather than wind), reasonably high nutrient concentrations can be used.

Salt Buildup

There has been a lot of emphasis placed on salt buildup on the surface of growing medium, without any explanation of how or why it happens. The media that are prone to salt buildup are those that have high water-holding capacity, such as rockwool, fine sand, potting mixes, sawdust and peat moss, in which the water moves easily by capillary action (or transfer from particle to particle). What is happening is that the nutrient solution at the surface of the medium is drying out through surface evaporation. As the surface of the medium dries out the less soluble salts such as calcium and magnesium phosphates and calcium sulphates come out of solution as a white cake. They are extremely difficult to redissolve and regular flushing with water will do very little. Even hot water does not dissolve them very well.

The only answer is to stop the salts building up in the first place by reducing the evaporation of water at the surface of the medium. This can be done by using simple techniques such as covering the top of the media with coarse gravel, plastic or weedstop material, or by lightly spraying the top of the medium with fresh water at least once a week, depending on the severity of the problem.

Flushing With Water

There is much talk about regularly flushing the medium with fresh water, but this can be very dangerous to plants. The plants undergo severe stress when the nutrient concentration is changed rapidly, particularly where high atmospheric temperature or hot dry winds occur, because the lower nutrient concentrations will cause the plant to take up excessive water into the plant cells, bloat them, and even rupture the cell walls, causing severe wilting. In the case of tomatoes this shows up as splitting of the fruit when they are ready to be harvested; in the case of strawberries the fruit becomes very watery and lacks flavour.

The reverse effect occurs when fresh nutrient solution is applied. The nutrient salt concentration is higher in the medium than exists in the plant, and consequently water is sucked out of the plant. The plant becomes short of water, transpiration is restricted, and the plant is again under stress.

Frequency of Feeding

This must match the rate at which the plant is using the nutrients. Long periods between feeds can stress the plant as the medium dries out. The aim should be to maintain a consistent moisture and nutrient concentration in the medium; hence particle size and choice of growing media are important factors. Gravel does not hold very much water because it is dependent on the surface area of the particles, since the water is held mainly on the surface of the particles. As the gravel becomes finer the surface area increases, hence its water-holding capacity increases. But as the water-holding capacity increases, the drainage or aeration decreases.

Gravels are very subject to wide fluctuations in moisture content, require regular watering and feeding, and have higher nutrient wastage. It is difficult to maintain a consistent moisture content between the top and bottom of the gravel or even across a section. Also, once it has dried out it is very difficult to re-wet effectively, hence the use of sprayers rather than drippers is preferred. This also applies to most growing media, but usually to a lesser extent. If drippers are used to feed the bed, channelling occurs, i.e. the nutrient solution does not spread out in the medium but runs straight through a fixed path or channel that provides least resistance.

A factor that contributes the greatest improvement to high yields and plant growth is the scheduling of watering and feeding. This means reducing the possibility of plant stress. It does not necessarily means that the stress is even visible or apparent at the time. Plant stress shows up in many ways, including flower drop, poor fruit set, bolting in lettuce, reduced size of fruit, distorted fruit, and increased root diseases—all of which reduce productivity. It is not just a matter of the frequency of feeding but the amount applied, and how it is applied. Some factors affecting the schedule include the amount of sunlight, humidity, wind velocity, temperature, the growing medium, and the stage of growth of the plant.

Testing Moisture Content

There are various methods and instruments for testing the level of moisture in the growing medium. If the grower is using bags or containers, then having one or two bags or containers sitting on a set of scales can be very effective, particularly if the weight is recorded regularly in conjunction with recording temperature, humidity, and even wind velocity. This way the grower starts to get the feel of what is happening and has a basis for the scheduling and quantity of nutrient feed required.

Tensiometers are used to measure the moisture content of the medium. This device is a sealed tube of water with a porous ceramic tip and a vacuum gauge. It acts as an artificial root, detecting moisture in a similar way to the roots of the plant. As the medium dries it exerts a negative pressure or suction on the tube of water through the ceramic tip, which is measured on the vacuum gauge. As the medium moisture is depleted the gauge reading increases. Tensiometers are relatively inexpensive, but require periodic maintenance such as refilling the water reservoir.

There are also many other more expensive pieces of equipment such as neutron probes, soil capacitance probes, time domain reflectrometry, and thermal conductivity probes. These are more sensitive and require regular calibration and maintenance.

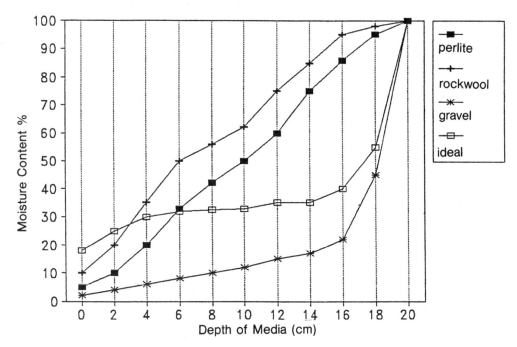

Moisture content of media at various depths

Feeding Control

Simple devices such as light sensors or humidity sensors combined with a controller can be equally effective. Daily manual setting of feeding frequency can be very accurate, even when based only on a simple thermometer and humidistat. In other words, if the temperature in the morning is about 15°C and relative humidity is 90%, the frequency of feeding is reduced. If the humidity is low, if it is windy, or the temperature is higher, then the frequency of feeding is increased.

It is very important to maintain consistent moisture, root aeration and nutrient concentration. At all times, the medium should be slightly moist, but not wet. If the medium starts to show a green growth on the surface then this indicates that it is consistently too wet.

The choice of a suitable growing medium should not be simply a matter of price or what is readily available. Very often a slightly more expensive medium will save money overall. The scheduling and frequency of feeding will contribute significantly to improvement in productivity. This is one area in which the grower's expertise is most important.

6 Controlling the Environment

The major factors that influence plant growth are the interaction of the plants' genetic makeup and the 'environment'. The grower has very little control over the genetics of the plant but he can exercise some control over the environment.

Most growers show no originality when looking to provide protection to their crops. They tend to move from growing outdoors without any protection to polyhouses which fully enclose their crop.

Windbreaks

The first stage in protecting crops is the use of a windbreak. The material used should allow air to pass through it and simply reduce the velocity of the wind. The barrier must be high enough and strong enough to do its job effectively.

Many lettuce growers build windbreaks 7 m or more in height, using commercial wind break fabric meshing. Other growers plant trees and bushes to reduce the effects of the prevailing winds. Some growers even go to the trouble of covering their growing areas with bird netting material which allows air movement but reduces the velocity and direction of the winds.

Rain and Hail

The next stage is providing protection from rain and hail. This allows the grower to work with a degree of comfort and at the same time

prevents the nutrient solution from being diluted or changed, resulting in crop damage. Many lettuce growers have installed clear plastic covers 5-6 metres above their crops, in the form of a pitched roof. This allows them to maintain their production when the soil growers have been washed out, and consequently, they gain the advantage of the higher prices during these periods.

Temperature Control

In areas where frosts or low temperatures occur, full enclosures such as polyhouses can be used to help maintain better growing temperatures. However, a problem with polyhouses is that humidity tends to increase and fungal diseases may be encouraged. Moisture condensation inside the polyhouse can also lead to water droplets falling on the plants, particularly flowers, as soon as the shed starts to warm up in the morning. This causes water marking on the petals and leaves, which is similar to scorching of the leaves. Hence, roll up curtains on the ends and sides of the shed are advisable in conjunction with shadecloth or windbreak material to assist air movement during the heat of the day.

While increased temperature can improve plant growth, enclosed polyhouses can become ovens in which the plants literally cook. Optimum growing temperatures are normally between 20°C and 30°C. Plant growth and pollination will slow down considerably once the temperature exceeds 30°C and the quality of flowers and fruit is seriously affected. Polyhouses introduce a whole new set of conditions and problems which the grower must learn to control.

Simple Structures

A structure which has given exceptional results with a wide range of crops, including lettuce, strawberries, tomatoes and cucumbers, is an area covered with bird netting on its top and sides. It is especially suitable for areas which experience high temperatures and low rainfall. While the side facing the prevailing hot winds usually requires a windbreak material, this structure provides good frost protection, remains cooler even on the hotter days, but is warmer on cooler days.

Fogging

Another method for controlling the growing environment is the application of fogging. A fogging system uses moderately high water pressure (60 psi) and nozzles to produce an ultra fine mist or fog. In summer the fog quickly evaporates, cooling and humidifying the area. In winter it maintains humidity levels and assists with frost control. The important feature of fogging is that it does not wet the foliage, and consequently, the normal problem of fungus diseases associated with wet foliage are reduced.

The most important reason for using a fogging system is to reduce plant stress commonly associated with extremes of temperature and low air humidity. Almost all of the water loss from a plant is through the tiny pores (stomata) in the leaves. The plant also breathes carbon dioxide through these pores. A plant that is not suffering stress will have these pores fully open and operating efficiently. The pores open and close in response to changes in light, humidity, carbon dioxide levels, and temperature.

If the plant is under stress from high temperatures or low air humidity, the water loss from the plant becomes excessive. As the air gets drier more water is drawn from the plant. Up to a point, the plant can cope with this, but when the demand of the air for water exceeds that which the plant can supply, the pores of the leaves tend to close up and carbon dioxide intake is reduced, hence limiting photosynthesis and growth. Fogging reduces this stress and keeps the plant operating efficiently.

Fogging also helps reduce the temperature of the air through evaporative cooling. As each gram of water evaporates it extracts 540 calories of heat from the air. In conditions of low humidity and high temperatures, this can mean a temperature reduction of about 10°C in a growing shed. In conditions of high humidity and low temperature, fogging aids in frost control because it holds the temperature above freezing point (in this case the energy is provided by the water in the fog).

A problem with fogging is that the water supply must be free of suspended solids which can cause the jets to block up; hence filtered water should be used. Spraying water is less demanding on the degree of filtration required but the water consumption increases dramatically, and the incidence of water marking and fungal diseases also increases. Water supplies with high levels of dissolved salts are particularly prone to causing nozzle blockages and leaving salt residues on leaves. This can be alleviated to a large extent by providing appropriate ventilation and fresh air which carries the 'salt dust' away.

In enclosed environments, the higher humidity may cause condensation as the temperature falls, and the amount and timing of fogging should be reduced to compensate for this.

Evaporative Cooling

The conventional cooling system in greenhouses is the use of a water-saturated evaporative cooling pad. A fan is used to blow (or suck) air over the pad to increase the humidity and decrease the temperature. However, the energy required for the large fans is much higher than for fogging equipment, and fans are less effective in covering the whole area.

Heat Pumps

In totally enclosed polyhouses or environmentally controlled sheds, heating in winter and cooling in summer can be very important. Also, in certain circumstances, it may be advisable to heat the nutrient solution and at other times to cool it down. Very few people realise that the reverse cycle air conditioner is one of the most efficient sources of heating. Most think of it as a cooling unit. For every kilowatt of electricity consumed it can return up to 5 kilowatts of heat. Conventional reverse cycle air conditioners are air-to-air heat pumps. In hydroponics, the heat pumps are air-to-water, in that the heat is taken out of the air and transferred to water through a heat exchanger. The heated water may then be used to heat the nutrient solution in a tank.

The heat pump uses refrigerant gas to extract heat from the air. The refrigerant gas is compressed and passes through the heat exchanger to heat the water. After losing its heat to the water, the condensed refrigerant gas passes through an expansion valve. At this reduced pressure, the refrigerant is evaporated by the heat from the warm air. The hot low pressure refrigerant is then compressed again to repeat the cycle.

While heat pumps are very efficient to operate, they can be very expensive and the water temperature achieved is normally about 50°C.

Root Zone Warming

While there are many claims that heating the nutrient solution during the cooler periods is beneficial, this takes very little account of the system being used. As anyone involved in propagation of seedlings or cuttings will tell you, bottom heating (or heating the root system) induces good root development. With bottom heating, the root zone temperature is normally maintained at 15°C to 22°C. A feature of bottom heating is that the warm air created above the media moves by convection past the plants. In this way the plants are warmed, and top growth is improved.

When plants are grown in a polyhouse or reasonably protected environment, root warming will also result in the plants being warmer. However, if the plants are grown out in the open, the roots may be warm but the leaves will be cold. This means that the root system will tend to grow but the leaves and foliage will be almost

dormant, and the dark reaction of photosynthesis will be very slow. Root zone warming will only be effective if the atmospheric temperature (the ambient growing temperature) is also increased. It is most effective when the root zone is about 5°C higher than the ambient air temperature. Taking this a step further, nutrient solution heating and root zone warming during the cooler weather is most effective as the ambient air temperature is rising or falling, such as at sunrise or sunset, and the air temperature is marginally higher or lower than the root zone. In other words, root zone warming extends the growing period by a few hours during the day, and this may be worthwhile.

While many NFT growers look to root zone warming to improve growth, there is very little effect. Because NFT systems rely on a thin film of nutrient to bathe the roots of the plant, the warm nutrient will only be effective for the first few metres before the solution temperature falls to the atmospheric ambient temperature. With a medium in the system, the heated nutrient must warm the medium as well as the roots. The medium acts like a heat sink or a cold sink— it takes a lot of heat to warm it up, and it must lose a lot of heat to cool down. The greater the difference between the root temperature and the atmospheric temperature, the greater is the rate of heat loss, and hence the less effective heating the nutrient solution becomes.

Thermal Screens

Thermal screens are widely used in Europe, and their use in greenhouses is gaining popularity amongst commercial hydroponic growers in Australia. They allow the grower to exercise greater control over the greenhouse environment, and they lower the cost of heating by reducing the volume of air that must be heated.

The aluminised screens consist of thin strips of aluminium knitted into a polyester or polyethylene fabric. They are installed with the aluminium side facing upward in the greenhouse. The aluminium reflects both solar and long wave heat radiation. The percentage of aluminised strips determines the shade value so that there is sufficient light for plant growth.

The most commonly used screens allow air

to move through the screen. In very hot weather the greenhouse remains cool, and in winter the warm air is retained below the screen, condensation is reduced, and humidity is retained. These are expensive compared to the conventional white screen fabrics.

White screen fabrics also reflect solar radiation but tend to break down after about 12 months. They are much cheaper than aluminised screens, very effectively retain heat at night, reduce the level of condensation, maintain reasonably high levels of humidity, and provide good light levels. Moveable shade screens make it possible to shade only as necessary.

A major advantage of thermal screens is their ability to slow down the rapid heating and cooling of the greenhouse in the morning and at night.

Carbon Dioxide enrichment

Carbon dioxide is a vital component for plant growth. The plant takes carbon dioxide in through the leaves and converts it to sugars by the process of photosynthesis. In polyhouses or enclosed environmental sheds, the plants will rapidly deplete the air of the essential carbon dioxide, and growth stops. Carbon dioxide is replaced by the introduction of fresh air or the use of heaters or carbon dioxide generators. While the old-fashioned grower was never aware of what he was doing when he burnt wood in an open drum or slow combustion stove in his greenhouses, he inadvertently provided the plants with carbon dioxide, as well as warmth.

Today we can use carbon dioxide from bottles with precision control to give optimum levels of the gas in polyhouses. Levels between 1000 and 2000 ppm in the air optimise plant growth and development. Carbon dioxide injection into the air is particularly popular in Europe.

While this technical sophistication is very beneficial to plant growth very few growers take advantage of the use of inexpensive fans to circulate air in their polyhouses. Air movement or circulation is equivalent to carbon dioxide injection because it replaces the stale air around the leaves with fresh carbon dioxide-rich air. It also helps keep the plants cool in hot weather because of the evaporative effect at the surface of the leaves. Even when ambient temperatures are as high as 35°C–40°C, the leaf temperature may be as low as 25°C–30°C when the air is moving across the leaves. The use of fans or natural air movement across the plants also reduces the incidence of fungal diseases.

Latent Energy Sources

While very few growers have ever heard of latent heat or latent energy systems, these systems have a number of potential uses for hydroponics. In particular, they can be used to maintain the temperatures around the root zone and the nutrient solution at steady and acceptable levels. The principles behind the use of latent energy systems have been well established, even though their application has been slow to start.

If we take a block of ice and allow it to melt, the temperature of the ice starts to increase slowly, remains steady for a long period at 0°C, then as it turns to water the temperature starts to rise again. This occurs because of the latent heat of freezing. In other words, it takes a lot of energy for water (a liquid) to change its state to ice (a solid). As the ice melts and changes from a solid to a liquid, it takes up energy from its surrounds (i.e. it reduces the temperature of its surrounds). Hence we have what is referred to as a latent energy system.

Instead of using water which forms ice at 0°C, we replace it with some other solution which changes to a solid at say 20°C. In other words as the temperature rises it does so slowly, then it holds this temperature of 20°C for a long period and then slowly starts to rise again. As the temperature starts to fall it does so gradually, remains constant for a long period at 20°C, and then continues slowly falling again. We have now a very efficient heat sink.

A number of growers have experimented with using a large bed of gravel through which they draw air into a polyhouse or enclosed area to cool the incoming air. During the day the gravel warms up, so that at night the air drawn over the gravel is warmed. In this way the temperature in the polyhouse or enclosed area remains fairly constant. The problem is that this requires a very large bed of gravel, and the efficiency of the system is low. Replacing the gravel with a latent heat material, or phase change material, which absorbs energy and holds it more efficiently at a specific temperature provides a very effective heat sink or energy storage system.

Ice is a naturally occurring phase change material that has been used throughout the world in cool storage systems. Its limitation for use in horticulture and hydroponics is its operating temperature. Newer phase change materials operate at temperatures more suitable to greenhouse conditions. These are generally poured into tubes or encapsulated, and are then placed under the channels or growing tables or stacked around the walls of a polyhouse in bundles, and water or air is drawn across them.

The application of this technology is still in its infancy, but shows great promise.

Light

While they may not know it, many growers do not supply their plants with sufficient light. They underestimate the effect that the cover and the framework can have on their crop. This applies particularly to tomato, strawberry and carnation growers. The effect of a close windbreak can cause shadowing, resulting in poor flowering and fruit production. In the case of carnations, the plants can become spindly, and no matter what nutrient mix is used, the stems remain very weak.

The amount of light required by plants is very deceptive. While our eyes adjust easily to light, plants do not. If you look carefully at a crop, the differences in light intensity in places like corners or one side of the polyhouse are visible in the plants.

The poly cover used can have a very detrimental effect on the crop. This may not show up immediately but may take a year or so as dust and algae accumulate on the surface. Heavy steel frames can also cause shadows, resulting in uneven growth, flowering and fruiting. It is advisable to ask the supplier if you can look at an existing setup in order to check out any new cover or structure by using a light meter or even a simple camera with an inbuilt light meter.

Plants' responses to light

Different plants require different levels of light intensity. Plants in low levels of light are often deeper green in colour compared to those grown in full light. The plants' simplest response to low light levels is to produce higher levels of the green pigment in their leaves (chlorophyll). However, lower levels of light also reduce the yield of flowers and fruit, as well as causing stem elongation (i.e. an increase in the distance between stem nodes).

It is particularly interesting to see the difference caused by reduced light levels in the red lettuce varieties. The colour of the lettuce is very intense in high light levels and falls off sharply after a few overcast days.

Until recently, commercial growers and hobbyists have been limited in the types of crops that they could grow using natural daylight. The normal types of household lights, which include incandescent and fluorescent lights, are not suitable for growing most vegetables or flowers. However, recent advances in lighting technology have meant that newly developed lights can be used for a wide range of applications, including the controlled production of cuttings and seedlings and the induction and forcing of flowering in many plants. The enriched ultraviolet (UV) component is very important in boosting photosynthesis and therefore the overall growth rate of the plant.

Composition of Light

Two factors contribute to the importance of the new lighting technology. The first is the lights' highly efficient conversion of energy from electricity to light energy. The new lights can deliver up to sixty percent more light while consuming about thirty percent less electricity.

The second factor is the wavelengths of the light produced. Think of someone playing a musical instrument. The sound can be almost deafening or it may be so quiet that it is hardly discernible. This is equivalent to the intensity of the light, either very bright or just visible. There are many lights that seem to provide high light intensity but have the wrong wavelength or spectrum for the plants. This is similar to tuning your radio onto a particular station. Unless you choose the correct frequency you will not hear the radio station. Similarly, if the light does not have the correct frequencies then the plant cannot be in tune with it. The sensitivity of plants to different colours of visible light is very different from our own eyes.

The light intensity of sunlight reaching a plant depends upon what the light passes through (haze, cloud, shadecloth, etc) and the position of the sun in the sky. At midday a ray of sunlight strikes the earth close to a perpendicular angle and hence is more intense than early in the morning when it strikes the earth at a shallow angle. Hence, artificial lighting can be used to give a more consistent intensity all the time resulting in increased growth. However, most plants need a rest from light to complete the process of photosynthesis or what are commonly called the 'dark reactions'. Some plants don't require this period of darkness.

Incandescent Lights

These are the common household bulbs. They are relatively cheap and produce a lot of heat; hence energy-wise they are very inefficient in their use of electricity. The intensity of the light is very low compared to the more modern lights. If the intensity is boosted then the amount of heat generated is enormous. The light spectrum tends to produce high levels of orange to red, which is desired for flower initiation.

Fluorescent Lights

These are the standard tubular lights. They give off very little heat and consequently are very efficient. The light spectrum is generally concentrated in the ultraviolet range. Growlight tubes are widely used for aquarium and indoor plant lighting. They will keep plants alive but not growing vigorously. Special grow lights have a very good spectrum for plants, but the light is not concentrated and is spread over the length of the tube. The normal wattage of these lights is about 40 watts, which is very low. Plants grown under fluorescent lights tend to be long and spindly and have long internodes.

Mercury Vapour Lights

This was the favoured light for many years, particularly for vegetative plant growth, because it produces high light intensities in the ultraviolet range. Mercury vapour is less effective than natural daylight for the initiation of flowering buds and flower development because it is deficient in the orange or yellow range. Because of its drawbacks, mercury vapour was super-seded in the 1980s by the metal halide and high pressure sodium lights.

Metal Halide Lights

Metal halide lights produce a very concentrated light and are highly suited to greenhouses and grow rooms. The light spectrum produced has high intensity in both the ultraviolet and orange range, making it suitable for encouraging strong vegetative growth, short internodes, increased branching and flower initiation.

Metal halide lights are basically mercury vapour lights with sodium added to widen the spectrum. The standard lights are 400 watt and 1000 watt sizes. The 400 watts are generally preferred because they have a longer lifespan (about 2 years). The uncoated lights tend to have a more concentrated light compared to the phosphor coated lights, which produce a more uniform brightness. Like fluorescent tubes, metal halides require a special transformer and starter circuits.

High Pressure Sodium Lights

These lights are ideal for encouraging flower bud initiation and development because they produce a high intensity of light in the orange-yellow spectrum and have a high radiant efficiency. However, if used throughout the growth phase, the stems of the plants tend to become elongated and the internodal length of the stems is increased.

These lamps are commonly available in 400 watt and 1000 watt sizes. They require their own transformer and starter circuits and are not generally interchangeable with metal halide lights. High pressure sodium lights are frequently used in conjunction with metal halide lights in horticultural applications because they reinforce and balance each other.

Plant lighting is becoming more important in horticultural practices as growers become more familiar with it and understand the benefits that they can derive from it. To grow plants successfully, it is necessary to provide an optimal environment. This includes providing the ideal growing medium, nutrients, water, temperature, air movement, and light. Hydroponics, in conjunction with effective light sources, assists in the development of strong healthy plants all year round.

Sanitation Systems

It is vital in any hydroponic system that the roots of the plant are maintained in a healthy condition. Good root aeration goes a long way in keeping the root system healthy. Water sterilisation is also a very important sanitation measure.

a) Chlorination

Sterilise your water supply
Water should be sterilised before it is used in the hydroponic system to prevent the intro- duction of water-borne diseases. It is particularly important to sterilise dam water. This can be done by adding sodium hypochlorite or calcium hypochlorite to the water supply. In some cases this may involve the use of storage tanks which can be used to hold the sterilised water.

Many growers use town water which has already been treated by the local water authority. However, it is advisable to check the chlorine levels in this water on a regular basis, and if necessary store it prior to use until the chlorine level has fallen to an acceptable level. The acceptable level is about 2–4 parts per million. A number of growers have had serious problems because they did not check their town water supply and added more chlorine, which damaged the roots of their plants.

Keep the nutrient solution free of pathogens
Chlorine compounds are generally added to give a level of about 2–4 parts per million of available chlorine. This corresponds to about 5 grams of the chlorine compounds in 1000 litres of water. The level can be tested using a simple pool test kit, and it is a safe and effective technique for maintaining a clean system.

If a system is heavily contaminated with decomposing or dead organic material, the chlorine is burnt off very quickly. As the nutrient solution is cleaned, it starts to take a lot longer to burn up the chlorine. Hence, while in the initial stages it may be necessary to add chlorine every day, within a week it should only be necessary to add chlorine every three to four days or even once a week to maintain the slightest trace of chlorine in the system. This is why it is so important to carry out regular testing of the chlorine levels.

It is important not to confuse chlorine with the chloride level which is normally present as common salt. Common salt is not effective as a sterilising agent.

b) The ORP Generator
The ORP Generator is an Australian research development, based on well established principles, and is ideally suited to hydroponic systems including Nutrient Flow Techniques (NFT systems) and Flow Through techniques, with or without the use of a growing medium. It increases the ORP (oxidation-reduction) potential of the nutrient solution sufficiently to inhibit and kill fungi and bacteria. The ORP Generator is simply fitted into the line before the pump or filter, or it may be suspended in the tank.

What is ORP?
The acronym 'ORP' stands for Oxidation Reduction Potential—a mouthful that may not mean very much until you understand the individual terms that make it up.

Oxidation is a process that we are all familiar with. When you touch a lighted match to a piece of paper, the resulting fire is oxidisation in action. The ash that remains is oxidised residue. The ORP Generator simply oxidises or burns up the fungi and bacteria present in the nutrient solution in a similar fashion to pool chlorine.

In chemical terms oxidation is a process of electron transfer. Recent medical evidence has shown that free radicals attack and destroy cancer-producing components. When an atom 'A' takes an electron from atom 'B' an oxidisation reaction takes place. Atom 'A' is an oxidising agent; and atom 'B' is being oxidised.

Reduction is the opposite of oxidation. Every action must have an equal and opposite reaction. In reduction, atom 'A' gives an electron to atom 'B'. In this case atom 'A' is the reducing agent; atom 'B' has been reduced.

Potential is the capability of doing work or performing an action. The higher this potential, the greater is its ability to perform. Consider, for example, the water in a dam—it has builtup energy which is released if we put a hole in the wall of the dam. The higher the water level, the greater is the pressure of the water which will gush out.

The electrical current involved in the operation of the ORP Generator is extremely small and uses about 1 kilowatt for every 15 hours of operation for about 40,000 plants. Its action is almost instantaneous and the ORP generated continues to operate even after the nutrient solution has left the generator.

The ORP Generator seems to work in two ways. It tends to reduce the pathogen level but at the same time it stimulates improved plant growth and the plants' resistance to the pathogens. The improved growth may be due to a number of factors, such as increases in the level of dissolved oxygen, or by making the nutrients more easily assimilated by the plants.

ORP Trials

The ORP Generator has been used over an extended period; in each trial there have been no signs of root diseases. In one particular example, a lettuce crop was severely infected by Pythium and Phytophthora. The plants were wilting badly when subjected to the slightest stress, the root system was virtually non-existent, and the roots which did exist were dark brown. The grower believed that he had lost his crop. However, within 24 hours after an ORP generator was installed, the lettuce started to develop new roots, and within a week the crop had recovered and developed long, strong white roots.

Maintenance

The ORP unit is based on electrolysis and during its operation there may be a buildup of some compounds on one of the electrodes, particularly if the pH regularly rises above pH 6.2. The residue is easily removed and this should be done about once a week, at the same time as the filter is cleaned.

c) UV Sterilisers

UV Sterilisers are units which are installed in line. The ultraviolet light generated sterilises the solution, thus destroying pathogens. They are very effective provided the flow rate allows adequate time for the ultraviolet light to do its job. It can also cause soluble iron compounds to be converted to insoluble iron compounds. Hence it is advisable to add iron salts on a regular basis. The suppliers of these units should be able to advise on the correct flow rates and the number of units required for your system.

The nutrient solution formula used can also assist in reducing the level of pathogens present in the system and keeping them under control.

7 Choosing a System

There is no perfect system that lends itself to all crops, so the choice of system depends on the grower and the crop that is being grown. There are some systems that are suitable for a number of different crops and others that are designed around one crop.

Consider, for example, lettuce in NFT systems. In this system the spacing of the holes and the distance between channels is very important. If specialty lettuce are being grown, the distance between the holes is smaller and the channels can be set closely together, allowing more channels to fit on the bench. If hearted lettuce are being grown, the holes along the channels are further apart and the spacing between channels is larger.

However, if the lettuces are to be grown in an open channel with gravel medium, then there is no constraint on the types of lettuce being grown, and the grower is free to space the plants as required. This also helps the grower establish the market because any type of lettuce may be grown. In fact, with few or no modifications the same system may be used to grow parsley, spring onions, chives, silver beet, cucumbers, cherry tomatoes, strawberries and other crops.

It is also important to remember that what may be a good system in one area does not mean that it is the best system. An expensive medium may be suitable in a particular area because the quality of the produce is good and there is a better price paid in that area for quality produce.

In many rural areas, the cost of transporting produce from city markets and the reduction in quality caused by handling in transport may give the grower a decided advantage, and in order to be able to supply quality produce consistently, the grower may elect to use a more expensive technique such as growing lettuce in gravel or an NFT system.

However, in rural areas, power failures and interruptions may be a problem, and this would be another point in favour of a gravel system. On a simpler level, there may be fluctuations in the type of lettuce required throughout the year or a demand for other produce such as herbs. A gravel system allows the grower to mix and match the produce according to changes in the market, whereas an NFT system would be restrictive.

While NFT systems have many advantages, they can also be very restrictive. If a grower has gone to the trouble of cutting holes in the pipes to suit a particular variety or type of tomato, then this could be a disadvantage when a new or different variety which requires different spacing becomes available. Even if the grower simply wants to change to cherry tomatoes from the standard full-sized varieties or vice versa, the spacing between the plants needs to be different for optimal production. In such cases, channels based on Panda film (black and white poly) may be more suitable.

Many growers get into trouble because they see a particular system and decide to use it without really working out if it is best for them. For a small fee, they could have discussed their options with a hydroponic consultant, and made a balanced decision. A major problem with many potential growers is that they have no idea what they want to grow, hence it is very difficult to help them. What system can a consultant recommend to a grower who wants to grow lettuce, tomatoes, and strawberries on a commercial basis? They all involve different systems and requirements.

Available markets

Many textbooks talk about finding out if there is a market and checking out the existing market for the produce. Growers will never know how big the market is until they start to supply produce for it, and then they will quickly learn what the market wants, how much it wants, and how good they are at selling their produce. Hence my suggestion is to start small, get the feel of what you are doing and your potential market, and expand if there is real potential. It is very important that you have adequate funds to continue in the event of a crop failure for any number of reasons.

Finding out

If you had heard of hydroponics and thought that you would like to try it out, where would you start? Of course you could travel to Holland, America, Japan or just about any country, and while you may have a very pleasant trip, you are likely to come back completely confused. Probably the systems that impressed you most were the most expensive to set up and in all probability the least profitable. A prime example of this is where the operation looks very impressive in terms of size and lush plant growth, but to a trained eye the plants have too much foliage growth and too little fruit and hence must have low profitablility.

Seeking to find some complex, expensive and technologically superior form of growing plants is not a good way to approach hydroponics. A much better understanding is obtained by studying the growth of plants in soil, as all hydroponic systems copy and emulate the soil, but with the advantage of freedom from soil-borne diseases and pests. Hydroponics means simply providing the plant with support,

nutrients, moisture, oxygen for the roots, warmth and light. Plants or crops can also be grown out of season if you are prepared to provide the correct conditions of warmth, daylength, light intensity, humidity, air movement, etc. This requires a thorough understanding of your crop and its requirements as well as a market that is prepared to pay the higher price for your produce.

Where to start

The first thing is to decide what to grow. The next thing is to work out whether you can sell it and where you are going to sell it. This is very different from finding out if a market exists. Tomatoes are a prime example. There are growers who produce tomatoes and sell them all year round at premium prices, and others in the same area who find it difficult to sell any, even at low prices. You must not only be able to grow the produce but you must also market your produce. It is easy to find growers who became disillusioned because they expected to be able to sit back and have customers come to them. It just does not happen like that.

How do you find out what system to use? You can either experiment with different systems or call in someone with the expertise. Simply copying someone else's system is a very good way to make major mistakes.

Hydroponics can be simple. Media-based non-recirculating systems are generally the most forgiving and the most versatile. They typically consist of boxes, bags or beds filled with a medium such as gravel, sand, scoria, or even potting mix, and a feed system involving a tank, a small pump, and a feeder or dripper line. From my experience, long beds or channels are easier to set up and look after than boxes or bags with individual drippers. The beds or troughs can be converted to an NFT system once the grower gains confidence.

Media-based non-recirculating systems are suitable for a number of crops including tomatoes, capsicums, cucumbers, eggplants, zucchinis, most flowers including roses and carnations, herbs, radishes and root crops. Media-based recirculating systems are also used for lettuce, cucumbers, capsicums, egg-plants, strawberries, roses, herbs and roses.

Small NFT systems are much more difficult to control and manage than larger NFT systems. Hence, if you are considering a large scale operation, then the NFT system has many advantages. NFT systems are typically used for lettuce, tomatoes, cucumbers, capsicums and short-term strawberry crops.

Types of systems

No Medium

Systems which do not use a growing medium are usually expensive to set up compared to media-based systems, and require a high level of expertise to operate effectively. However, once the techniques involved in the system have been mastered they are very effective. They are usually designed with a particular crop in mind and are not suitable for growing other crops unless modifications are made. These systems are not recommended for long-term crops such as carnations and are more suited to short-term crops such as lettuce and single-season strawberry crops. Electricity is a major operating cost since the pump must operate continuously, although media replacement costs and handling are eliminated.

With Medium

The choice of the growing media is extremely important. For containers, a number of commercial growers use polystyrene foam boxes, while others use nursery bags.

Separate drippers are required for each container and it is very difficult to obtain a consistent moisture content in every container. To overcome this problem, the system which is preferred is a trough which may be up to 50 m long and 300 mm wide, filled with the growing medium, and fed by dripper tubing lying on top of the growing medium. In the case of carnations, the beds are usually 900 mm wide, and dripper tubing or sprayers may be used. The beds are fed daily or a number of times per day. Short regular feeds are preferred and will give more consistent growth.

Media Selection

While gravel or sand is generally the cheapest and most readily available growing medium,

after you have moved 15 tonnes or more, then you may not believe it was the best choice after all. Alternative materials should be considered, depending on the crop grown and the system being used. Small additions or combinations of support and growing medium can give surprising advantages. Despite gravel or coarse sand being readily available, it may pay to get a load of scoria at a slightly higher price, as it confers a number of benefits including reduced work in handling.

Many books talk about NFT systems with thin films of nutrient flowing down channels and being recirculated continuously. They discuss flow rates and minimum and maximum slopes. Yet, there are nutrient systems being operated successfully in which the nutrient solution is recirculated on an intermittent basis (without any medium), half an hour to one hour on and half an hour to one hour off. The benches are level and nutrient solution is retained in the channel to a depth of up to 50 mm.

There are many different techniques which can be used to suit a particular application or a particular crop, but more importantly they should suit the grower's circumstances and conditions. Some fundamental goals include:

a) adequate nutrient solution and root aeration;

b) unrestricted root growth—avoid crowding of roots into pipes, pots, or channels that are too small and cause the plant to become root bound;

c) avoiding disease contamination by sterilising the nutrient solution by the use of low levels of chlorine or an ORP Generator;

d) feeding the plants regularly with short cycles.

All of these are aimed at eliminating undue stress on the plants.

Water Supply

If the water supply is suitable for drinking or for irrigating soil crops then it should be suitable for hydroponics. The most important test to carry out is conductivity. This will tell you the level of total dissolved salts. If it is above 500 parts per million then you are likely to have problems with it or it may need treating. A full analysis is important because there may be unusually high levels of a particular mineral salt such as sodium, calcium, or one of the trace elements. It is very unlikely that you would have to make any modifications to a nutrient formula based on the analytical results.

Providing that the water is reasonably good, the next important factor is its sterility or freedom from pathogens. The water used for hydroponics should be sterilised before it is used. This usually involves the addition of common pool chlorine at the rate of about 6 grams per 1000 litres of water, and the water is allowed to stand for about one day. This applies particularly to dam water. I consider a standard pool test kit as essential; although it is useless for testing the pH, it is ideal for testing chlorine levels.

If you use chlorine regularly to sterilise your water supply and your nutrient solution, you will certainly have very few problems of disease or algae in your system. If you are using town water, you should test it regularly for chlorine content. The level of chlorine that you should maintain in your system is the faintest trace, in other words, the chlorine test gives a very faint colour response which is just discernible. An ORP Generator will also help you maintain the sterility of the nutrient solution.

The next important factor is the clarity of the water or the level of suspended solids. This is frequently a problem with dam waters. Suspended solids should be removed by treating the water with lime or even a mild alum treatment. If the water is only slightly milky then these solids will drop out with the addition of nutrients, and can cause a sludge to build up at the bottom of the nutrient tank, blocking the feeders or drippers. An efficient filter in the system overcomes this problem.

Sterile System

It is well established that good healthy plants will grow and produce well even if pathogens exist in the nutrient solution. Maintaining a completely sterile environment can frequently cause devastating results, as the plants cannot build up their immune system to cope with pathogen attack. Frequently the techniques for maintaining the sterile environment can be worse than the cure. Plants are very much like you or I—if they have been under stress then their ability

to resist attack is reduced.

Tip burn in lettuce has been blamed on many factors including calcium deficiency. However, most nutrient formulations are adequately supplied with calcium. Plant uptake of nutrients and water takes place through the roots. If the roots are under stress, nutrient uptake is reduced. Some of the factors causing root stress are diseases or pathogens, very high or low root temperatures, excessive movement of the plants caused by winds, high or low nutrient strength or inconsistent levels of watering and feeding, sudden changes in pH or high or low pH levels.

The size of the tank

The optimum size of the nutrient tank is normally about 1 litre for every 4 lettuce plants or 3 litres for plants such as tomatoes. However, this is a rough guide. What determines the tank size is the rate at which the plants can transpire water, and that depends very much on environmental and operating conditions and most importantly the type of system. The optimum is about 4 days' supply of nutrient solution.

With recirculating systems the larger the tank, the more control can be exercised over the system. A large tank will reduce temperature fluctuations, the pH and conductivity will remain more steady, and plant stresses will be reduced. However, if the tank is too large, nutrient deficiencies can occur, particularly iron deficiency.

Nutrient Selection

A single pack nutrient which is complete, balanced and specifically designed for the particular crop is the easiest to use. The dry nutrient is weighed out and added slowly (over a few minutes) to the tank as a dry powder while the tank is being filled or agitated. A good single pack nutrient if correctly formulated will be completely soluble with possibly a trace of sediment which is removed by the filter.

Some growers use an injector system which pumps concentrated nutrient into a water line, and then this feed is sent to the crop. Normally a two-part nutrient pack is used, employing two separate feeding tanks marked A & B. An injection system is less precise, and the pH of the feed is more variable.

Where the grower uses automatic dosing equipment, it is advisable to install two concentrated nutrient tanks from which the nutrient concentrates are dispensed into the main nutrient tank. This requires a two-part nutrient pack nutrient. Many growers have turned off the automatic dosing system and gone to manual dosing because when things go wrong they can go terribly wrong, and manual dosing gives the grower a better feel for what the crop is doing. For example, if nutrient uptake slows down, then the grower knows immediately and can seek a a cause such as root disease, cool weather, etc.

Cost of Setting Up

The setup cost for a non-recirculating system is usually a third or a quarter of the cost of setting up in NFT. The operating cost of the two systems is very similar in that the NFT system uses more electricity whereas the non-recirculating system requires changing the growing medium every year or two depending on the crop grown, although the medium may only need topping up after some crops.

While the NFT system can be operated using a smaller tank, it generally must be dug into the ground, whereas the tank can be above ground with the non-recirculating system However, there is very little difference in cost for the slightly larger tank. With NFT systems, nutrient supply and return pipework is usually underground.

Based on current prices, the cost of 100 m of a channel system including pump, filter, growing medium, growing bed and feeder lines is usually much less than a similar NFT system with 100 m of growing area including PVC channels, pumps, filters, piping supports, and feeder and return lines.

Conclusion

There are a number of crops such as lettuce for which the NFT system is ideal. It has a number of advantages when used correctly and when the grower has learned how to use it.

For most crops, including tomatoes, herbs, capsicums, cucumbers, eggplants, okra, root crops (e.g. radish and garlic), carnations (and flowers in general), a static system using the channel system with a growing medium has many advantages, including simplicity and the low cost of setting up and operating.

PART II

8 Capsicums

Capsicums, also called peppers and chillies, belong to the Solanaceae family. They are not related to the true pepper, *Piper nigrum*, which provides the common black pepper for table use.

Capsicums are thought to have originated in Peru. The Spaniards and the Portugese introduced capsicums to the New World tropics in pre-Columbian times.

Capsicums are a rich source of vitamin C and vitamin A. Green capsicums and red chillies have very high levels of vitamin A; red capsicums are very high in ascorbic acid (vitamin C).

They are a warm season vegetable, requiring a relatively long frost-free growing period for maximum production. Supplies of capsicums come from Queensland throughout the year, and from NSW during summer and autumn. Prices tend to be relatively constant throughout the year.

Most growers consider capsicums to be a good stable crop with a fairly consistent price and good returns. For this reason they are often grown in conjunction with tomatoes: although tomatoes can provide higher returns, the prices tend to fluctuate widely according to over or under supply of markets.

Morphology

The capsicum genus contains a wide range of plant types which vary greatly in the shape and pungency of the fruit. They are either annuals or perennials, according to climatic conditions, and may be either cross-pollinated or self-fertilising. Capsicums normally take 11 to 13 weeks from transplanting to maturity.

Like tomatoes, capsicums show phases of vegetative and fruit growth interspersed in time as the lateral buds resume growth when a terminal meristem is induced to flower.

Soil-grown plants develop a strong, moderately extensive tap root. When transplanted, the root system becomes very branched and vigorous.

The flowers are only open for 24 to 30 hours, and adverse conditions during this period can affect fruit set.

Varieties

There are two main types of capsicums:
1. Mild or sweet capsicums (Bell capsicums)
2. Hot or pungent capsicums (Chillies)

The degree of pungency is determined by the amount and location of the compound Capsaicin, which varies from sweet to hot to very hot.

In Spain the sweet or mild types are referred to as pimento. In Australia, however, pimento refers to a single type of thick-fleshed, bright red, sweet capsicum.

It is best to avoid growing two varieties of capsicums at the same time because of the possibility of cross-pollination. If a hot and a sweet capsicum are grown together then all of the crop may be hot.

Bell capsicum

This is the normal sweet pepper or capsicum. It is a very important fresh market variety. The fruit are large, 8-10 cm in diameter, 10-13 cm long, block-shaped with three to four lobes and are thick fleshed. The fruit is generally used green but sometimes it is used in the full ripe red stage. It generally requires from 11 to 13 weeks from transplanting to harvest.

Commonly-grown varieties include Green Giant, Yolo Wonder, Californian Wonder, Northern Bell and Emerald Giant. The F1 hybrids such as Alliance, Domino, Melody are now gaining popularity because of their large size and thick flesh.

Chilli

The chilli plant usually has pendant, red, thin-fleshed fruit. The fruit is distinctly pungent and is used mainly for flavouring. The fruit ranges from small cherry-like fruit which tend to be very hot through conical-shaped forms to slender fruit up to 20 cm long. They normally take 110 to 150 days from transplanting to harvest.

Two important varieties are Long Red Cayenne and Red Chilli. The small hot chilli is a popular variety and is a very heavy producer.

Paprika

The paprika fruit is normally dehydrated and crushed or diced. The dark red flesh has little or no pungency and the fruit is grown specifically for processing.

Pimiento

The fruit are smooth, conical or heart-shaped, 7.5-10 cm long, pointed at the blossom end with very thick, sweet, red to yellowish-coloured flesh. The fruit is used for canning, flavouring pimento cheese and processed meats and stuffing olives.

They normally take about 80 days from transplanting to harvest.

Temperature

Temperature is critical for maximum fruit production. Light frosts during the growing period can injure or even kill plants.

The optimum monthly average temperature for sweet capsicum is 21°C to 24°C, with a minimum of 18°C and a maximum of 28°C. Hot peppers require higher average temperatures: the optimum monthly average temperature is 21°C to 31°C, with a minimum of 18°C and a maximum of 35°C.

Some of the longer-growing varieties, including Pimiento and Tabasco, require considerably higher average temperatures and are more sensitive to lower temperatures.

As the plants are being established, higher temperatures will retard flower production and favour better leaf development.

Capsaicin development is most rapid at temperatures between 30°C and 35°C. However, very high day temperatures (32°C and over) can stress the plant to wilting point, causing blossom, fruit, and leaf drop.

The effect of temperature on flowering

It has been shown that more flowers develop if capsicums are grown at 12°C compared to 18°C at night for 25 days at the commencement of the third true leaf stage.

The capsicum flower is normally open only for about 24 to 30 hours and flowering is adversely affected on dull or wet days.

The effect of temperature on fruit set

Temperature is critical for fruit set. Fruit set is poor when day temperatures exceed 32°C and night temperatures fall below 15°C. Fruit which has been set at a mean temperature of 27°C are likely to be small and poorly shaped because of heat injury to blossoms. Above 35°C few, if any, fruit will set, especially if the air is very dry or if drying winds prevail. Small-fruited varieties are more tolerant of high temperatures and moisture stress than large-fruited varieties.

When the fruit reach the mature green stage, red colour develops best at 18°C to 24°C, regardless of whether the fruit is still on the plant or in storage. If temperatures are above 28°C during the colouring period, the red colour develops a yellowish cast. When the temperature falls below 18°C colour development decreases, stopping completely at about 13°C. As a consequence, capsicum colour poorly during autumn and winter.

Growth cycle

The growth cycle generally follows the same pattern for all types of capsicums although the ambient temperature and the root zone temperature will affect the growth cycle.

1. Planting to emergence: 8–12 days.
2. Emergence to transplanting: 36–60 days.
3. Transplanting to first harvest: 75–150 days. First harvest day varies from 75 days for Bell types, to 110 days for green mature chilli types and 150 days to ripe red capsicums.
4. Duration of harvest varies.

Propagation

Propagation media
Hydroponically-grown capsicums are usually propagated in a standard propagation medium containing sand, peat moss and perlite. The seeds are germinated in seeding trays containing square or round plugs at least 2.5 cm diameter.

Enviropeat, a media made from crushed coconut shells, has produced exceptionally good results. It promotes very good root development and is free from diseases. Depending on the system, rockwool propagation blocks are also sometimes used.

Peat pots, about 5 cm square filled with propagation medium, are also ideal for seed germination because they allow the seedlings to become well developed before transplanting. Also, because the pot is planted with the seedling, plants rarely suffer transplant shock.

Germination
Capsicum seeds germinate within 8 to 10 days at temperatures between 24 and 30°C. The minimum germination temperature is 15°C: at this temperature seeds take about 26 days to germinate. Once the temperature rises to 35°C the germination rate falls dramatically.

The moisture content of the germination medium can be kept reasonably low and if maintained slightly on the dry side will generally give improved germination rates. Soaking the seeds in 1% sodium hypochlorite solution for 5 minutes stimulates germination and promotes rapid early growth.

After emergence, seedlings are grown with the aid of protective heating before hardening off prior to planting out. At this stage temperatures should be in the range of 18 to 24°C.

Transplanting

The seedlings should not be allowed to become root bound. They can be transplanted into progressively larger containers before they are transferred into the hydroponic system. This reduces the time required in the hydroponic system and increases crop turnaround.

Capsicum seedlings should be hardened off carefully. For best results transplanting should take place after the medium has reached at least 18°C. The transplants should be placed in a protected position and night temperatures maintained at a minimum of 18°C.

The seedlings normally take 8 to 12 weeks from seeding to transplanting, depending on growing conditions.

About 450 g of seed (at 160 seeds per gram) is needed to produce 30,000 to 35,000 plants.

Spacing

Most hydroponic capsicum cropping is based on single or double row planting. Single row crops are planted at 30 cm intervals in rows spaced 90 cm apart.

Double row plantings are normally done in summer to reduce the incidence of sunburn. The rows are about 40 cm apart with 100 cm between the aisles.

Chilli and pimiento capsicums can be planted in clumps with 3 plants per clump and each clump spaced 30 cm apart. Depending on the growing conditions, increased plant spacing will reduce the incidence of fungal diseases.

Nutrition

Capsicums are not as heavy feeders as tomatoes although they do require a well-balanced plant food. They also require good root aeration or high oxygen content in the nutrient solution.

Nitrogen has been found to significantly affect fruit set. High nitrogen levels have been found to reduce sunburn, although the incidence of blossom end rot may be increased. Inconsistent feeding and low levels of calcium in the nutrient solution also increases the plants' susceptibility to blossom end rot.

pH range

The optimum pH of the nutrient solution is 5.5 to 6.5 with preference for the higher pH level. However, lower pH values tend to reduce the incidence of root diseases.

Watering

It is important to avoid overwatering and feeding because capsicums are susceptible to root diseases such as Pythium and Phytophthora. An erratic moisture supply during fruit development may also cause blossom end rot, shedding of the fruit and flowers, and stunted plant growth.

Training

Yields may be increased by topping the seedlings, i.e. the top of the plant is pinched out. Topping increases the number of side branches close to the ground, giving more flowers and a concentrated fruit set.

To top the seedlings, remove 10–20 cm of top growth when the seedlings are 50 cm tall. Plant development can be adversely affected by more severe topping.

Harvesting

The fruit is normally ready to harvest 14 to 15 weeks after transplanting. The stage at which the fruit is picked depends on the market requirements. The fresh market trade prefers sweet bell capsicums as a mature green fruit. There is less demand for semi-coloured fruit and only sporadic requirement for the full red fruit.

Green bell capsicums are ready for harvesting when the fruit is firm and fully developed; the colour has changed from light green to dark glossy green; and the flesh is succulent and sweet. Red bell capsicums are harvested when red pigment begins to show on the point of the fruit. Chillies and paprikas are picked when they are fully mature and red.

The fruit is snapped off the bush by hand. Ripe capsicums hold better on the bush than tomatoes, hence picking can be done at intervals of 7 to 10 days. They will continue to bear fruit until they are affected by frosts or extremes of temperature.

Most capsicums are marketed in 18-litre (half bushel) fibreboard cartons. When properly filled the carton will hold about 5 kg of fruit; cartons filled with smaller varieties will hold about 6 kg.

Optimum storage conditions for capsicums are 7°C temperature and 95% relative humidity. In these condition they will keep for up to 2 to 3 weeks. Washing the fruit in a very dilute hypochlorite solution (6 ml per litre) prior to packing will remove some of the field heat and reduce the incidence of post harvest diseases.

Yields
High: 10 kg per 3 plants.
Average: 10 kg per 10 plants.
Poor: 10 kg per 20 plants.
Average 8.75 tonne per hectare.

Hydroponic Culture

Hydroponic systems used for growing capsicums are very similar to those used for tomatoes and cucumbers. One of the differences is that capsicums are generally supported by the use of side wires, whereas cucumbers and most types of tomatoes are supported by tying the plant from above.

There is no single best technique for hydroponic capsicum culture, although some methods are more forgiving. In particular, there are very few growers who would advocate nutrient flow systems with any long-term crop such as capsicums because the risks are too high, particularly for the inexperienced.

Non-recirculating Systems

Bag systems
The bag system is commonly used by commercial capsicum growers. Plants are grown in 15–20-litre black plastic polythene bags filled with a growing medium. The nutrient solution is delivered through a common feeder line with a minimum of 1 dripper per bag. The length of each row of bags is 40–50 m.

The most commonly used medium is washed coarse sand. However, the weight of the filled bags, and the physical effort required in laying them out and cleaning up the media after the crop has finished can be a problem.

Alternative media are scoria or volcanic rock, rice hulls, sawdust, bagasse, perlite and potting mix. Perlite is more expensive but it has the advantage of being lightweight and hence is easier to work with and clean up.

One problem with using bags is that the roots tend to concentrate at the bottom and around the inside of the bags, resulting in root burn and plant stress on hot days. For this reason, short wide bags provide better growing conditions than both tall thin bags and standard nursery bags containing the same amount of growing medium. Short wide bags also give more consistent moisture content through the medium compared to tall thin bags.

Many growers have found pillow-shaped bags promote consistent growth and production. The pillows are made from Panda tubing (black and white coextruded polythene film) and measure about 60 cm long, 15 cm deep and 30 cm wide. Alternatively, sheets of Panda film can be wrapped around the medium with the unjoined edges being folded and tucked under the medium.

Channel systems

Channels or troughs are also used for growing capsicums and are generally much easier to work with than bags. The system consists of a long narrow bed measuring up to 10 m or more in length and about 300 mm wide. The bed is filled with a growing medium to a depth of about 10 to 15 cm, depending on the waterholding capacity of the media used. A perlite or sawdust bed need only be about 10 cm deep while fine gravel or coarse sand would need to be about 15 cm deep. (Increasing the depth of the bed gives the plant greater support and provides the plant with an increased reserve of moisture and nutrient.)

The bed should have a slight even slope from top to bottom. Even when the ground is not perfectly level drainage holes should be made at the lowest points.

The nutrient solution is intermittently pumped from a bulk nutrient storage tank to the bed, using dripper tubes (T tape or similar) with a feed rate of about 4 litres/metre/hour. The dripper tubes are laid on top of the bed. T tape gives good results but the feeder holes tend to be too far apart. Alternatively, sprayers or drippers may be inserted into the feed line but this involves a lot of work. The simplest feed line is similar to T tape but the holes are spaced about 30 mm apart.

The nutrient solution should be filtered before it is pumped to the bed and it is important to flush the line regularly, e.g. once a day, with fresh water to prevent the nutrients blocking the holes as the solution dries out.

The frequency of feeding varies according to the water-holding capacity of the medium. The crop is fed 2–4 times each day if perlite is used; crops growing in gravel or coarse sand will need to be fed 4–10 times each day. The length of time for feeding is normally 5–10 minutes, sometimes with an extra water feed in the middle of the day.

The bed is fed with the nutrient solution until a very slight excess of solution goes to waste. If the medium becomes very wet, the duration or frequency of feeding should be reduced.

The grower has two controls over the amount of nutrient solution supplied to the plants: the duration of the feeding time and the frequency or number of feeds given to the plants. Feeding the plants for a shorter time but increasing the number of feeds per day is preferable to giving the plants one or two feeds per day but for long periods. The amount and regularity of the feeds is determined by the season, temperature, humidity, the amount of air movement, and even more importantly the growing medium used. After some simple preliminary trials are carried out, the feeding is controlled by a timer.

Advantages of the channel system:
a) It is less labour intensive than bags, both when laying out the system and cleaning up after the crop is finished.
b) Crops can be grown at higher densities and there is less restriction on root development.
c) Watering and feeding are more easily controlled.

Rockwool systems

Rockwool slabs are not generally used for capsicum growing. Although the slabs are easy to lay out and clean up, the financial outlay—including the cost of the material and delivery—

is not justified by the returns from the crop. To be considered viable, the rockwool would need to be used for two or more seasons and this may cause a number of problems. The rockwool would need to be sterilised before it is re-used and the old spent roots removed to prevent root diseases occurring. Another problem is disposal of the used slabs. However, the use of granulated rockwool in pillow-type bags may be worth trying.

Recirculating Systems

The major reason for using a recirculating system is to reduce the labour and cost involved in filling and cleaning bags or beds. Another advantage is the shorter turnaround: once the crop is finished, the next crop can immediately be planted into the system, although this is not a critical factor with long-season crops like capsicums.

The power consumption required for a recirculating system is very much higher than for non-recirculating systems. If one of the reasons for choosing a recirculating system was to reduce nutrient wastage then the potential grower will be sadly disillusioned since the non-recirculating system is no more wasteful than a recirculating system. In fact an advantage of a non-recirculating system is that the plants are being supplied with fresh nutrient solution on a regular basis and nutrient imbalances are less likely, especially if some nutrient solution is allowed to go to waste each feeding.

Problems occur more rapidly in recirculating systems, hence they require greater expertise to manage correctly. On the one hand they provide the grower with more control over the growing of the crop but on the other hand things can go wrong and they do so more quickly. The other factor is that the cost of running the system continuously is more expensive and power failures can wipe out a crop very easily. Unlike lettuce which can be put back into production quickly and income generated within a few weeks, capsicums are a comparatively long-term crop which cannot be replaced quickly and income may be lost for long periods.

Some recirculating systems use plastic channels with a medium, such as gravel, placed in the bottom of the channel to keep the root system more open and better aerated.

Channelling for recirculating systems can be very expensive and sealing the channels against leakages can be difficult. The channels must be large enough to cope with a root system that can grow very vigorously. The channels or pipes must be at least 120 mm diameter, and preferably 150 mm in diameter. Rectangular channels 150 mm wide and 100 mm deep are preferable to round pipes.

If plastic film channels or gutters are used, the floor must be levelled to give a slight slope, without any undulations which can cause pooling. The slope used is dependent on the rate of nutrient flow. High flow rates require less slope than low flow rates. The standard slope is normally 2 in 100. A high flow rate, about 2–4 litres per minute per channel, is preferred.

Many NFT growers use capillary matting in the bottom of the trough to help the young seedlings obtain moisture and nutrients when planted out. An alternative method is to lay a piece of string along the bottom of the channel—this helps to direct the nutrient solution to the roots of the young seedling. Another method is to sit the seedlings on a small piece of blotting paper, tissue or paper towelling.

Cultural Problems

Nutrient Problems

Nitrogen
In nitrogen-deficient plants, growth is seriously restricted and the foliage, particularly the older leaves, tend to be yellow-green in colour. Since nitrogen is fairly mobile in the plant it generally moves from the older leaves to the newer young leaves and shoots. Seriously affected plants will be stunted and will produce small fruits.

Phosphorus
While growth is restricted in plants suffering from low levels of phosphorus, the foliage tends to remain glossy and dark green in colour although the leaves are narrower. Fruit shape and size is also affected. Phosphorus deficiencies generally occur during the cooler weather, particularly when nights are cold.

High levels of phosphorus have been found to improve the rate of fruit ripening by up to a week.

Potassium

The lack of potassium appears as a bronzing of the leaves. Growth is restricted and small reddish-brown spots develop on mature leaves with some interveinal and marginal yellowing.

Deficiency symptoms are often accentuated by high levels of nitrogen in the nutrient solution. Yields are adversely affected by both high and low levels of potassium. High levels of magnesium can also depress the uptake of potassium by the plant.

Sulphur

Many nutrient formulae are low in sulphur. Sulphur deficiencies disorders can be confused with nitrogen deficiencies in that the leaves tend to be yellowish-green in colour.

Calcium

Calcium deficiencies show up as yellowing of the margins of the young leaves and pale brown sunken areas on the fruit. Growth and yields are affected by calcium deficiencies.

Magnesium

The older leaves tend to develop a yellow-green chlorotic colour between the veins which may stay deep green. Since magnesium is relatively mobile within the plant, deficiencies tend to show up on the older leaves. Capsicums are particularly sensitive to low magnesium levels: the fruits are small and sparse.

Iron

This is a common problem because it drops out of solution very easily and deficiencies are induced by a high manganese to iron ratio. The youngest leaves become yellow and interveinal yellowing develops near the base of the older leaves. Iron is not very mobile within the plant and deficiencies show up mainly in the younger leaves. The roots appear to be blackened at the tips and stunted.

Pests and Diseases

The most common pests of capsicums are Queensland fruit flies, budworms, aphids and spider mites. The diseases which attack capsicums include mosaic virus, powdery mildew, Anthracnose, bacterial spot and bacterial soft rot.

9 Carnations

Although carnations are grown all over the world, they have been bred for the more temperate climates. In warmer climates, flower quality and plant health is adversely affected, giving rise to smaller flowers with shorter and weaker stems, and a greater incidence of disease problems. Under warmer conditions, it is very important to provide good air movement through the crop, and planting density should be reduced. This is particularly important for carnations grown under greenhouse conditions.

Carnations are susceptible to root diseases, particularly fusarium wilt, hence the systems used do not involve the recirculation of the nutrient solution.

Commercial carnations will flower continuously for up to two years; after this they begin to decline and should be replaced. It is not uncommon in Victoria for the plants to produce well for up to three years, while growers in New South Wales are doing well if their plants produce for two years, and northern Queensland growers are lucky if their plants last much more than 12 months. As the plants get older the problems caused by pests and diseases increases and the plants become tall and straggly.

Growers generally start to replant in February or later in order to have young vigorous plants flowering during winter or early spring, depending on the climate.

The flowers are damaged by frosts, high temperatures and severe winds; therefore they are usually grown in greenhouses or polyhouses.

Varieties

Most modern commercial carnations are Sims varieties or developments from these. In particular, the Mediterranean varieties, which are available in a wide diversity of colours and types, are extremely popular in Australia. These carnations are distinguished from the normal garden varieties by long flower stems, erect growth habit, and continuous flower production.

The Bulgarian varieties, although producing very large perfumed flowers, have been found to be unsuited to commercial production because they do not yield very well.

While the standard and spray carnations are the most popular carnations, the mini carnation is becoming increasingly popular for use in posies.

Temperature

The recommended greenhouse temperatures for carnations are 12.5°C at night and 19°C during the day. The maximum day temperature should be 21°C. At higher temperatures flower size and the number of petals are reduced, and the stems become longer and weaker. Good air movement in the greenhouse during the day will reduce the temperature of the plant material, hence exhaust fans and lower plant densities will improve the quality of the flowers.

Temperature fluctuations of more than 6°C in one hour, which may occur if the shed is completely or even partly closed during fine but cloudy weather, will increase the incidence of calyx splitting and spindly growth. The problem of hollow flowers is also caused by high temperatures and high light intensities.

If air movement and ventilation is poor, a thin layer of white shading may be necessary to keep the temperature down in summer. This should be removed as soon as the ambient day temperatures start to fall.

Spray carnations require a slightly higher growing temperature than standard carnations. In summer the spray carnations can withstand temperatures up to 6°C higher, and shading is not usually needed.

While heating is beneficial to the plant in winter, the increased yields may not justify either the capital cost of the installation or the running costs. However, taking the chill off the crop during winter results in earlier spring flowering flushes, and will generally pay dividends.

Lighting and temperature

Carnations are a long day plant, i.e. flowering is promoted by long hours of daylight and is slowed down by short hours of daylight. Extending daylength with lighting will help but may not be justified commercially.

Higher yields are obtained when the light intensity and daylength are increased. Hence the ridge of the greenhouse should be true north-south, with the beds running in the same direction to take advantage of maximum light, particularly when polythene covering is used.

Ventilation

Very few growers have any concept of good air movement. The ideal air flow around the plants is about 4-7 km per hour. With good air movement and ventilation (not draughts) the quality of the flowers and stem thickness are greatly increased, especially in the summer months. This corresponds to the cooling effect of air moving across the plant and the exchange of gases from the leaves, which is equivalent to increasing the carbon dioxide levels in the greenhouse. The effect of increasing the levels of carbon dioxide has been shown to improve the yields of carnations as well as their quality.

Propagation

The importance of obtaining good clean virus and disease-free stock cannot be over-emphasised. Most growers purchase their young plants from recognised suppliers as rooted or unrooted cuttings, which are taken from the terminal parts of the mother plants. (Note that certain carnation plants are covered by plant protection rights.)

The cuttings should be clean, strong and well-developed, and between 100 mm and 150 mm long. Spindly and weak cuttings should be rejected. The cuttings may be stored at 0°C for up to three months in polythene bags, provided they are first washed in a dilute solution of sodium hypochlorite (2 ml per litre) and then treated with a fungicide.

Maintaining sterility during propagation is critical. When getting ready to propagate the cuttings it is advisable to recut the stem and immediately dip the cutting into a hormone gel, liquid or powder and then insert it into a sterile growing media. A very good propagation media is Enviropeat, which is crushed coconut shell.

To prevent diseases, the cuttings should be misted regularly with sterilised water until they have formed roots. Feeding may then be commenced, using a well-balanced nutrient solution. This will give strong healthy plants.

Many of the plants supplied by commercial nurseries are very weak and tender. They should be watered and fed with a good complete nutrient for a few days before they are planted out. They should also be washed in a fungicide solution to prevent and inhibit diseases that may come with the plants.

Feeding

The nutrient balance is critical to the continued production of marketable flowers. High levels of nitrogen will push the plant into vegetative growth, while high potassium and phosphorus levels will assist flowering at the expense of future vegetative growth. Low levels of phosphorus will affect the colour of the flowers.

Many growers tend to feed their plants using a shot-gun approach: they use high nitrogen nutrients to boost foliage growth, followed by high phosphorus and potassium nutrients to stimulate flowering. This gives rise to massive flushes of growth followed by flowers with long spindly stems. It is better to feed the plants the same nutrient consistently. Very few growers seem to realise that flower bud development starts long before the buds are observed.

It is not necessary to change the nutrient concentration or its contents in summer and winter because the increased watering in summer supplies more total nutrients, and the opposite occurs during winter, i.e. slower growth in winter corresponds to less frequent watering.

Some growers conduct leaf analyses to determine the plants' requirements and then modify their nutrient solution to make the adjustments. This is costly and does nothing. All the leaf analysis determines is those elements which the plant has taken up through the roots. If the nutrient solution is well balanced then all the required elements are present in the nutrient solution around the roots of the plant. If a leaf analysis shows a deficiency then this is generally best corrected by foliar feeding. While the nutrient solution around the roots of the plant may be complete and contain all the essential nutrient elements in balanced quantities, other factors can contribute to the uptake of nutrients. Some of these factors include root zone temperature, root aeration, pH, and moisture content of the media.

It is advisable to take samples of the drainage water as it leaves the bed and check that the conductivity and pH is the same as that going into the bed. If the conductivity is higher, this indicates that salts are building up in the growing media and the nutrient feed concentration may need to be reduced and the amount of nutrient going to waste may need to be increased slightly. If the nutrient concentration is lower, this indicates that the plants may be feeding more heavily and are looking for nutrients. It is also advisable to check the volume of nutrient going to waste.

pH control

The pH of the nutrient and the growing media should be maintained between pH 5.5 and 6.5. At this level all the major elements and the trace elements are available to the plant. Some growers go to a great deal of trouble to adjust the nutrient to some specified figure. In doing so they create other problems, such as causing many of the trace elements, especially iron, to become insoluble. However because most growers use a non-recirculating system, they use freshly made-up nutrients; hence deficiencies are seldom experienced.

Watering

Consistent moisture content of the growing media is essential to produce good quality flowers. A number of growers use overhead watering sprayers after the new plants have been planted. They may use the overhead watering system for two to three weeks until the young plants have become well established. At the same time they use the feeder system for supplying nutrients to the young plants.

The most satisfactory method of watering is the use of seepage hoses between two rows of plants in the beds. This ensures more consistent watering over the entire bed, with the moisture having time to slowly spread through the growing medium.

Other types of watering systems may create problems. Drippers tend to wet the bed in a series of cone formations which spread out at the bottom of the bed. Microtubes tend to block up easily and apply different amounts of water over the bed. Although sprayers distribute the water over the entire bed, they also tend to wet the lower leaves of the plant foliage, providing ideal conditions for fungal diseases.

If drippers are used, a strip of blotter-type material placed under each dripper point will help to distribute the nutrient solution more evenly. The blotting paper technique also helps to attract media-borne pests such as cutworms, particularly in beds filled with potting-type or soilless mixes. The insects will congregate under the paper and can be found and disposed of early in the morning.

Drainage and media

A well-drained medium which provides good root aeration is essential because of the carnations' susceptibility to root and crown diseases. Because of these problems carnations should never be grown hydroponically in a recirculating system. The medium should be maintained on the moist side of dry at all times. In other words, use regular short bursts of feeding and watering. The best advice to any commercial grower is if you think the plants need feeding and watering then leave it until later in the day or possibly the next day.

With media such as coarse sand or gravel, the bed tends to be unevenly wet and will dry out quickly, so the depth of the bed needs to be much greater than perlite or rockwool beds. Once gravel or sand beds dry out, they are difficult to rewet evenly, so sprayers are frequently used in conjunction with drippers. The sprayers are also used to provide foliar feeding.

Perlite, perlite mixes, rockwool and soilless potting mixes tend to produce consistent moisture distribution throughout the bed, but once they dry out they are also difficult to wet.

Plant spacing

In the early stages of growth, the spacing of the plants does not greatly influence the production of flowers. However, as the plants get older and the density increases, air movement between the plants and light penetration through the canopy is reduced. These factors give rise to longer and more spindly growth, softer buds, irregular flushes, and increased disease and pest problems.

At higher densities of planting it is more difficult to spray the plants effectively for pests and diseases. The normal spacing is 200 mm by 200 mm to obtain good air movement and maximum yields. While an increased spacing of 250 mm by 250 mm may not increase yields per square metre over a given period, it can increase the production of consistent quality flowers and extend the plants' productive life. A good grower can expect yields exceeding 300 blooms per square metre in an eighteen month period.

Training

While it is a common practice to pinch back the young plants to five or six nodes to help strengthen the plant and form the foundation of the growing plant, this may not be as beneficial as often assumed. Trials have indicated that this gives rise to an initial heavy flush followed by a decrease in flower production and overall yields because the next flush is delayed. Higher yields and more consistent production can be obtained by firstly removing the apical shoots, and then removing two to three of the developing lateral shoots.

Removal of the terminal growth (pinching) of young carnation plants encourages the buds in the axils of the leaves to break and develop more uniformly, thus producing a bushy plant, particularly under high light conditions.

When starting off from cuttings the plants are pinched back to two nodes in the early stages to induce branching. The apical stem is again pinched back, leaving five to six nodes in order to spread the flush and delay the growth of laterals.

Pinching does, however, delay flowering and may reduce the productive life of the crop, depending on the climatic conditions. It is generally sufficient to pinch only once, and should a second pinching be required it is preferable to increase the plant spacing or reduce plant density.

The first crop of flowers is usually of a higher quality and while the plants will continue to produce flowers, they are usually produced in flushes, particularly in spring and summer. The flushes may be reduced to give consistent flowering by using a well-developed complete and balanced nutrient in conjunction with regular watering and feeding. If the plants are stressed at any stage the frequency of watering and feeding can be reduced to help initiate flowering, but unless the stress is relieved then the flowers formed may become distorted, small, and with weak stems.

Disbudding is the removal of lateral buds from the lower parts of the stem and its purpose is to improve the size of the terminal flower. In the case of spray carnations the terminal bud may be removed to ensure more uniform flowering.

It is important to note that any plant material taken from the plant should be collected and disposed of.

Harvesting

Flowers should be cut at the correct stage of development to optimise their vase life, and this will depend on the grower's market and his treatment of the flowers after harvesting.

Carnations are generally picked by snapping the stems at a leaf node. This is preferable to cutting because the cut stems are more susceptible to dieback and diseases.

There are a number of vegetative lateral shoots on the flower stem which, if left on the plant, will develop into flower stems. Cutting long stems may result in the removal of these lateral shoots and hence reduce the total yield of flowers from the crop, as well as the quality of the flowers. However, cutting long stems also helps to keep the carnation bush open and induces new fresh lateral growth, thus increasing the density of the plants and stimulating fresh new growth and vigour.

After harvesting, the flowers should be placed in water, preferably in a cool room at 5 to 8°C, to remove field heat. The use of a cut flower food and preserver is recommended to reduce the bacterial infection of the freshly cut stems and to maintain the turgidity of the plants.

The flowers are graded on stem length and quality and are then bunched, tied and sleeved.

Storage

Carnations can be stored dry for a period of two to four weeks at a temperature of 0°C to 5°C without deteriorating. The flowers should be cooled to 5°C, and if they are to be stored in boxes, the boxes should be wrapped in polythene film to maintain a humid atmosphere around the flowers before cooling down to 0°C.

If the flowers have been stored for any length of time then the stems should be recut and placed in a cut flower preservative.

Hydroponic Culture

Non-recirculating Systems

All systems used for carnation growing have one thing in common—the susceptibility of the carnation to root diseases, particularly Fusarium wilt. Hence, most systems used do not involve the recirculation of the nutrient solution. Instead, most systems involve a flow-through principle in which a growing medium is used to support the plant and the nutrient is added on a regular basis to replace the water and nutrient used by the plants. A small amount of nutrient is allowed to go to waste or flow through the system. While this may seem to be wasteful it is no more wasteful than a recirculating system. In a recirculating system the nutrient solution is dumped on a regular basis, maybe once every month or two. In a flow-through system the plants obtain fresh nutrient solution at each feeding and a small amount of excess (about 5 to 10%) is allowed to flow through. The amount that is wasted in either system depends on the purity of the water used.

The most common system used for growing carnations is beds or polystyrene boxes filled with inert growing media such as scoria, perlite, coarse sand, rockwool or soilless mix.

The alternative to the bed or tray system is the use of rockwool or perlite pillows, which are normally 750 mm long, 300 mm wide, and 75 mm deep. Each bag holds eight to ten plants. In this system, two or three bags or slabs are laid across each row. Some growers only use two rows of rockwool slabs or perlite bags to form up their beds and then leave a space between the rows. They claim that the lower density planting gives better air movement between the plants, and thus improves the yield per plant and the quality and vase life of the flowers.

Some growers use beds that are 40 to 50 m long by 900 mm wide; the depth depends on the growing medium used. The beds are constructed from bricks, fibro sheeting or cliplock roofing. A layer of gravel is placed on the base and the bed is then filled with a potting or soilless mixture.

Other growers use polystyrene tomato boxes with drainage holes at the bottom or at one end. The problem with polystyrene boxes with holes at the bottom is that the nutrient solution tends to channel through the medium and run out through the drainage holes. This results in uneven wetting of the medium, as well as excessive nutrient wastage when trying to wet out the bed effectively.

Most carnation growers set their rows up so that they are 900 mm wide, with an aisle spacing of about 600 mm. This is a convenient width for picking and working on the crop. The standard support wire mesh used is available in a 900 mm width.

The actual width and length of the bed is at the discretion of the grower and the level of risk that he is prepared to accept of losing his crop through diseases. Long beds have the advantage that the watering and feeding is more controlled and consistent, and there is less chance of losing a crop because a dripper has become blocked. However, the chances of losing the entire crop through diseases becomes greater. With smaller and shorter beds losses from diseases are minimised, but it is difficult to control the moisture content of each bed, particularly if polystyrene tomato boxes are used. In long beds the bed may have wet spots, especially at the drainage end. This can be overcome by shortening the bed or providing drainage points along the bed.

Special attention must be paid to the cost of the growing medium. In situations where quality is important and the customer is prepared to pay a higher price then perlite growbags or rockwool may be justified. Soilless mixes can produce high quality carnations but they are very susceptible to disease contamination and tend to pack down with time, thus reducing root aeration and increasing the waterholding capacity. When this occurs the quality of the flowers tends to gradually deteriorate.

Soilless mixes need to be fumigated and resterilised, prior to replanting. This may involve the use of steam or fumigant gases to destroy pathogens; however, this is an expensive operation and is not always effective.

In order to reduce the risk of root diseases, good root aeration is critical. The frequency of feeding will depend on the waterholding capacity of the growing medium and its drainage properties. In general, feeding is normally carried out two to three times per week. However,

shorter and more frequent feeding and watering is preferred. The aim of feeding is to maintain as consistent moisture levels as possible to avoid stressing the plants.

Most growers use a large nutrient tank to feed their crop. This gives the grower better control over the nutrient being fed to the plants. Some growers use a nutrient injection system which pumps concentrated nutrient into the water supply, hence feeding can be a hit and miss affair. It is preferable to use an automatic controller which controls the time and frequency of feeding. The controller not only saves labour and is less time consuming, it is also more reliable. Depending on the size of the operation, a multistage automatic controller may be required. Additional features such as temperature and light level sensors may be built into the controller.

Setting up
The growing areas are usually 900 mm wide and the aisle spacing is normally about 600 mm wide. Coarse gravel is placed in the aisles.

If beds are used, they are formed up and filled with the growing medium after first putting down plastic sheeting with gravel placed on top for drainage. If polystyrene boxes are used, they are normally filled up and transported to the area. The boxes may be placed on a bed of gravel or raised off the ground with bricks. If perlite grow bags or rockwool slabs are used, the base is prepared with a slope to the centre of the row and covered with plastic or weedstop material and a thin layer of gravel. The grow bags or rockwool slabs are then laid down on the base.

The next step is to install the feeder system. If beds or boxes are used, this may consist of T tape or seepage tubing. However, some growers prefer to use sprayers instead of seepage tubing. In this case, they use PVC tubing and insert the sprayers or drippers into the line. This helps to maintain even watering and wetting out of the medium, particularly while the plants are young. If perlite grow bags or rockwool are used, most growers use standard 13 mm polythene tubing and insert microtube feeder or dripper tubes (usually two or three dripper tubes) into the polythene piping; the other ends are inserted into the bags or onto the rockwool slab. Most growers have a tap or valve at the end of each growing section so that they can turn the feed system off or on as required.

If perlite grow bags are used, it is advisable to cut the top out, leaving a strap across the middle of the bag for side support. This makes it easier to plant and space the plants. The other advantage it offers is that T tape or seepage tubing may be used, which makes setting up easier than if dripper tubes are used.

The medium is thoroughly soaked before planting. The grower then sets up the support meshing (usually wire mesh 900 mm wide, with a 100 mm mesh size) by using star pickets or similar side supports and strainers. The meshing is put in place as the crop grows. The first level of support mesh is usually placed 200 mm to 250 mm from the top of the bed. As the plants grow the next layer is placed about 300 mm above the first layer of mesh, and additional layers are added as the plants grow. The usual number of support mesh layers is normally three or four.

Cultural Problems

Physiological Symptoms

Calyx splitting
Calyx splitting is very common in the Sims varieties of carnations and occurs mainly in the spring and autumn. It can be caused by a number of factors including rapid temperature fluctuations, low light levels, boron deficiency, excessive levels of nitrogen, and moisture variations in the bed.

Slow bud opening
Sleepiness or slow bud opening in carnations can be caused by high levels of ethylene, resulting from the decay of vegetative matter; after replacing old polythene igloo covers with new material; or during cold weather. Some growers have claimed that spraying Foliar K, which is a high nitrogen, phosphorus and potassium nutrient, has been effective in breaking dormany.

Weak stems
Weak stems are generally caused by low light levels, which may occur during extended periods of overcast weather or poor transmittance of light through the plastic cover of the greenhouse. It is also associated with excessively high levels of

nitrogen in the nutrients used, and if night temperatures are consistently high.

Aborted flower buds
The abortion of flower buds is associated with a deficiency of both calcium and boron, as well as a damaged root system (caused by high nutrient concentrations, diseases, very low pH of the growing medium, etc).

Bull heads
Malformed 'bull heads' occur when there has been a sudden drop in temperature at the bud initiation stage.

Calyx tip dieback
This can occur when the plant is stressed, which may be caused by low moisture content of the growing media; Botyritis disease (grey mould); or low levels of calcium and potassium in the nutrient solution. It can also occur if overhead watering is used.

Grassiness
Grassiness occurs when the plant remains in the vegetative stage, producing many branches without flowers. While the actual cause is not precisely known, it is usually associated with high temperatures or high levels of nitrogen. It is frequently considered to be genetically related and occurs in a particular colour and variety at any one time and may only last for a short period.

A similar problem which appears to be genetically related is when the apical leaves become very distorted and the flower buds are small, distorted and empty. This may occur in a particular colour, variety or batch of plants. It appears that some strains of plants have a very high demand for boron at certain stages of growth. Soluble boron may be applied by foliar feeding to correct the problem which normally lasts for about two to four weeks and then may correct itself.

Splitting of the nodes
Splitting of the nodes and bushy growth caused by new shoots developing through the split is also usually associated with a deficiency of boron. The flower quality in affected plants is also generally poor. The deficiency of boron can be caused by several factors including low

concentrations of boron in the nutrient, high levels of calcium in the nutrient, and high pH of the nutrient solution. Some varieties require higher levels of boron.

This type of problem may also occur when the nutrient is supplied as two separate parts at different times or the use of a 'shotgun' approach to feeding whereby the grower is constantly playing with adding one form of nutrient to correct a problem and then another form of fertiliser or nutrient to correct the problems he has created. A well balanced and complete nutrient designed for carnations from a reputable supplier will justify the slightly higher costs of the commercial nutrient.

Discoloured and distorted leaves

Small narrow leaves with the edges folding in are attributable to low levels of nitrogen. The leaves tend to lose their bluish or glaucous appearance, and in severe cases the leaves may become pale and turn brownish. Infrequent or irregular watering and open media can also cause this problem. In the case of the media, the water and nutrients supplied to the plant may not wet the media effectively and run straight through the bed. If the bed has dried out the growing media may in fact repel water and be difficult to rewet. In such cases growers usually blame the nutrient first rather than their inability to maintain a consistent and regular watering and feeding schedule.

Nutrient Problems

Boron

This seems to be the most common deficiency that occurs in carnations. Some varieties are more susceptible than others. It shows up as shortening and thickening of leaves, malformed flower buds, and deformed flowers with fewer petals which may be distorted. The branching stems at the top of the plant become distorted and very bunched as a result of the loss of the apical buds. This problem seems to occur during summer and autumn, particularly when the growth is very vigorous.

Calcium

Calcium deficiencies usually show up as the tips of the leaves turn yellow and die. The production

of blooms is affected in mature plants. Side shoots are often pale and thin, and an excessive number of side shoots may develop.

A deficiency in calcium often occurs when the pH of the media is below 5, and seems to occur most frequently when two-part nutrients are used to feed the crop. It also occurs when a newly planted crop begins to make rapid growth, and reflects a low calcium level in the stock plants rather than a deficiency in the new media.

Increased levels of calcium tend to cause splitting of the calyx, particularly in the Sims variety of carnation. This is attributed to the calcium interfering with the uptake of boron by the plants.

Phosphorus

In plants suffering from a phosphorus deficiency the newer foliage tends to be dark green in colour, while the oldest leaves become pale green, develop pale brown areas, and wither.

At low levels of phosphorus the young vegetative shoots are blue-green in colour and exceptionally narrow. Plants grown on low levels of phosphorus tend to have shorter internodes and produce fewer sideshoots.

Potassium

The most common symptom is tip burn on the lower and upper foliage. Leaf spotting is very characteristic of low levels of potassium, particularly with the Sims varieties.

Iron

In iron-deficient plants, the younger leaves become yellow and almost white. The edges of the leaves start to pale, while the midrib is a mottled green colour.

Pests and Diseases

Carnations are subject to an array of fungal diseases which attack the roots and stems in particular. The most serious soil-borne diseases of carnations are Fusarium wilt, Rhizoctonia stem rot and Sclerotium collar rot. Other common diseases are rust, Alternaria leaf spot, Botryitis, ring spot, Phytophthora, Septoria leaf spot and Pseudomonas.

The most common insect pests which attack carnations are red spider mites, thrips, aphids and Heliothus caterpillars. It is important to remember that more than one disease or pest may be present at any time.

There is no substitute for hygiene when growing carnations and prevention is often easier than trying to cure the problem once it is present. This includes using footbaths when entering glasshouses, and washing hands and sterilising equipment before and after handling plant material. Some growers take a lot of trouble to protect their crops, using shadecloth around the outside of the sheds and across the door openings.

In order to maintain healthy plants it is essential to remove those parts of the plant that have been infested with a disease, and in the case of vascular diseases it is important to destroy the plant and treat the surrounding area.

Fungus diseases are spread by spores which may be carried in water, by the wind or on shoes. The spores can survive for long periods—even years in the case of some soil-borne diseases. In cases where a crop has been severely infected with a wilt disease, such as Fusarium, disinfestation will not eradicate it from the growing medium since the roots and the disease can penetrate deeply into the medium. In these cases it is important to separate the growing medium from the soil and preferably dispose of it when the crop is finished. It is also advisable to spray the inside of the greenhouse or igloo thoroughly with dilute formalin solution or dilute liquid chlorine solution before replanting. Sterilisation of the medium cannot be relied upon to provide more than temporary control since reinfestation from the water supply and other host plants is almost inevitable.

10 Cucumbers

There is evidence that shows cucumbers have been cultivated for at least 3000 years. They were cultivated in France in the 9th century, in England in the 1300s, and by the American Indians by 1539.

Over the last 60 years there have been a number of significant developments in the breeding and cultivation of cucumbers. During the 1930s new varieties were introduced with improved vigour and fruit and greater disease tolerance and resistance. In 1945 the earliest monoecious hybrids (plants with both female and male flowers on the same plant) were introduced to commercial cultivation. These plants exhibited hybrid vigour and multiple disease tolerance but acceptance by growers was limited because of high seed costs associated with hand pollination in seed production. A major breakthrough came in the 1960s with the development of the first gynoecious lines (plants with female flowers only) and a new technique for maintaining seed of gynoecious lines. Since then numerous hybrids have been introduced to the commercial market.

During the last ten years continental cucumbers have grown in acceptance from being a novelty vegetable to a major vegetable crop in a number of areas. In the last three years, production has accelerated to the point where overproduction is occurring and prices are falling in the peak growing season.

The techniques used for hydroponic cucumber production often involve a polyhouse. This protects the plants from rain, wind, hail, extremes of temperature, etc. The systems used include:

a) the nutrient film technique, involving nutrient recirculation without a support medium;

b) nutrient flow technique, involving recirculation of the nutrient and a support growing medium. This technique is increasing in popularity because it provides the benefits of recirculation systems and growing media;

c) trays, troughs or bags, using a growing medium such as gravel, rockwool, sand, scoria, etc. and non-recirculation of the nutrient solution. This is the most popular technique at present.

Varieties

Pickling cucumbers
Pickling cucumbers are processed from both fresh and brined cucumbers. The most popular cucumber for pickling is cylindrical in shape with blocky (flattened) ends, has a length to diameter of about 2.9, and is a uniform medium green colour. Popular varieties include Calypso, Flurry and Fancipak hybrids.

Slicing cucumbers
Slicing cucumbers, commonly referred to as English cucumbers, are used almost exclusively as fresh salad cucumbers. Traditionally, these fruit are more attractive in appearance, distinctly dark greener in colour, and larger in size compared to other types of cucumbers. Varieties include Crystal Salad, Green Gem, Redlands Long White and Marketmore.

Hybrid Long Salad

In recent years long green trellis cucumbers have grown in popularity and are now a major glasshouse crop in Victoria and South Australia.

They are generally classified as hybrids and include the Lebanese and telegraph (or continental) cucumbers. They are often referred to as 'burpless' cucumbers because they tend to be less acidic than the English cucumbers.

They are one of the new breed of seedless parthenocarpic cucumbers so it is important to keep the plants isolated from outside pollen sources, otherwise deformed fruit will occur.

Popular varieties are Sprint 400, Sofia (continental), Pigal (Lebanese), Monarch, Jordan and Jade (Lebanese types), and Burpless Tasty Green.

Plant Types

Gynoecious plants express female flowers for an all female phenotype; in other words these plants only bear female blooms. Predominantly female (PF) phenotypes are commonly produced by crossing gynoecious (female flowering plants) with monoecious lines (plants with both male and female flowers). The number of male flowers borne on the plants may range from zero to a large number, depending on variety and climatic conditions. Cool weather tends to induce male dominance.

Monoecious plants have separate male and female flowers on the same plant. These phenotypes produce numerous male flowers compared to the number of female flowers borne on the plant. In the initial phase only male flowers are produced; in the second and longest phase both male and female flowers are produced; and finally in the third phase only female flowers are produced. The length of each phase is dependent on environment and genetic background.

Hermaphroditic phenotypes produce perfect (bisexual) flowers. This genotype will sometimes react to environmental conditions to produce low numbers of male flowers.

In parthenocarpic cucumbers, the fruit develop without being pollinated, consequently the fruit are seedless or bear infertile seeds. Lebanese and continental cucumbers are parthenocarpic.

Environmental factors

Environmental factors can have a profound effect on cucumber yields and quality. High temperatures and long days induce male flower development, while low temperatures and short days favour female flower production in monoecious varieties. Good growth conditions such as high light intensity and warm temperatures generally enhance femaleness in PF (predominantly female flower) hybrids while environmental stresses encourage the development of higher numbers of male flowers in the PF hybrids.

In some varieties, including Lebanese cucumbers, pollination and fertilisation will result in deformed fruit. It is essential therefore, to keep these plants isolated from other pollen sources.

Temperature

Cucumbers are a warm season crop which require a root zone temperature of at least 15°C for germination and growth. For most varieties optimum temperatures are 18°C at night and 24°C–26°C during the day—at these temperatures the crop can be harvested in 44–55 days.

Lebanese and continental cucumbers are particularly sensitive to low temperatures. During vegetative growth temperatures below 19°C to 20°C at night and 23°C to 24°C during the day can result in the formation of unwanted male flowers. Fruit formation is adversely affected by temperatures dropping below 17°C to 18°C at night and 23°C–24°C during the day.

Propagation

Seed should be purchased from reliable suppliers and breeders. Immature seed, variations in seed consignments due to genetic drift, and poor quality parent stock will adversely the performance of a crop.

The minimum temperature for germination is 15°C with an optimum range of 15°C to 25°C and a maximum of 41°C.

Seeding must be uniform and consistent to achieve maximum yields. Most growers sow the cucumber seeds directly into the growing medium or in 2.5 cm pots filled with perlite, vermiculite and peat moss or a similar soilless propagation medium. Once established, the seedlings can be transferred into the growing medium, although this needs to be done with care because the seedlings are sensitive to root damage during transplanting.

The seeds of Lebanese and continental cucumbers are very expensive so it is important to ensure that each seed germinates and losses are reduced in transplanting. They are best propagated in peat pots filled with propagation medium so they can be transplanted with the propagation medium intact and undisturbed around their roots.

Plant Spacing

Plant spacing varies between cultivars. As a general guide, plants are grown 22.5 cm to 30 cm apart with rows spacings of 1 to 1.5 m. This gives about 25,000 plants per hectare.

Growing Media

If the plants are grown in media-based systems, the growing medium used must be open textured and provide good root aeration. The root systems of cucumber plants are very extensive and if damaged will adversely affect plant growth, flowering and fruiting. Media with small fine particles are less likely to damage plants, especially during the early stages of growth.

Nutrition

Cucumbers have a reasonably high requirement for nutrients. The newer specialist cucumbers have a much greater requirement for water and nutrient requirements than the traditional cucumber varieties.

The nutrient concentration is normally maintained at about 1700 uS. However, environmental factors are very important and it is up to the grower to determine the concentration that optimises cucumber production under his particular microclimate. Generally under high temperature conditions the nutrient concentration is lower; the concentration is usually raised where the growing temperature is lower.

pH range

The recommended pH for cucumber growing is between pH 5.5 and 6.8. High pH tends to produce symptoms of iron deficiency.

Watering

Cucumbers are very sensitive to water on their leaves because this can spread various diseases to the foliage and fruit. They are also sensitive to water marking on the leaves which reduces their potential to produce sugars and photo-synthates. However, cucumber plants should never be allowed to wilt if maximum yields of marketable fruit is desired.

Training

Pruning is one of the most time consuming tasks in growing cucumbers. The plants grow rapidly and need pruning and training by removing the lower leaves and laterals every 7 to 10 days. They are normally trained up strings to a height of about 2 metres (see diagram page 62).

Hydroponic Culture

NFT systems

The early hydroponic cucumber growers used the nutrient film technique but they generally found the system difficult to control effectively. Nowadays, there is a lot more information and assistance available to growers using this system. The main advantages of NFT for the commercial grower are that replanting is quick and no media is required. While the technique sounds simple, it can present a number of problems. As with any long-term crop, if problems occur with this system the entire season's crop can be wiped out or yields severely reduced. With most NFT systems the grower must monitor and watch the crop very carefully because problems can arise quickly, e.g. the pump may break down, the water supply could be cut off, the pH or nutrient concentration may change, or water-borne diseases may rapidly spread.

NFT systems used for growing cucumbers require a level base or floor, or one which has a slight slope such as 1 in 100, which is lower than the level used for most NFT systems. The nutrient tank must be dug into the ground so that the nutrient solution will flow back into it. The alternative to sinking a tank into the ground is to use a collection sump and pump the recirculated nutrient back up into a tank at ground level.

The original channels used for cucumbers consisted of black polythene formed into a triangle with the top edges clipped or clamped together on both sides of the plant stem. Some growers formed the trough by using black plastic suspended between two wires and clamped the plastic to the strained wire supports. A capillary mat was used to assist the flow of the nutrient solution (without the matting the nutrient would flow snake-like down the trough, hence some plants would miss out on the nutrient). A few growers have used cliplock guttering to shape the base of the gully and to provide a more even slope.

Currently the most common channels used are PVC piping, such as the round 150 mm stormwater pipes or rectangular PVC channels which are 150 mm wide and 100 mm high. While many growers have tried to use smaller pipes they inevitably get into trouble as the roots fill up the channel and the nutrient solution banks up and overflows. Another problem with smaller pipes is that the nutrient flow must be reduced as the plant grows.

PVC piping is expensive but it is very durable and will last a number of years. In comparison, the black polythene was a reasonably inexpensive material and at the time it was in vogue a number of growers spent large sums of money on environmentally controlled sheds, concrete floors, and

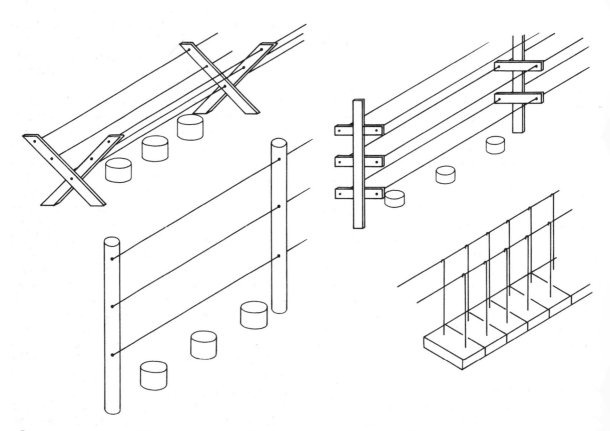

Crop support systems. There are a number of techniques used to support tall plants such as cucumbers, tomatoes and capsicums in hydroponics.

sophisticated controllers of pH and conductivity. The newer Aquachannel, a rigid ultraviolet light stabilised PVC plastic, offers a number of advantages: it is relatively inexpensive; it is easy to form into shape; and it is more resistant to breakdown caused by ultraviolet light.

A problem with most NFT systems is that the solution in the channels or troughs can become very hot, particularly in the summer months. The resulting oxygen depletion around the root system can increase the potential for root problems such as root diseases. Some of the ways of overcoming this problem are to increase the tank size, keep the tank cool, increase the rate of flow down the channel, and to use shorter gullies. If possible, the ambient temperature should also be reduced to a maximum of 25°C to 30°C.

NFT with media

These systems involve the use of channels or gullies which are similar to those used for the NFT system. The open channels contain a coarse medium such as gravel, which is generally pushed to one side of the channel, and into which the cucumber seedlings are planted. This ensures that the nutrient does not pool up in the channels and that there is good drainage or root aeration. The nutrient solution is collected at the ends of the gullies and flows into the nutrient tank which is dug into the ground.

The nutrient is recirculated at intermittent intervals to reduce operational costs. The nutrient may be pumped for 20 minutes on and 20 minutes off. Most growers work out a sequence depending on the temperature and climatic conditions.

This system has many of the benefits of the NFT system and fewer problems. It gives the grower greater control over the aeration of the root system. The amount of medium used is minimal, thereby reducing the labour involved in preparing the channels and in cleaning up after the crop is finished. When spread out on the bottom of the channel the medium is only about 1 to 2 cm deep.

Bed or channel systems

This system is a flow-through system involving non-recirculation of the nutrient, using an inert support or growing medium. A major advantage of a growing medium is that it acts as a buffer against pH changes and nutrient concentration variations, and offers some protection against pump breakdown, electricity cut off, etc. Many new growers prefer using this system.

Suitable growing containers include polystyrene boxes, black or white polythene growing bags (these are particularly suitable for uneven ground or steep slopes), and preformed channels or troughs made from polythene or similar materials.

At least one or two drippers are used to supply the nutrient solution to each bag or box. If channels or troughs are used, the solution is fed through a dripper or seepage tube which runs the full length of the channel.

The nutrient solution is made up once or twice a week, checked for conductivity and pH, and fed to the plants as required. It is never advisable to make up a large volume of nutrient solution which is to be used for more than one week.

Although these systems are classified as 'go-to-waste systems', the amount of nutrient solution used is only sufficient to keep the bed moist and to replenish what the plants have used up. A slight excess (about 5%) is also required to give the medium a moderate flush at each watering to avoid a buildup of salts.

In winter most growers water or feed their plants about 2 to 3 times per day for about 10 to 15 minutes at each feeding. In summer the rate may be increased to about 6 times per day for about 10 minutes each time. A medium which has high water-holding capacity, such as rockwool, may only need to be fed and watered once a day, or possibly twice a day in summer, with very little nutrient solution going to waste. However, a medium which has a poor water-holding capacity, such as gravel or sand, will need to be watered and fed at least 6 to 8 times per day for very short periods in summer, with up to 10% of the nutrient solution going to waste. It is very hard to be precise about the frequency of watering and feeding because of the differences in the water-holding capacity of the different growing media, the rate of flow of the nutrient from the feeder tubes, drippers, etc, and the microclimate of the area.

In areas where the water supply is high in soluble salts it is very important to allow a larger amount of nutrient solution than normal to go to waste to avoid excessive salts building up.

Bag system

Many growers use pillow-shaped black poly-thene growing bags filled with pine sawdust as a growing medium for Lebanese cucumbers. The bags are about 60 cm long, 30 cm wide and 125 mm deep, and hold about 40 litres of sawdust. Each bag will take 2 to 3 cucumber plants.

The bags are laid end to end to form a row. A feeder line of 13 mm black polythene tubing is laid on top of the bags, with a microtube dripper to each plant.

A problem that can occur with this set-up is that some bags tend to be very moist while others may be very dry. This can be overcome by using a long trough or bed system with a feeder line laid on top of the medium.

The nutrient solution may consist of a two-part mix which is made up as concentrates and pumped into the water supply. Smaller growers usually make up the nutrient solution in a holding tank and then pump the solution to the plants. Many of the larger growers are moving to the use of large nutrient storage tanks because the local water supply and pressures cannot cope with their demands. It must be borne in mind that these growers may have up to 20 sheds, each measuring 50 m long by 12.5 m wide, with each shed holding about 1000 plants. Cucumber plants require almost twice as much water as tomato plants grown under the same conditions. The conductivity reading used by these growers is about 12 CF units. The conductivity used can be adjusted to suit the growing conditions. Higher conductivities are used where stable environmental conditions exist.

Many of these systems are fed automatically and feeding is controlled by environmental conditions such as humidity and light. On an overcast day the light controller will sense that the light levels are lower and the controller will decrease the number of feeds per day.

There are a number of problems associated with the use of pine sawdust. Sawdust tends to hold excessive amounts of water, and root diseases are prevalent, especially stem rot, crown rot, Pythium and Phytophthora. In trials using troughs instead of bags, the incidence of disease was reduced considerably. Also opening up the sawdust by combining it with sterilised seed hulls gave better drainage and hence better root aeration.

Another problem occurs as the sawdust decomposes and releases tannins which can be toxic to the plants. Some growers treat the sawdust with a solution of iron chelate before planting out. The iron reacts with the tannins in the sawdust and seals off the sawdust, slowing down the decomposition rate, as well as providing a ready source of iron for the plants.

Perlite has also been used as a growing medium but it tends to be very expensive in comparison to sawdust and some growers find that their yields are not much higher. A major problem with local perlite is the large proportion of fines contained in the commercial product.

Rockwool is also expensive and the water-holding capacity is generally too high for growing cucumbers. However, imported rockwools with better drainage characteristics are becoming available. Trials on these materials have indicated improved crop performance and yields.

Starting out

If I were starting out in cucumber growing and did not know a great deal about hydroponics, I would set up a trough system and use a medium such as a potting-type soilless medium (preferably sterilised) without added fertilisers, and send some nutrient to waste just to get the feel of hydroponic growing. This medium has many of the advantages of soil: it has a good buffering and water-holding capacity, and it tends to remain cool. It will help you appreciate how just how small a quantity of water and nutrients are required for hydroponic growing.

The main problems encountered with this medium are that it will pack down with time, resulting in reduced root aeration; it can be a source of root diseases; it tends to accumulate salts, resulting in salt buildup; and it can bind some of the nutrients, giving unpredictable growth or more importantly inconsistent growth, flowering, and fruiting. Most salt buildup in the medium is a result of exposure to the air, such as occurs in open beds, resulting in evaporation of the nutrient. A medium which is open and aerated and is wet on the base but dry on the surface does not tend to have salt buildup. Media such as crushed peanut shells or seed hulls are very good, being lightweight and reasonably free of most diseases.

Sawdust is another good medium to start off with, but the type and source is critical. Most pine sawdusts are satisfactory and preferably they should have been exposed to the weather and undergone some composting. Many of the local timbers contain resins that will restrict or hinder growth, and these should be avoided. It is a good practice to trial the medium in one bed or row before using it for full scale production. The best size of sawdust particles is 6–10 mm diameter with a minimum of fines.

Some growers have opted for washed coarse sands or fine gravels with some success. It is important to find out exactly where they have been mined. Sands that have come from rivers subject to tidal flow are frequently contaminated with salt which is extremely difficult to remove. While you may consider that gravel is inert and therefore suitable for growing plants, there have been a number of cases in which the gravel dissolved in the nutrient solution and seriously affected plant growth.

A common problem with sands or gravels is that they can contain nematodes and pathogens such as fungal root diseases. It is always advisable to sterilise these media with liquid chlorine (at the rate of 20 to 30 ppm or 100 ml per 1000 litres of water) by flushing it through the beds or troughs, and allowing a few days for it to do its job. Other methods of sterilising include:
1. chemical sterilisers, e.g. chlorine, bromine, formalin.
2. steam sterilisation.

The water-holding capacity of the medium will depend on the distribution of the particle sizes. It is important when using a medium in a non-recirculating system for cucumber production to use a medium with good water-holding capacity and which is reasonably fine for the roots to hold onto. Coarse sand and gravel have a very low water-holding capacity, whereas the finer sands have a higher water-holding capacity (but poorer aeration). Coarse sand or gravel will be better for the plant during the later stages of plant growth, while the finer media are better during the early stages of plant development. If coarse media is used, frequent but short feeds will be needed to prevent the media drying out and to maintain a consistent moisture supply for the plants. The major problem with sand and gravel is that all the moisture is held on the surface of the particles and is very easily depleted, particularly as the cucumber plants are very thirsty when reaching maturity.

In order to provide the cucumber plant with a good supply of water and nutrient it is important that each plant has a minimum of 20 litres of sand (or gravel), preferably in a larger diameter bag or container. It is often advisable to incorporate some Enviropeat, peat moss, or sawdust with the sand to help improve its properties.

Some growers prefer to use rockwool or perlite as the growing medium. While these growing media are more expensive, in some cases the cost can be justified. In particular, many smaller growers in rural areas tend to use rockwool or perlite bags because they can obtain relatively high prices for their produce. Both media are lightweight and are very convenient to use. Rockwool is available in convenient sized slabs or wrapping, while perlite is packaged in bags. The bags and slabs are very easy to lay out—even a very large area can be covered in a single day. Perlite offers an advantage over rockwool in that the roots can be removed from the perlite before replanting. The standard bag size for the perlite is 25 litres (or approximately 700 mm long, 300 mm wide, and 75 mm deep). The perlite bags or rockwool slabs are lined up end to end to form a single row. The bags are suitable for growing two or three plants per bag. If slabs are used, the preferred number is two plants per slab.

When using rockwool slabs it is preferable to start the seeds in rockwool propagation blocks; the seedling is then transferred into a 75 mm rockwool cube. The seedling can be maintained in the rockwool cube until it is well developed. The cube is placed on top of the rockwool slab and the plant is watered and fed by individual drippers at each cube. While the technique of using rockwool blocks on top of the slabs tends to be relatively expensive, it cuts down on the time required by the plant in the growing slab before it begins flowering and fruiting. Another major advantage of this technique is the improved root aeration as a result of the increased height of the root system. The economics of this system requires that the slab must be used for growing at least two, and preferably three crops.

When using perlite grow bags it is not advisable to start the cucumber seeds in rockwool. When the seedling is planted out, the perlite drags the water out of the rockwool, causing the seedling to wilt badly. The cucumber seedling is normally started off in a medium such as perlite, or a propagation medium of peat moss, sand, vermiculite mix.

Cultural Problems

Cucumbers are very susceptible to a wide range of bacterial and fungal diseases. Growers are usually not very concerned about leaf blemishes because they do not directly affect the market value of the crop. This attitude ignores the fact that the leaves are indicative of the plant's health and have a significant effect on fruit production and quality. If the leaves are not healthy then fewer or poorer fruit will be formed. Generally leaf symptoms are only apparent after nutritional and other problems have become serious.

Diseases tend to be more prevalent during moist humid weather or when the cucumbers are grown in a poorly ventilated polyhouse. Powdery mildew, downy mildew and Botrytis commonly occur in these conditions. Other diseases which affect cucumbers are gummy stem blight, Anthracnose, Fusarium wilt, bacterial leaf spot and angular leaf spot.

Two-spotted mite is a major pest of greenhouse cucumbers. Aphids and caterpillars may also be a problem.

It is also important to note that cucumbers are very sensitive to herbicides and careful attention must be paid to the use of weed control sprays when cleaning up around the polyhouse or growing area.

Nutrient Problems

Nitrogen
Low levels of nitrogen tend to produce short and pale green fruit. The new leaves are pale yellow and small, while the older leaves become yellow and die prematurely.

Phosphorus
Low levels of phosphorus will seriously restrict growth and fruit production. The young leaves are small and dull green in colour. Brown areas tend to develop between the veins on mature leaves and the leaves die prematurely.

Potassium
With low levels of potassium growth may not be affected but the yields of fruit may be reduced. The leaves tend to curl downwards and a yellow margin develops and spreads between the veins. The older leaves tend to scorch easily in hot weather. The fruit may become poorly developed at the stem end and slightly swollen at the tip.

Calcium
The growing leaves develop a cupped appearance and the margins of the younger leaves become scorched when the nutrient solution has low levels of calcium. It is difficult to rejuvenate these leaves because calcium is relatively immobile in the plant. The growing points of the plant may suffer and die. Similar symptoms occur when the plants are grown in very hot humid conditions or if the growing medium has become dry.

Magnesium
With low levels of magnesium initially the leaves turn yellow between the veins. Finally the whole leaf will turn yellow. The symptoms are most obvious in the older leaves

Iron
This is the most common of all the mineral deficiencies and cucumbers show the effects of low levels very rapidly. The younger leaves turn pale yellow, almost white, in colour, and are reduced in size. A temporary deficiency can occur if the roots are damaged by pests or diseases or when the growing medium has a high water-holding capacity.

Manganese
While low manganese levels do present problems, with the leaves turning a pale yellow colour, toxicities are generally a more significant threat to plant health, and can be a common problem in some areas. Excess levels of manganese show up as black spots in the veins

of the lower leaves as well as yellow spots on the leaves.

Copper
The leaf size and the fruit yields are drastically affected by low levels of copper. The mature leaves develop a mottled appearance, and the leaf margins become pale green. Flowering is also restricted and the few fruit that do form tend to be poorly developed with small sunken brown spots on the skin.

Boron
Low levels or unsuitable forms of boron can severely affect the plant. The growing tip may die and the new growth tends to be twisted, distorted and knurled. The fruit tends to develop corky streaks which extend along the fruit.

Molybdenum
A deficiency of molybdenum causes stunting and yellowing of leaves; in severe cases the leaf edges die.

11 Lettuce

Lettuce is an indispensable part of most salads. It is a summer flowering plant which produces vegetative growth in the cooler months and flowers under conditions of long, warm days. In hot dry weather or when the plant is under stress the plant is inclined to run to seed.

While lettuce is not generally considered to be a difficult crop to grow on a small scale or as a one-off crop, as a business venture lettuce cultivation can be fraught with problems if maximum output is to be achieved and consistent quality and yields are to be maintained. These goals can be achieved through hydroponics, providing the grower gains experience in the basic growing techniques, as well as in the more complex operations such as timing and scheduling of seeding, transplanting and harvesting.

The gap between peak maturity and starting to run to seed may be as short as one week. It is very important, therefore, to know exactly when to harvest to achieve high quality, well-developed lettuce. Many hydroponic growers pick their lettuce too early, resulting in poor handling characteristics, more open lettuce with unfilled heads, and poor market acceptance. These growers will start to be displaced as the market becomes more competitive.

Market competition has put greater pressure on growers to perform, improve their technique, and use better nutrient formulations. Backyard nutrient formulators and amateur chemists have tended to go by the wayside. Many growers spend much of their time making up their own nutrients without the skills or knowledge to formulate or test nutrients effectively. The various agricultural departments have tended to sponsor this concept, not realising or appreciating that the growers do not have the same expertise. Hence the quality of the lettuce grown in many areas has suffered.

Any person considering the production of hydroponic lettuce should realise that it is a mass production technique in which volume is critical and profit margins are small, except when market prices are high. It is important to establish yourself as a quality producer because when prices are low you will still get your sales and cash flow. Hence consistent size, shape, quality and volume are very important. If the lettuce are consistent in shape and size then the entire bench can be picked when the lettuce are ready. But if the crop is inconsistent then picking is selective, leaving the immature lettuce to develop further. This ties up the bench and slows down production; hence labour costs will increase rapidly.

The aim of commercial production is to bring the lettuce to market size in the shortest possible time at the lowest possible cost. In hydroponics it is possible to produce up to 10 crops per year compared to two to three crops when grown in the soil. The main reason for the increased number of crops is that with hydroponics as soon as one crop is finished then the next one can be started. Another special feature of hydroponic lettuce growing is that production is carried out at a convenient height (bench height).

Varieties

There are four major types of lettuce:
1. Butterhead
2. Crisphead
3. Looseleaf
4. Cos or Romaine

Butterhead and crisphead are the most commonly grown commercial varieties.

Butterhead
Butterhead lettuce varieties are all very similar. The leaves are small, soft and smooth-edged and have a subtle, sweet taste. They are very fast-growing warm climate plants that can be grown throughout the year. They do exceptionally well in hydroponic systems and do not bolt easily. They tend to have better storage characteristics than the crisphead varieties.

Crisphead
Crisphead lettuce are renowned for their large firm hearts. They tend to be less resistant to bolting than the butterheads.

The major difference between crisphead varieties is the sowing times. Great Lakes is an excellent hot weather variety and can be sown all year round in warmer climates. However, it is not a very popular variety for hydroponics.

Imperial 847 is normally sown in spring and summer. Imperial Triumph is normally sown in autumn and winter for winter harvesting. Narromar has been bred for winter cropping and is slightly slower in maturing.

The most common varieties grown at present in hydroponics are Fame, Classic, El Toro and Narromar.

Crispheads were originally developed to withstand summer conditions in California and other areas in the southern states of America. Many growers experience difficulties in growing the crispheads in hydroponics because they tend to bolt easily during periods of warmer weather. The other problem is that the lettuce tends to be more open than conventional soil-grown lettuce, particularly in the Tweed Valley. This is most likely due to the nutrient formulation used in the area.

Looseleaf
The looseleaf varieties are grown by a number of commercial growers because they are faster growing and turnaround is faster. Some growers can achieve up to nine or ten crops per year.

Looseleaf lettuce are also popular amongst consumers because they are smaller and more tender than the hearted lettuce. They also tend to stay fresh longer if the plants are sold with the roots intact.

Cos
Cos lettuce are a tall, open-headed, oblong lettuce. The long, slender, slightly folded leaves are thicker and tastier than other types of lettuce. They usually take eight to ten weeks to mature, and can be grown all year round in the tropics. They are not very popular in hydroponics because they are slower growing than other varieties and tend to have a very large root system which can block the channel.

While one grower may be successful with certain varieties, another grower in the same area may have difficulty growing and marketing those same varieties. This can be attributed to different microclimates and to the grower's expertise in harvesting at the optimum maturity.

Growers should constantly evaluate different varieties to find out which is the best variety at any particular time. Many growers have found that El Toro respond well in cool conditions but if the plants run too far into spring (or early warm conditions occur) then they can bolt or become very open. However if the variety is grown in warmer weather they can respond well. Hence variations in growing temperature over the growth cycle can have a very significant effect on the plants' development. Growers who take regular records of temperature, humidity, nutrient concentration, pH, etc., can start to pick up patterns of growth and development in different varieties at different times.

The Protected Environment

While the myth that lettuce cannot be grown under a polyhouse covering is generally believed, it is based on the failure of a few growers to do it successfully. It is simply a matter of modifying growing techniques and understanding the effects of nutrient modification on plant growth. When grown successfully, lettuce grown under these conditions are slightly softer, have a far superior taste, and are more consistent in quality. The other major advantage of using a covered environment is providing protection from frosts, rain, birds, etc.

Lettuce is probably one of the most responsive crops to carbon dioxide enrichment, which can be provided in the polyhouse environment. Yields may be increased by up to 100% and the crop may mature at least a week or two earlier than other lettuce. Carbon dioxide enrichment also increases the solids content of the lettuce, especially under low light conditions.

Air movement (not wind) is critical in the production of high quality lettuce—good air movement will provide similar results to carbon dioxide enrichment.

Wind protection is also vital for commercial production of lettuce, otherwise plants may suffer from tip burn. However wind protection in the form of windbreaks may encourage a greater incidence of fungal diseases such as powdery mildew.

A northeast facing site is favoured for quality production.

Temperature

The preferred growing conditions are warm days with temperatures of 18°C to 25°C and cool nights of 3°C to 15°C. They grow best when the temperature variation between day and night is 5°C to 8°C. However, breeding has lead to the development of varieties which can tolerate higher temperatures. Hence selection of varieties suited to your location and microclimate is very important.

Propagation

The seed raising stage usually takes two to three weeks, although it can take up to six weeks, depending on temperature. It is one of the most important operations in the production of hydroponic lettuce. If the seedlings are strong and healthy, they can be transferred into the hydroponic system without problems. Weak, spindly seedlings will not grow into top quality lettuce so culling inferior seedlings will more than pay for itself. If you have to throw away a high percentage of your crop four or even six weeks later, lettuce growing becomes a very expensive exercise.

A major consideration in the seed-raising operation is the provision of suitable environmental conditions, including humidity, temperature, watering, feeding, and protection from winds. One of the most important factors is a good watering or misting system to prevent the seedlings drying out and to maintain a consistent moisture content in the seed-raising medium. Hence most seedlings are raised in a polyhouse on benches with mist spraying and regular feeding with nutrient solution.

Most hydroponic lettuce growers use a standard seeding mix of peat moss, vermiculite and sand, with slow release fertilisers such as gypsum, blood and bone and superphosphate added to the mix. However, a number of growers are now starting to use Enviropeat, a crushed coconut shell material which provides good results and is fairly inexpensive.

The lettuce seeds are irregular in shape and are difficult to sow mechanically. Seeding is usually done with a vacuum seeder. Because of the small size and shape of the seeds it is difficult to place individual seeds in each cell. Many growers now used pelletised seed to ensure that there is only one seed per cell in the seedling trays. While pelletised seeds are more expensive, the additional cost can be justified. When the seeds have germinated it is advisable to separate any doubles and leave an individual plant in each cell.

If the seeds are simply sprinkled onto a gemination medium in a tray, many seeds will end up in clusters. This will induce poor germination and irregular sized seedlings which will mature at different times. Consistency in size and growth is essential if operating costs are to be kept to a minimum.

While rockwool propagation blocks are a good medium for germinating the seeds, they can be difficult to seed out automatically. The major advantage of rockwool propagation blocks is that the seedling stays in the block during transplanting so the plant does not suffer any transfer shock and is stable and self-supporting in the channel.

Seeding must be done every week, or sometimes even twice a week, to keep the growing channels full. As the lettuce are harvested they are replaced with new seedlings. It is very important to develop a planting schedule so that a continuous supply of lettuce is maintained. This schedule can make or break the operation.

The seedlings are normally hardened off before they are transferred into the hydroponic system. This simply means they are left outside in the sun for about a week.

The watering of the seeds and seedlings is a most important part of the development of good strong seedlings. Most growers use straight water for watering and misting. However, I prefer to use a nutrient solution for watering and misting the seedlings. The normal nutrient strength used in these circumstances is about 1500 uS/sq cm. If the seedlings are overwatered, they will grow slowly and become pale and yellow. If the seed raising mix is allowed to dry out or the seedlings are underwatered they will turn a very dark green colour and the leaves become thick and dense.

Transplanting

Lettuce have a tendency to bolt (go to seed) before the plant reaches maturity. While this problem is reduced using hydroponics, it still occurs and to a large extent is caused by transplanting at the wrong time or by the seedling suffering some form of transplant shock. Hence it is very important to keep the plant growing quickly and without any setbacks. It is also very important to select strong, healthy, well-developed seedlings when planting out into troughs or channels, otherwise harvesting will be spread out because of inconsistencies in the rate of growth.

Bare rooting the seedlings may give rise to transplant shock which can delay harvesting by up to a week or more. This can mean the difference between producing an extra crop or two in the year.

Nursery system

Some growers transfer their seedlings into a nursery area for one or two weeks. This usually involves the use of 50 mm PVC piping, with 30 mm holes cut into the pipes into which the seedlings are inserted. The nutrient solution is pumped through the pipes continuously using the NFT system. When the seedlings have increased in size they are transferred into the main system.

The idea behind this practice is that the plants will not tie up the main system and hence turn-around time is shorter. This involves considerable double-handling and expertise is required to schedule the operation. Since the developed seedlings are much larger than younger seedlings, the number of seedlings that the grower can carry and handle is reduced. A normal seedling tray is about 60 cm by 30 cm and holds 196 seedlings. However, the same-sized tray would hold only about 100 developed seedlings.

There are a couple of other problems with this practice. The developed seedlings have a greater chance of suffering from transplanting shock compared to young seedlings. Another problem that is frequently encountered is that the seedlings may have to stay in the pipes for longer than anticipated. When this happens, the roots may clog up the pipes and cause the nutrient solution to pour out of the holes.

Some growers use 2 inch (50 cm) nursery pots to hold the seedlings in the NFT channels. The pots are filled with a medium such as gravel or potting mix. However, the pots are fairly expensive and reasonably large amounts of media are required. Root development tends to be restricted and the seedlings are prone to damping off and other diseases.

NFT Cups

Many growers are now using disposable NFT cups which have been specifically designed for lettuce production. The cup is placed in the holes of the NFT channel and is secured by clipping the corners into the hole. The lettuce seedling plug is then pushed firmly into the cup until the bottom roots contact the nutrient solution. The cups provide support for seedlings and do not restrict the growth and development of the root system. The lettuce grown in these cups are sold with the roots intact and with the cup still on them. A major advantage of these cups is that the plants have less tip burn than those grown directly in the channels.

Hydroponic culture

The systems used for lettuce production are in a constant state of flux as new ideas and techniques are tried. There is certainly no consistency between growers as to the best method or the best system. In the early '70s growers were using the NFT system, based on the use of the 'Super Six' fibro sheets. When the fibro sheeting products went off the market, growers used 100 mm round plastic PVC pipes which were cut lengthwise in half and filled with a gravel support medium. This system was very popular but had a number of limitations including the cost of media replacement and the work involved in cleaning the gravel after harvesting. A number of growers went back to the NFT system, this time using the rectangular downpipes. This was followed by the development of plastic channels with removable lids. These systems all have two features in common: they all involve the recirculation of the nutrient solution and the plants are grown on tables or benches for convenience of harvesting.

To say that one system is better than another raises questions relating to the grower's expertise, the market that is being supplied, the cost effectiveness of the system, and the characteristics of the system. If the grower is interested in volume then the NFT systems will speed up crop turnaround. This assumes that the grower is producing consistent lettuce which can be harvested in one batch. If the grower has to waste time picking and choosing when harvesting then the advantages gained by this system are easily lost. Since the system is continuously recirculating, power costs are very important and any time wasted or delays in harvesting become much more critical than systems using intermittent cycling. Another problem with NFT systems is that the lettuce will not survive for very long in the event of a pump or power failure, especially if the grower is absent when the problem occurs or if day temperatures are high.

The length of the NFT channels varies from 3 m to 18 m. The value of increasing the length of the channels depends very much on nutrient flow rates and the degree of aeration of the nutrient. Many of the earlier growers using gravel in the half pipes had micro tube feeders and found it necessary to use another micro tube feeder halfway along the channel. All new systems use capillary tubing which give higher flow rates when used with very coarse gravel media and this overcomes the problems encountered by the early growers.

It is much cheaper to set up systems using 18 m channels than say 6 m or even 3 m channels. The spacing between the supports is normally about 1.2 m which means that every 6 m bench requires 6 supports, whereas an 18 m bench requires 16 supports, hence saving two supports for every three lengths of 6 m benching.

The benches are normally 1.2 m wide and the lettuce are picked from both sides of the bench. The number of channels across a bench will depend on the type of lettuce being grown. For mignonettes and butterhead lettuce (or the smaller lettuce) the number of channels is normally between six and nine across the bench. However, with the headed lettuce the grower usually uses five or six channels across the bench. If the channels are spaced too close together, air movement is restricted, resulting in a higher incidence of fungal diseases. Close spacing also makes it difficult to effectively spray the plants.

There is no hard and fast rule for the spacing distance between the plants in the channel. Normally butterhead and mignonette lettuce are spaced at 20 to 25 cm intervals, whereas the headed lettuce require a spacing between 25 and 30 cm.

The slope of the channels should be consistent and normally is about 2 in 100. There are some growers who recommend a greater slope, resulting in faster flow of the nutrient solution

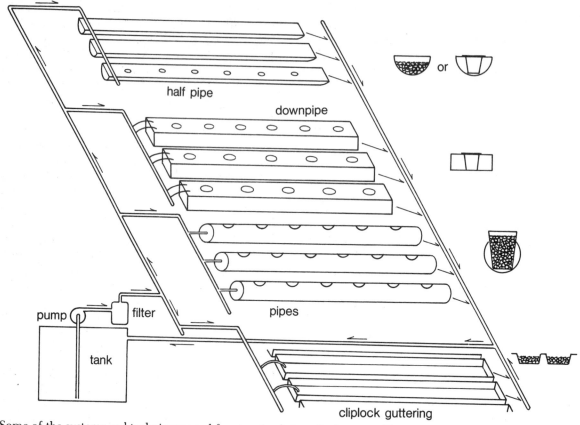

Some of the systems and techniques used for growing lettuce hydroponically

down the channel. A similar effect is achieved by increasing the flow rate at the inlet. A fast flow of about 2 litres per minute is generally acceptable.

The slope is important in that a slow flow rate will allow the nutrient solution in the channels to warm up faster in hot weather. This means that the plants at the beginning of the channels will reduce the dissolved oxygen in the nutrient solution (as will higher temperatures). In other words, in hot weather the rate of nutrient flow should be increased. In hot weather it is also very important to pump air into the nutrient solution. An air venturi in the tank, as well as a good cascade of returning nutrient will assist greatly. However, one of the best techniques for improving root aeration is to stop the pump for short periods and allow the nutrient solution to drain away from the roots of the plants before starting up the pump again. Nothing improves plant growth like good root aeration.

There are a number of nutrient flow systems

in which the channels have no slope at all and the growers adjust the level of the nutrient solution to whatever height they choose. These channels are frequently 18 m long.

With lettuce it is important that if one intends using a growing medium in a recirculating system, the medium must drain freely. Hence coarse gravel is normally used. However, a lightweight inert medium is preferable, such as expanded clay, expanded earth or pumice. Perlite, vermiculite or sawdust should not be used for recirculating systems.

Other systems

Many growers are currently using the standard 110 mm round PVC pipes cut in half and filled with a gravel medium. However, a number of these growers are considering eliminating the gravel and changing to NFT systems because of the various problems involved in the use of gravel. As well as the problems of sterilising the media, cleaning up after harvesting, and the sheer physical labour involved in handling the gravel, a factor which has contributed to this change is the problem encountered by restaurants and hotels in disposing of the root system containing gravel particles, especially when sink disposal units are used.

Another problem with gravel systems is that in hot weather the gravel tends to heat up quickly and actually holds the warmth (acting as a heat sink). This can be an advantage in autumn and spring but is detrimental in summer. As the nutrient solution heats up the oxygen tends to be expelled from solution and when the root zone temperature exceeds 30°C growth may be retarded and the roots damaged, giving rise to diseases.

However, gravel systems do have a number of advantages. They tend to be easier to manage and control, and with less variations in pH and conductivity. The gravel systems also allow the grower to have greater control over root aeration by simply modifying the cycle of pumping and draining.

Occasionally growers are doing their own thing. One grower is using a hanging bag system and having a lot of success. This may be due to the nutrient formulation being used, the method of growing, or the grower's expertise. He was growing under cover which also may have helped. He claimed that more lettuce could be grown in a smaller area compared to the half pipe system. One of the disadvantages of this system is the problem of cleaning up the bags after harvesting the crop. Because lettuce is a short-term crop, the media in the hanging bags has to be replaced every few months (i.e. after two to three crops) because of the excessive root mass and the problem of disease.

Some growers have used a full pipe with a smaller diameter than 110 mm and cut holes in the pipe to grow the plants. In most cases the small pipes have not proved to be very successful because when the plants grow the root system fills up the pipe and the nutrient flow is restricted. The nutrient can be modified to give a small root mass, but many growers would find this system restrictive, and a larger diameter pipe is generally preferred.

Some growers using the smaller pipes have very little slope on their pipes and hold a reservoir of solution in the pipes at all times. They use an intermittent flow cycle. The lettuce seedlings may be started off in rockwool propagation blocks or the seedlings may be transferred into small nursery pots (about 2.5 cm diameter) with a gravel support medium. The bottom of the pot is cut away to allow the roots of the lettuce to escape easily.

Many growers have set up using the rectangular 100 mm by 50 mm plastic downpipes with a nutrient flow technique. However, a number of problems can occur during the initial period of setting up. One problem is that the nutrient does not spread out in a film across the bottom of the pipe; instead the nutrient tends to run in rivulets. Once the lettuce is established this is not a problem, but in the early stages it causes inconsistent growth patterns over the bed. This can be overcome by using a wetting agent to help spread the nutrient film.

A few years ago, the plastic manufacturers introduced channels with removable lids. The main advantage of these pipes is that they have a V shaped bottom or ribs which centralise the flow of nutrient down the centre of the channel. This is very important, particularly when the seedling plant is just introduced to the channel. The fact that the lid is removable is also very convenient for cleaning and sterilising. However, most growers do not go to the trouble of removing the lids.

It is unfortunate that these channels were introduced at a time when there was a large number of systems already set up. Many growers have now reverted back to the 100 mm by 50 mm plastic downpipe channels because the pipes with the removable lids did not live up to expectations; they are also much more expensive. In areas where growers have established their markets and are exanding their operations, the preferred systems are the rectangular channels used in conjunction with the disposable NFT cups.

Nutrition

Consistent lettuce production is, to a large extent, dependent on the use of a good nutrient solution. A poorly formulated nutrient can induce the crop to bolt or encourage the development of very tender open-hearted lettuce. Many lettuce growers blame every problem that they have on the nutrient they have purchased. Those who make up their own blame all their problems on diseases, weather or variety. While both groups of growers may be correct, it is true that the nutrient formulation can have a significant effect on the performance of the crop. Unlike crops such as tomatoes or cucumbers which are slower growing and allow time for the grower to modify the nutrient balance, the fast growth rate of lettuce crops means it is more difficult to remedy nutrient problems.

Adjusting the pH

It is important that the pH of the nutrient solution remains steady. The optimum pH for hydroponic growing is pH 6.2. However a range between pH 5.5 and pH 6.5 will encourage steady growth. Most nutrient solutions will tend to stabilise at a given pH, depending on the nutrient formulation and the water supply. Many growers force problems on themselves by trying to make the nutrient maintain a particular pH. Many of the older growers ignore pH, provided that it does not rise too high, and consider conductivity to be the most important factor.

Problems tend to occur more frequently when the pH is high than when it is low. Many growers are their own worst enemy as they constantly try to adjust the pH to some arbitrary pH figure. Phosphoric acid is generally better than nitric acid for adjusting the pH down because it has a better buffering effect. Not only is nitric acid more dangerous to handle but it is very easy to overshoot the mark and drop the pH too quickly. Rubber gloves should be used when handling nitric acid or phosphoric acid and the acid should be diluted to give a 5% solution in water. Another good acid is acetic acid or vinegar (preferably white vinegar). Sulphuric acid, while not widely used, is usually readily available and offers benefits in that it helps to build up the sulphur content of the nutrient which most hydroponic nutrients are usually low in.

If the pH is too low it may be adjusted using an alkali such as potassium hydroxide or caustic potash. Care must be exercised in using potassium hydroxide since it is caustic. Other alkalis that can be used include caustic soda (sodium hydroxide), lime, washing soda (sodium carbonate) and baking soda (sodium bicar-

bonate). They should be dissolved in water to give a five percent (5%) solution. Sodium bicarbonate is preferred because it gives a better buffering effect.

It is interesting to hear growers complain that when they dilute the acid or alkali it takes too much solution to adjust the pH. The reason for the dilution is so that the nutrient pH is adjusted slowly and has time to come to equilibrium and avoids overshooting the required pH. Rapid adjustments frequently cause the trace elements to drop out of solution, resulting in deficiency problems.

Harvesting

It is very difficult to tell a grower when to harvest lettuce. Generally the buyers know what they want but there is no generally accepted standard. When starting out the best thing to do is to take along what you believe is required and discuss it with the buyer or alternatively go to the markets and look at what stage of growth obtains the best prices.

Many growers go through their tables and choose the lettuce that are ready, leaving behind those that have not developed as well. The grower will follow up a few days later and again select the developed lettuce. However, it is more efficient if the entire table can be cleared when harvesting. This is only possible if the initial seedlings had been consistent in size, shape and quality, hence the techniques used in raising the seedlings are critical and this is where most growers create their own problems.

Lettuce should be harvested in the coolest part of the day to prevent moisture loss and wilting. They should then be cooled quickly to remove field heat. While lettuce are normally graded and packed directly into cartons in the field, they may be kept cool by damping down with water.

The crisphead lettuce are often cut manually with a sharp knife and packed directly into the carton. Because the plant is clean and free of dirt, the leaves generally do not need to be washed or trimmed.

Some growers wrap the root system in plastic film and this can extend the shelf life of the lettuce considerably. Mignonette and butter lettuce are normally harvested with the roots intact—this also helps to preserve their shelf life.

Storage

Harvested lettuce should be stored at 1°C and a relative humidity of 95%. The temperature of the harvested lettuce should be reduced quickly to remove the field heat. Under good storage conditions, lettuce can be kept for up to three weeks.

Marketing

Most smaller hydroponic lettuce growers market and sell their produce direct to green grocers, restaurants, hotels and shops. The larger lettuce growers tend to supply their lettuce under contract to chain stores and restaurants. Most tend to avoid the produce markets because the prices tend to be lower and fluctuate widely. Furthermore, agents at the markets have a very poor reputation and their charges are considered excessive for the service offered.

Shops are usually happy to pay a slight premium for better quality, fresher lettuce, particularly in rural areas.

A product which is gaining popularity with restaurants, hotels and the export market is 'mesclun'. These are salad bowl mixes consisting of lettuce leaves, herbs and edible flowers. The leaves and flowers are chopped up and packaged in convenient-sized 500 g or 1 kg packs, or into 5 kg boxes. The lettuce used in the salad bowl mix includes Red Coral, Green Coral, Royal Oakleaf, Red Oakleaf, Frisee, Green Oakleaf, Monet, Mignonette, Regency, Cos, Buttercrunch and Red Sangria. The herbs grown for the salad bowl include Rocquet (Aragula), Milbuna, Mizuna, Nasturtiums and Calendula. The seeds are available from local suppliers such as Royal Sluis, South Pacific, Yates and New World Seeds.

We established a very good market at one stage with packets of lettuce leaves which were sold to specialist shops and restaurants. Unfortunately, we had to pull out of this market because we could not cope with the quantities needed. The lettuce were stored and sold directly from refrigerated cool cabinets in the shops. It saved the shops considerable space, as well as providing ease of storage. The lettuce could be stored for up to 4 weeks or more.

Another benefit of this marketing strategy was that the lettuce plants continued to be productive for more than 2 months because only the young fresh leaves were picked as they grew. Hence, the labour involved in seeding, replanting, harvesting, cleaning up the system, etc. was drastically reduced and the area required was much lower. The lettuce plants were taken out of the system when the stalks were about 45 cm tall. The cost of packaging and handling was high but this was recouped in the selling price.

Cultural Problems

Nutrient Problems

Nitrogen
Low nitrogen uptake by plants results in restricted growth and development, with the leaves being pale or yellow green in colour. The lettuce is underdeveloped, and the crisphead varieties often fail to develop hearts.

Phosphorus
During winter the leaf colour of phosphorus-deficient lettuce remains green, although plants grow more slowly and the crop develops unevenly. In summer the effects of low phosphorus are more obvious with the plants yellowing and large brown areas developing between the veins and spreading to the leaf margins.

Potassium
Indications of low levels of potassium generally become apparent as the plants mature. The outer leaves turn yellow and the plants may collapse rapidly in warm weather, followed by infection with the fungal disease, Botrytis. In cases of very low levels of potassium in the nutrient or slow uptake, brown areas develop on the margins of the leaves and may be mistaken for tip burn. The surrounding tissue may become yellow.

Calcium
When the nutrient contains low levels of calcium the plants are usually stunted and small dark brown areas develop on the margins of the leaves and also between the veins. The inner leaves can become twisted and cupped, and the edges of the leaves may appear scorched. This frequently leads to an infection of black bacterial slime inside the head of the lettuce.

Boron

The leaves tend to be dark green and somewhat leathery when the nutrient contains low levels of boron, and in extreme cases the growing point may die or become knurled and twisted. The crisphead lettuce may fail to form hearts.

With high levels of boron in the nutrient solution the leaves develop symptoms of tip burn (scorching on the margins of the leaves), particularly when the plant is under stress or under conditions of high humidity.

Molybdenum

Low levels of molybdenum are more of a problem during the seedling stage, particularly when the seedlings have been propagated in a peat media with overhead watering and the pH of the media is acidic. The symptoms are very pale green lettuce seedlings that fail to develop properly and unevenly when planted out into the hydroponic system.

Hygiene

Strict crop hygiene is the best means of combating diseases and pests in the system. Hygiene should start at the seedling stage, hence the seedlings should be grown on wire mesh benches or the seedling trays suspended on a frame.

If gravel is used in the system it should be stored on concrete or heavy duty plastic sheeting, making sure that it is thoroughly washed and sterilised before use. The gravel should be changed regularly, for example after every third crop, to avoid contamination and disease. Most gravel growers allow the gravel to dry out for several hours before replanting. In fact exposure to direct sun while drying out will help to sterilise the gravel because of the rise in temperature of the dry gravel.

Growers using the nutrient flow technique usually disconnect the return channel and flush the channels with water, followed by sterilisation with dilute chlorine solution. Allowing the channels to dry out for about one day in the hot sun will help sterilise the system and cause any algae to dry out and flake off the inside of the channels. Some growers use a 2% formalin solution to disinfect the channels, seedling trays, benches and equipment.

The simple rule of removing dead or decaying organic matter from the plant as well as around the plant is very important. The area under benches and in the aisles should be free of grass and weeds, especially thistles. All too often growers forget that grasses and weeds act as hosts to many of the problem diseases and pests such as mites, thrips, aphids and mealy bugs. It is very important to be clean and tidy in your operation, and not to drop old leaves and rubbish on the ground.

Fungus spores may be borne by air or water. Good ventilation or air movement around the plant is essential to keep the leaves dry and hence slow down the germination of the fungus spores. Air movement is improved by removing the old and decaying leaves from the base of the plant, and by keeping the plants clean. Breaking the leaves away from the lettuce is preferred to cutting the leaves at the base. When the leaves are cut away there is a short part of the stem which dies, decays, and is a open source of infestation for the plant.

Fungus diseases such as Pythium and Phytophthora may also be introduced from the water supply. Many growers treat their water before it is used to make up the nutrient solution. To eliminate water-borne diseases the water supply can be dosed with sodium or calcium hypochlorite (pool chlorine) at about 6 to 12 parts per million, or about 10 grams per 1000 litres of water.

While it is difficult to eliminate flying insect pests they can be reduced by the use of mesh or windbreaks around the perimeter of the operation. The windbreak protects the crop from strong drying winds and flying insect pests, and also helps to maintain the humidity of the air within the operation.

Diseases

The most common diseases of lettuce are Anthracnose, bacterial spot, big vein, damping off (Pythium), downy mildew, grey mould, necrotic yellow, Phytophthora, Sclerotinia rot and Xanthamonas.

Pests

Insect pests of lettuce are aphids, caterpillars (including cabbage moth larvae, white butterfly larvae, cluster caterpillars, loopers, budworms and Heliothus larvae), leafminers and thrips.

Other Problems

Yellowing of lettuce
Factors which can contribute to this problem are:
a) genetic problems in the particular batch of seeds supplied or seedlings used.
b) the propagation medium used for raising the seedlings may retain too much water. The seed raising mix may help in raising the seedlings but once it is constantly wetted by the nutrient solution in the system it may induce stem and root diseases. The diseases may not be severe enough to kill the plant, although they may restrict efficient nutrient uptake.
c) consistent overcast weather. This can reduce the amount of solar radiation and affect chlorophyll production.
d) pH rising above 6.7 causing iron to drop out of solution. While the iron may have been present as iron chelate, it will still come out of the nutrient at the higher pH levels. Other factors which contribute to iron dropping out of solution includes high levels of nutrient aeration and light.
e) low nutrient concentrations. This will contribute to deficiencies if any nutrient is at its lower limits, e.g. magnesium. Low nutrient concentrations cause deficiencies to show up more rapidly because the concentrations are closer to the limiting levels, particularly if the plant's uptake of a specific element suddenly increases. This can be accentuated by (f).
f) periods of heavy rain. This dilutes the nutrient solution, and more importantly, the roots of the plants are constantly standing in fresh water without nutrients for long periods. Rain frequently carries fungus spores which may inhibit the plants' growth.
g) slowing down of the nutrient flow caused by a blocked or dirty filter or feeder tubes. This can result in reduced root aeration, inefficient nutrient uptake, or excessive heating up of the nutrient solution in the channels.
h) nutrient solution concentrations becoming unbalanced and requiring changing.
i) roots becoming coated with contaminants such as algae and residues, and the root system becoming matted or interlocked.

Bolting
This is a common problem with crisphead lettuce in that they fail to heart and they run to seed prematurely. It is associated with the variety being grown out of season, nutrient or pH imbalances, and unseasonal changes in weather conditions (especially sudden warm to hot days).

Tip Burn
This is a physiological disorder which occurs for a number of reasons. The disorder has two basic causes:
1. The roots cannot take up enough water to reach the extremities of the plant (the tips of the leaves).
2. Weaknesses in the cell walls.

The first cause can be the result of a damaged root system; damage caused by movement or plant shock due to winds tugging at the lettuce and moving the roots; high nutrient concentration or sudden changes in nutrient concentrations; nutrient imbalances such as potassium levels, calcium levels, excessively high nitrogen levels; hot dry winds; drying out of the root system; high nutrient temperatures (low oxygen levels); high carbon dioxide buildup in the nutrient solution; incorrect pH levels; and constant pH changes.

Weaknesses in the cells walls can be caused by very rapid growth, calcium deficiencies, and moisture adsorption as a result of moisture sitting for extended periods on the edge of the leaves, giving rise to softening and possible fungal attack. Moisture on the leaves can create an osmotic potential difference between the new young tender plant cells at the tips of the leaves and the free water, thus causing the cells to bloat and rupture.

There are many factors that can cause tipburn and some lettuce varieties are more susceptible than others. Solving the problem of tip burn is not always a straightforward process. Accurate recording of prevailing conditions and factors can help to determine possible causes.

Two techniques used with the NFT systems to overcome the problem of tipburn during periods of high humidity are to reduce the nutrient concentration or to use a pumping cycle in which the nutrient flow stops for about 20 minutes each hour. A problem with the second technique is that on starting up again the feeding rate to individual channels may have to be readjusted.

12 Roses

Most commercial hydroponic rose production is carried out on a reasonably large scale by specialist growers. In these operations, a wide range of grades and varieties are grown to ensure the market can be supplied with flowers throughout the year.

The rose plant is classified as an evergreen shrub which becomes deciduous when temperatures drop below 12°C. Roses are more exacting in their requirements for light, temperature, humidity and general maintenance than most other crops. For this reason most hydroponic growers use a polyhouse which will provide conditions suited to year round production of high quality flowers.

Roses grown in the right conditions can live up to 35 years or more. However, most commercial hydroponic growers give their plants a life span of about five years.

Varieties

Miniature Roses

The miniature rose plant is a small bushy plant 45 to 65 cm tall, although commercial plants may reach 150 cm in height. The buds are perfect miniature replicas of the larger-growing hybrid tea bush rose. The flowers are single, semi-double or double, and some are scented. The colour range is excellent and the majority flower from spring to autumn.

Miniature flowering bush roses may also be sold as patio, Chinese or fairy roses. Their habit of growth is short and bushy, making them ideal for narrow beds or on benching. Most miniatures have a long flowering period, often from seven to eight months, so it is possible to use them to supplement other crop sales.

After a few years, commercial growers often sell the plants to nurseries so that they can bring in fresh plant stock to replace the older and less vigorous plants.

Floribunda Roses

Floribunda roses, also known as polyanthus roses, are compact bushy plants growing to a height of 1–1.3 m. They flower prolifically in clusters of up to 50 blooms per stem from spring to autumn, and are borne on the current year's wood. They are available as single, semi-double or double forms.

Old varieties have flattish flowers. The more recent varieties resemble the hybrid tea roses, but have longer and broader petals and a higher centre. The flowers are available in a good colour range and most are fragrant. The plants have attractive foliage, and are generally free of diseases.

Hybrid Tea Roses

The hybrid tea rose has a taller and sparser habit than the floribunda rose; the height ranges from 1.2 m to 1.8 m. They have a remontant flowering habit, a very wide range of flower colours, and many are scented. The blooms are carried on new season's growth, and range from solitary blooms up to eight flowers per stem. Flowering can be extended well into autumn, providing correct summer pruning is carried out.

Grandiflora Roses
These plants are the result of a cross between hybrid tea and hybrid floribunda roses. They are very vigorous bush roses, often growing in excess of 2 m tall. The foliage is good; the plants have good disease resistance; and the flowers have a high centre, similar to the hybrid tea roses.

Most commercial growers favour the hybrid tea and the floribunda roses for commercial cut flower production.

Temperature

The rose is classified as an evergreen shrub which becomes deciduous when temperatures fall below 12°C during winter. At 15°C and above the plant will continue to grow and produce flowers. Optimal growth occurs at temperatures of 25 to 30°C with night temperatures of 15.5°C. Low night temperatures can drastically reduce growth and continued low temperatures will delay flowering, and possibly prevent flowering.

Other adverse effects caused by low temperatures include the development of excessive numbers of petals, and poor colouring, shape ('cabbage head' formation) and keeping quality. At low temperatures the colour of dark red roses can intensify to the point where blueing starts to occur.

At high summer temperatures (above 27°C) flowering is very rapid, the buds open quickly, and the flowers have a shorter life. If temperatures remain high, flower size is reduced, the petal count is low, petal colour is paler, keeping quality is poor, and the stems are thin and soft.

It is extremely important to avoid rapid changes of temperatures and cold draughts since this can lead to defoliation of the plants. Fan and pad cooling has been used for a number of years to reduce stress on the plants during periods of high temperatures. High pressure mist systems can also be installed to provide summer cooling and humidity control.

Since the highest prices are obtained in winter, additional heating should be provided and, if possible, a thermal screen which can be drawn over the crop at night to conserve heat.

Humidity

Reputedly roses require relatively low humidity. Misting, particularly during the warmer part of the day, can cool the plant and reduce transpiration stress. Misting and spraying the plants with water also reduces the incidence of red spider mite, although excess moisture will induce foliage diseases such as downy mildew and black spot.

In high greenhouses fans may be used to create air movement which helps keep the plants cool, reduces pockets of high humidity, and keeps the leaves dry (thereby reducing the incidence of diseases).

Ventilation

Air exchange in the greenhouse is vitally important, especially in daylight hours. Early in the mornings the carbon dioxide levels in closed greenhouses have been found to be extremely low and at levels which are limiting to growth. It is advantageous to use some form of internal heating which produces carbon dioxide, such as oil or gas heating.

In winter, early closing of the greenhouse to retain the day heat can be detrimental because the plants are still photosynthesising at the low light level and carbon dioxide depletion can take place rapidly, thus restricting growth. Closing ventilators early also leads to increased fungal disease problems because water condenses on the leaves as the warm moist air cools down.

Lighting

Flowering and the rate of growth is directly related to light intensity and duration. Hence many overseas growers plant the roses in double rows, 600 mm apart with 300 mm between plants and an aisle spacing of 700 mm. They have found that this spacing maximises winter light and provides increased yields.

Flower production can be significantly improved by the application of supplementary lighting, particularly with the short-stemmed varieties. The benefits of lighting will depend very much on the prevailing weather conditions during winter, such as the number of overcast days. Sodium vapour lights have produced the best results, and research has shown that high pressure sodium lights which provide 350-500 foot candles for 16 hours per day will increase production by up to 25 percent. A 1000 watt light will cover an area of 15 square metres (170 square feet).

Growers often paint their polyhouses with white paint in summer to reduce light and heat. As the intensity of light increases in spring, it is advisable to use a light application of shading compound to paint the polyhouse or glasshouse. As summer approaches the level of shading compound can be increased. Sudden applications of high levels of shading compounds can reduce or delay flower production when applied early in the season.

Propagation

It is important to note that many rose cultivars are protected by plant variety rights, and approval must be obtained before these plants are propagated.

There are several techniques used for propagating roses:
1. Seeds: Plants grown from seed do not breed true to type but are useful for breeding new cultivars.
2. Cuttings: Some cutting-grown cultivars do not produce a strong root system, but the plants are true to type.
3. Budding: This is the main method of commercial propagation, using vigorous, disease-tolerant understock plants.
4. Grafting: Grafted plants are seldom used for greenhouse cut flower production because a substantial amount of time is required between planting and flower production.

Budding

On a commercial basis, budding is by far the most important method used to produce new plants for cut flower production. Long shoots or whips produced by the stock plants are cut and tied into bundles and taken to the propagation shed. The shoots are then dethorned and sterilised in chlorine solution before they are cut into short lengths. The cuttings or sticks are

de-eyed by removing all the bottom eyes (buds) and leaving the top three eyes. The cuttings are then planted out.

Once the root system is established (normally about five months) and the plants are about 15-25 cm tall, budding can take place if the bark 'slips' (i.e. it can be peeled away freely at the cambium layer). A T-shaped cut is placed well below the shoots that arise from the understock and a bud from the named cultivar is inserted into the T and is wrapped securely with budding tape. Three to four weeks after budding, the understock is cut above the inserted bud and the top broken over. After a further three weeks the tops are removed entirely from the plant. The budded plant is then dug up and washed, pruned to remove injured stems and roots, and finally graded. The plants can then be stored at 0-2°C until shipped to the grower.

Cuttings

Cuttings can be taken any time of the year depending on the intended planting date. The grower will need to take into account that a considerable amount of time is generally required to build the plant to sufficient size before harvesting of the flowers begins. Another problem with cuttings is that a large number of mother plants are required to produce a limited number of cuttings.

Cuttings are normally propagated using bottom heating at 18-21°C, as well as misting. Under these conditions the cuttings should begin to grow roots in about five to six weeks. The rooted cuttings are grown on with regular watering and feeding, and occasional pruning to train and shape the plant as required.

Propagating miniature roses

Miniature roses are normally propagated directly into a growing medium such as rockwool, without grafting new bud stock onto the mother stock. This cuts down on the time required before the rose comes into flower.

Transplanting

Roses normally take three years before they are ready to transplant as bare rooted plants into the hydroponic system. Transplanting is usually

Setting up an NFT system for growing lettuce

Above and right: Crisphead lettuce growing in
150 mm half-pipes and gravel

A large commercial hydroponic lettuce farm

Birdnetting over a lettuce crop

An NFT lettuce system using 3 m length pipes sloping to the centre

Propagating lettuce

Chinese vegetables growing in beds of perlite

Bulbs growing in beds of perlite

Propagation of roses in rockwool cubes

Carnations growing in beds filled with media

Gerberas growing in bags filled with scoria

Left: Roses growing in rockwool slabs

Strawberries in gravel and 110 mm pipes

Strawberries growing in an NFT system on benches

Left: Strawberries in rockwool inserted into 120 mm pipes

Below: Strawberries in full PVC pipes

done in late winter to early spring. The tops of the roses are chopped off about 70 cm from the crown of the plant. The roots are pruned about one month prior to lifting by running a mechanical digger through the roses.

Once the plants are lifted and bare rooted they may be kept for about three to four weeks in cool storage prior to replanting. The bare rooted plants are dipped in a clay solution to seal them against drying out.

Planting Bare Rooted Roses

These are normally planted out in June to August (i.e. the most dormant period). Night temperatures should be around 16°C at the time of planting.
1. Place the roots in water for several hours prior to planting to remove old soil.
2. Prior to planting, the growing medium should be sterilised with dilute chlorine solution. Roses have a very shallow root system so they should not be planted too deeply since this can cause stem rot. The roots should be distributed evenly and not twisted.
3. Space the plants to allow for ease of flower picking and spraying. Plant spacing should also provide good air movement around the plant and light penetration. The most common planting distance is 30.5 cm × 30.5 cm, with three rows across the bed.
4. Immediately after planting feed the plants with nutrient solution.

Building Up New Plants

Normally greenhouse roses do not build up a permanent structure. Shoots, known as basal or water shoots, grow from the base of the plant and terminate in a flower. After flower removal a shoot develops from the apical bud; this normally produces a flower, and so the plant builds up height. New basal shoots are also developing concurrently, so that after two seasons the original shoot is pruned out.

The object of any rose planting is to produce three to five working canes per plant. The ability of the grower to get dormant buds to break and develop into strong canes determines his success with a new crop.

New plants are often set in a warm room (24°C) for three to four days. During this time the buds swell and new feeder roots will grow.

Many growers root prune new cuttings by trimming off the last 2–3 cm of the roots. The canes of started eyes are also pruned back to about 15 cm; plants with dormant eyes are left unpruned.

Overhead watering and foliar feeding will help develop top growth in newly planted bushes. A very wet growing media at this stage will result in poor root development and possible root diseases.

Crop support

Although roses have firm stems they still need extra support. Usually this is done by placing stakes at both ends of the beds, stretching wire down either side of the bed, and supporting these with occasional cross pieces in the bed.

New shoots need to be tucked in and the flowers regularly disbudded to leave the apically dominant bud.

Nutrition of greenhouse roses

A well-balanced complete nutrient is critical to maintain the fine balance of good foliage growth and flower bud initiation. Roses are heavy feeders and the nutrient solution should be fed to the plants on a regular basis to maintain a steady moisture and nutrient concentration.

Excessive levels of ammonia-type nitrogen will give rise to ammonium toxicity, while low very levels will produce short stems. Excessive levels of potassium will result in blotchiness and leaf tip burn. Boron deficiency will lead to malformed flower buds.

pH range

The optimum pH level of the nutrient solution or media is 6.2 and should be held within the limits of pH 5.5 to pH 6.5. If the pH rises above pH 6.5 then growth slows and iron deficiencies may become apparent.

Root Aeration

A vital consideration in any hydroponic rose production unit is the provision of good root aeration or drainage of the growing media. Good root aeration and drainage are not synonomous. Good drainage is the presence of air pockets between the particles of the growing media while good root aeration is the availability of dissolved oxygen in the nutrient solution around the roots of the plant. It is also important to maintain a consistent moisture content of the growing media otherwise the leaves will fall off prematurely.

Training Plants

The growth and early cropping will be determined by the training and pruning applied to the young plants. The recommended practice is to build up the plants during summer and autumn and cut down on the wood during winter and spring. To build up a plant for production all new growth should be pinched back to the second 5-leaflet leaf when buds appear.

Two-year-old budded bushes already have the main framework of branches. The bud union should be level with the growing medium or just below the surface of the medium. The main branches are shortened to four to six buds from their base and weak shoots are removed.

The first shoots to develop will tend to run to flower on relatively short shoots, therefore the flower buds should be removed as soon as they are visible to encourage branching and foliage development before flowering is established. One shoot, however, can be left to flower to confirm variety and colour and then cut back to half its length.

Pruning is carried out each time the flowers are cut. The usual method is to cut the stem leaving two 5-leaflet leaves on its originating shoot. However in summer the plant may grow too tall so occasionally the flower stem is cut to one or two buds below its originating point (undercutting the knuckle).

In good growing conditions weak shoots and blind shoots (i.e. stems without buds) should be cut back to stimulate stronger growth. Under conditions of low light as much foliage as possible should be kept on the plant.

Strong basal shoots on vigorous cultivars can produce long flowering shoots. The flower stem is cut back to about half its length and the next flower from that stem is delayed or it can be stopped when half grown and then cut to stimulate branching and the production of two blooms.

When the crop is grown for continuous flowering (using heating) it is best to prune back the plant in late February and early March to obtain a good flush of growth in autumn and early winter. If there is no heating then it is best to rest the crop by allowing the medium to dry out. Pruning can then be carried out to stimulate rapid growth and flowering in spring. The flushes induced will continue at about two monthly intervals throughout the season.

Cutting, Pinching, Pruning

Strong flowering stems last only one, or possibly two, years in good condition. They are usually replaced with strong growth (water shoots) growing from near the base of the plant. The water shoots are usually reddish in colour with brittle thorns and smooth bark. Older wood is grey-green or yellowish-green with light brown thorns and the bark is often rough and flaky. The older stems produce spindly growth and poor quality flowers. The main object of pruning is to rejuvenate the plant by removing these old, diseased and worn-out stems. This will encourage strong healthy new growth to form.

There are basically two types of buds: round buds (flower buds) and pointed buds (foliage buds). All pointed buds are removed, as well as blind or weak shoots.

There are a number of successful growers who practise green pruning at the same time as they cut the flowers. Green pruning is the practice of removing the tops of the plants to a point where cutting and pinching can once again manage plant growth. This prevents the plants from becoming dormant before an annual pruning, hence the plants do not suffer from the normal severe pruning. However, overall production may suffer.

Most growers, however, prune severely once a year and believe that this is giving them higher overall production, even though their downtime is longer.

Irrespective of the system used it is important to take careful note of when pruning is carried out, the temperature patterns, varietal responses, and the time it takes to get back into production, so that in future the grower will have a basis for predicting flowering schedules.

Pruning Miniature Roses

Miniature roses should be pruned while they are dormant in early to mid winter to shape the bush and to stimulate new fresh water stems. Hard pruning is recommended and the bush should be pruned between 4 cm and 6 cm from the top of the media. The stems are cut back to outward pointing buds, removing spindly or crossing branches.

A second pruning in summer (late February) is often recommended to promote the development of a second crop of flower buds and to keep the plant growing vigorously until autumn. This should be a light trim to remove spent flower heads and to tidy up the bush. Many growers constantly light prune as they pick the flowers. This helps to keep the plant vigorous and producing new flower buds.

Harvesting

In summer roses should be cut twice a day to ensure that no flowers will open on the plant and be lost. In winter the flowers are harvested every second day.

Yellow roses are picked in the tight bud stage; red and pink roses are usually harvested as the calyx reflexes below a horizontal position and the first two petals begin to unfold. White cultivars are usually harvested at a more open stage than other cultivars. If the flowers are cut while they are too immature, the heads can droop producing a symptom known as 'bent neck' and the flowers never straighten up.

Roses cut at the right stage should last five to seven days at 1°C and 80% relative humidity, or even longer depending on the variety. It is very important to remove the field heat and to cool them down quickly once they have been picked and placed in fresh water or preserving solution.

When cutting roses it is common to cut to the second 5-leaflet leaf on the new wood. This will assure you of another rose within about seven weeks from this cut. The hooks produced by this type of cutting can be removed by cutting below the hooks in late winter and spring. Alternatively some growers soft pinch all breaks as they appear and cut the rose back below the pinch. This will tend to give long stems and higher quality flowers, but at the expense of reduced production.

Yields

Cultivar yields should be measured in the number of saleable stems per square metre of crop area. Most greenhouse rose growers do not exceed 20 blooms per plant per year, or about 220 blooms per square metre based on spacings of 30 cm between plants in two rows.

Post harvest handling

The stage of development at which the flower is cut has an important bearing on the longevity of the flower and the customers' satisfaction. Harvesting the flowers too early can result in bent necks.

It is important to remove the field heat from the cut flowers as soon as possible after cutting. For extended storage the cooled flowers may be placed in an airtight container and held for two weeks at 1°C or until needed. The stems should be recut when grading.

It is important to grade the flowers for stem length and consistency of quality. If you set your own standards fairly high then you will have very few problems in marketing your roses. If you tend to be lax then you will suffer when supplies of roses are plentiful.

Hydroponic Culture

Roses differ to many other crops grown in hydroponics in that the plant may last up to five years or more in the system. Rockwool is generally considered the best system for commercial rose production, although other systems are used.

Growing Roses in Rockwool

Rockwool is considered to be one of the best systems to use for hydroponic rose production. It is relatively easy to set up, and because the plants are grown in the system for three to five years, the cost is comparable to most other media.

The rockwool system is based on striking roses on their own root system in rockwool propagation blocks. The blocks are then transplanted into wrapped cubes, which are placed on top of 75 mm thick rockwool slabs. Currently rockwool slabs with a depth of 100 mm are preferred.

Propagating roses on their own roots can give substantial benefits. Propagation can be done at any time of the year, hence planting can be scheduled to improve profitability. For example, replanting can be done during the spring flush in order for the plants to be in full production for winter. Other benefits are that it is a cheaper method of propagation compared to budding, and the possibility of virus transmission through the root stock is eliminated. Rockwool is also suitable for root zone warming which can be used to increase winter production.

Propagating with Rockwool

• Propagation is best done using the larger propagation blocks, e.g. Growool PB35-57.
• Wet the blocks with water, insert the cutting into the blocks, and place them direct on a sterilised sand bed with bottom heating.
• The propagation blocks are then misted or fogged automatically.
• The use of a balanced nutrient solution will assist the cutting in getting started.
• The propagation cube and cutting are transferred into the wrapped Growool cube WC75-H35.
• Continue growing on the cutting in the cube using overhead misting and bottom heating, until at least several roots have emerged.

Setting up

The following system is based on unwrapped rockwool slabs. It has been very successful because it allows the rockwool to drain freely but at the same time provides good moisture retention. The excess nutrient can be collected in a sump and reused.

1. The growing area is levelled with a slope to one end.
2. The soil base is formed into wide beds. Each bed is about 150 mm high with a flattened top and a trough down the middle.
3. A 2 m wide sheet of Panda plastic film (black and white plastic film) is laid on top of the bed.
4. A porous drainage pipe is laid in the trough. If bottom heating is to be used, black polypipes are laid on top of the panda film.
5. The drainage and heating pipes are covered with coarse gravel to a depth of abot 30 mm.
6. The unwrapped rockwool slabs are laid in two rows on top of the gravel. The remainder of the panda film is then pulled over the slabs, forming a long thin envelope.

Layout

A typical layout is based on a 900 mm wide bed with two rows of wrapped rockwool slabs separated by 150 mm space down the centre of the bed.
1. The rows of slabs are laid down the centre of the bed.
2. Cut a hole for each cube in the top of the slab.
3. Planting is usually five plants per slab; that is, two rows of plants (two plants on one side of the slab and three plants on the other side), planted at 250 mm intervals along the rows.
4. Set up the irrigation system allowing one dripper per plant.
5. Wet out the slab with diluted nutrient solution.
6. The nutrient solution is used at every irrigation. It is preferable to feed in small quantities at frequent intervals. In summer this may be four or more times each day.

While rockwool is sterile at the time of packaging, it can be contaminated unless some basic sanitary precautions are followed:
• Discard or destroy any diseased or doubtful plants.
• Disinfect all knives, secateurs, etc.
• Avoid contact with soil and store slabs in a dry place off the ground.
• Sterilise all potentially infected feed water.
• Set up the growing area to avoid pooling of waste nutrient.

The same precautions apply to any other media that the grower intends using in a hydroponic system.

Other systems

Most other hydroponic systems use beds filled with media, and the nutrient solution is not recirculated.

Flood and Drain Systems

Flood and drain systems are not popular in Australia because of the problems that can occur from the spread of diseases. The other problem that flood and drain systems have is that they require large holding and storage tanks. To effectively flood a single bed requires a solution which is at least half the volume of the bed. Hence a bed 1 m wide, 50 m long and 20 cm deep will require a minimum of 5000 litres of nutrient solution for about 500 plants. In order to fill a bed of this size about 10 cubic metres of media such as gravel (about 15 tonnes of gravel), or about 150 tonnes for only ten beds will be required. As can be seen from these figures the volume of nutrient solution required and the physical labour involved is considerable compared to the use of rockwool or other media. The nutrient solution is usually dumped every six to eight weeks.

Run to Waste Systems

Growing media used in non-recirculating systems include rockwool, scoria, potting mixes, sand, gravel and perlite. The medium must be free draining, provide good root aeration, and have a good water-holding capacity. Miniature roses do best in a minimum of 2 litres of growing medium.

The beds are formed using polystyrene vegetable boxes or plastic growing pillows; alternatively long growing beds are used. Beds have a major advantage over other containers because they provide more consistent moisture levels. However long beds tend to have wet spots, resulting in uneven growth. A good length for the bed is usually about 10 m, depending on the evenness of the ground or the slope of the bed.

The bottom of the bed or container should be closed off and drainage holes placed 1–2 cm from the bottom to assist nutrient spread. One to two drippers or micro sprays are connected to each box or container.

Regular watering and feeding is essential, especially over summer. Any period of dryness will affect flowering and result in reduced growth and plant vigour. At each watering and feeding there should be a small excess of diluted nutrient allowed to go to waste (normally about 5%).

Nutrient Flow System

Few growers have tried growing roses in NFT without a media, and it certainly would not be recommended. The reasons are very simple:
• the root system is fibrous so the plants require a supportive medium;
• the pump would have to be operating most of the day which would make the operation very costly.

In comparison, media-based systems provide a number of advantages:
• the rose plant is long-lived so the medium is a very small part of the overall cost;
• a medium gives the grower more control over the watering, feeding, pH and root aeration;
• the maintenance costs of media-based systems are lower.

Cultural Problems

Roses are susceptible to the same pests and diseases in hydroponics as they are in soil. Aphids and thrips in particular can severely affect flowering so both should be controlled as soon as they are noticed. The diseases which can affect roses are Anthracnose, black spot, downy mildew, grey mould, powdery mildew, Verticillium wilt and wilt virus.

13 Strawberries

Strawberries are one of the most popular hydroponic crops. Compared to soil-grown strawberries, hydroponic growers find they can manage a much larger number of plants; the fruit stays clean because it is away from the soil; the fruit is easy to harvest because the plants are raised to a convenient height; spraying and cleaning up the crop is simplified; and the system can be controlled to give an extended picking season.

Strawberries offer quick returns on capital outlay. In particular, out-of-season fruit, which is produced between March and May, attracts very high prices. Most of the fruit produced is consumed as fresh fruit on the domestic market, and about 4 percent is used for processing. Australia is currently importing in excess of 2000 tons per year of processing grade strawberries.

While there are benefits to be gained from growing strawberries in hydroponics, new growers should be aware that it is a demanding occupation, both time and expense-wise. The grower must outlay a lot of money in purchasing and caring for the plants before they come into production.

Many growers experience problems because they do not understand the crop. The commercial strawberry is a highly bred plant selected for particular environments and growing habits; hence a certain level of expertise is required to successfully manage the crop. The growers' problems are also partly due to a lack of information about the techniques involved and the growth habits of specific varieties, particularly the more recently introduced Californian varieties.

Another problem is that many growers have copied other systems without any real understanding of the limitations and advantages of the system. Frequently this leads to disaster because they have not learnt the techniques required to manage the system. Like so many things in life the successful grower makes it look simple because he has learnt to manage his crop.

Cropping Habits

If you understand your plant you have a much better chance of producing high yields and good quality strawberries. Amateur growers can allow their plants to fruit at will, but professional commercial growers must plan and schedule their operations to achieve maximum cropping of good quality fruit to coincide with high market prices.

During summer, runners develop on the plant and roots form at the nodes. The runners are used as planting material. However, if the grower is looking to increase yields they should be removed so that the plant's energy is pushed into producing fruit for as long as possible.

Fruiting normally occurs in flushes from May through to February but the experienced grower, using a good nutrient, can reduce these flushes and have continuous cropping.

When the climatic conditions are hotter the cropping season tends to be shorter. Hence polyhouse protection, shading and climatic control during the hotter parts of the year can extend the cropping period.

Plant Development

Most varieties of strawberries are short day flowering plants. In other words cool temperatures and short hours of daylight induce flower bud formation and presage the onset of dormancy.

The main growing axis is a short stem, bearing leaves at the nodes and a bud in the axil of each leaf. As the daylight hours shorten to 11–13 hours per day many of the buds in the leaf axils turn into flower buds. The larger the size of the plant in autumn, the more flower clusters and fruit are produced next spring due to the extra sites for fruit induction. Flower trusses are initiated terminally but are displaced as new terminal buds are initiated. The length of the fruit stems tends to be shorter in autumn and longer in spring. In most varieties the later flowers do not develop into fruit because they are predominantly male flowers.

Differences in the size of the fruit are due to the number or seeds (or achenes) per fruit. Under conditions of poor pollination caused by frost damage, lack of bees, too much rain when the fruit is setting, or a nutrient deficiency, the fruit may become distorted and misshapen. The presence of the developing achenes is necessary to stimulate fruit growth and enlargement of the fruit.

Root development in soil-grown plants takes place mainly in autumn and spring when the water demand is at its lowest. In hydroponics the root system and the crown will continue to develop into late autumn and early winter because the system tends to retain more warmth. If the root system is kept cooler as summer approaches then fruiting will continue and the development of runners slowed.

While the plant normally has a dormancy period, a number of growers have the expertise to make their plants produce well past their normal seasonal production periods.

Temperature and Daylength

Most of the popular varieties prefer temperate conditions and have a chilling requirement which ensures growth and flowering occurs in an even cycle. If the plant's chilling requirement is not met excessive foliage may be produced at the expense of flowers and crop yields will generally suffer.

The period from first blossom to first ripe fruit is about 30 days, but will take longer at lower temperatures. The fruit generally has better flavour when the days are sunny and the nights are cool.

The firmness of the fruit changes during the season. Fruit grown at lower temperatures (i.e. 16°C to 20°C) is firmer and has better storage characteristics than fruit grown later in the season. Warm rainy weather also causes fruit to soften as the berries absorb water through the skin.

The mechanism for flower initiation is very complex, being both temperature and daylength dependent. Under warm or hot conditions, e.g. 27°C to 35°C, flowering will be inhibited regardless of daylength. Hence unusually warm winter periods can cause the plant to vegetate instead of forming flower buds with the result that the spring and summer yields may be reduced.

Varieties

Selecting the best cultivar depends primarily on local knowledge and trialling, the genetic makeup of the plant, and the microclimate of the growing area. Other factors to consider are yield, fruit size, flavour, seasonality, skin colour, disease resistance, handling and storage qualities and market requirements.

Most commercial strawberry cultivars are short day plants, i.e. flower bud initiation is induced by short days of less than 12 hours. In general, short day cultivars are more vegetative than the day neutral varieties, and have a tendency to produce more runners when daylength exceeds 12 hours under warm conditions. They respond to supplementary chilling for 2 weeks at 1°C. Short day varieties include Tioga, Torrey, Pajora and Earlisweet, which produce mainly in spring and early summer.

Day neutral varieties produce flowers, fruit and runners simultaneously, regardless of daylength provided the temperature remains reasonably stable. Cropping is generally continuous from spring through to autumn with several peak production periods occurring during the season. Under most temperature and light conditions they bloom and fruit on a six week cycle. From mid summer to early autumn flower production is poor.

In the first season, day neutral varieties will often flower without rooting and will not become dormant until short day conditions prevail, providing temperatures are favourable. At a mean temperature of 21°C flower bud formation is unaffected by daylength. They do not perform well when night temperatures exceed 23°C, or when day temperatures exceed 26°C. Smaller fruit may be produced in summer—this is directly related to high root zone temperatures. Some popular day neutral varieties are Selva, Tribute, Fern, Brighton and Aptos.

Long day varieties, also known as everbearers, flower in response to long daylength and generally produce few runners. They tend to produce a double crop or two harvesting periods, one in spring and the other in late summer to early winter. The combined yield is slightly less than the single season crop produced by the short day varieties. However, the returns may be greater because of higher market prices. Some long day varieties are Red Gauntlet, Tribute, Tristar, Ostara and Rabunda. In general they do not perform well in northern NSW and Queensland.

Torrey and Tioga are the most favoured varieties in coastal regions and some inland areas. Red Gauntlet is generally accepted as the best variety for tableland districts. The important varieties in Queensland are Tioga, Early Sweet and Queensland Red. Victorian growers prefer Tioga, Red Gauntlet and Torrey. There has been a growing interest in the Californian varieties such as Parker and Pajora.

Redland Crimson and Earlisweet are winter and spring bearers in southern Queensland, while the southern varieties produce fruit at other times of the year.

Some growers plant a mixture of varieties to spread out their harvesting period, but there are other ways of achieving the same ends. It is an advantage to grow both short day and day neutral varieties, provided conditions are suitable because the harvesting period can be extended.

Newer Varieties

Aptos

Aptos is a day neutral variety. Fresh runners tend to produce a compact bush while cooled stored plants produce a larger bush with more runners and delayed fruiting. The early fruit tend to ripen unevenly. The fruit can be damaged by rain and heat.

The fruit is produced about three months after planting and is borne continuously on a cyclical basis throughout summer and autumn. The fruit is firm, durable, medium to long, and blunt to ovoid to wedge shaped.

Pajaro

Pajaro is one of the most popular newer varieties. It is a short day variety and a late season producer. It has an extended fruiting pattern and produces consistent quality fruit. The flowers are highly self-fertile with ample pollen produced throughout the season.

The fruit are medium to long, conical-shaped, almost always smooth, usually hollow centred, and the primaries are frequently wedged in various degrees. The fruit skin colour is distinctly redder and darker than Tioga. The finish is particularly glossy and attractive with a tendency to light shoulder colour early in the season. The flesh colour is about the same as the skin, ranging to a lighter centre. It is a good fruit for shipping.

Summer planting produces high fruit yields in the following spring in southern Queensland.

Early fruiting due to early planting can produce fruit which has a white shoulder and fruit tip breakdown can occur. The plant produces a small bush and the fruit is susceptible to scorching and rain damage.

Parker

Parker is a popular short day plant which is usually grown for mid-season picking. It is a cross between Douglas and Tufts and is one of the parents of Pajaro.

Bushes are vigorous and open and plants will require wider spacing to allow for this vigour. Yields tend to be fairly good and plants have performed exceptionally well in winter planting as they produce late-season fruit.

The flowers are self-fertile but some of the early fruit tend to be malformed. The fruit is long and conical-shaped to long, flat and wedge-shaped, and varies in size throughout the season. The fruit is solid throughout, with a slightly darker colour than Tioga. The flesh is the same colour as the skin. Because the fruit are large and firm they are easy to pick, but they tend to be inconsistent in shape and may be difficult to pack into punnets.

The fruit is susceptible to rain damage. The plants tend to have fewer mite problems compared to other varieties.

Selva

Selva is a weak day neutral variety which is planted in late spring, summer and winter. It is an early producer and is less vigorous than some of the other varieties, although fruiting will commence about three months after planting provided satisfactory conditions prevail. The flowers are self-fertile with ample pollen throughout the season, hence there are few deformed fruit.

The fruit is firm and ranges in size from medium to long. The shape is conical, although some are flat and wedge-shaped, and have a lower moisture content. They are borne on a single stem well out from the plant, which allows for ease of picking. The fruit are much larger than Tioga and are borne in a range of sizes as the season advances.

The cool stored plants are planted in January to February, while the fresh runners are planted in mid March. The plants are more resistant to spring heat and rain than Aptos and can tolerate spring heat in northern NSW. However they are susceptible to powdery mildew and spotted mites. The early flowers are sometimes removed to improve fruit quality.

Toro

Toro is a short day variety which produces a medium-sized bush. The fruit tend to be soft, dark orange rather than deep red, and the flavour is average. Fruit is held away from the plant and is subject to weather damage.

Planting Material

The crop is started from fresh runners or cool stored frozen runners. Cool stored frozen runners are mature runners which are kept in the ground after completion of fresh runner digging. The dormant runners are dug up from the soil in late autumn or early winter and wrapped and stored at –1°C until required for planting out.

Cool stored runners are usually planted in summer to autumn, i.e. January through to May, although they can be planted at any suitable time. The first yield is usually light and occurs about five weeks after planting. Some growers deliberately time their planting to give a small late crop in late summer to early autumn. However, the main crop occurs in spring from well-developed crowns after a winter dormancy period.

The plants tend to produce a lot of runners in the first season, and these should be removed as soon as they occur.

There is an optimum period of freezing or cool storage for each variety that will return the highest yields. Fruit size may initially be high but fruit numbers may be lower when excessive cool storage has occurred.

Fresh runners are only available in early to late autumn for immediate planting. They have the advantage of producing a better developed crown which will give heavier early fruiting in late winter to early spring of high quality strawberries (that is, provided the crowns have time to develop before the onset of winter).

In Queensland runners are dug from mid-March to supply growers in warm sub-tropical areas. These plants are relatively immature and have a relatively low chilling requirement. Red Gauntlet or Earlisweet are often supplied in this way.

Victorian runners are generally dug later (in about mid to late April) and can be planted out in the warm coastal areas of NSW to produce out-of-season winter and early spring crops.

Opinions differ on which planting stock is better—fresh or cool stored runners—but frequently it is a matter of availability. Most suppliers have limited stocks and orders must be placed up to a year in advance for fresh runners.

Climatic variations from year to year can delay the harvesting of the runners, hence delays in replanting are common. A delay of up to one month can reduce the total yield by as much as 45 percent.

It is very important to select and use only good

healthy runners with a well developed root system and crown. The first and second plants on each runner are preferred as planting material.

Virus diseases can cause havoc to a crop, both in terms of plant growth and fruit production. The cost of the runners is a small part of the overall cost of producing strawberries and the extra cost of buying good quality certified virus free plants is far outweighed by the cost of bringing them into production. It is important to be ruthless in culling plants which do not grow actively in the early stages. In fact, some growers grow extra runners in a separate nursery area to replace those plants which are slow to start.

Planting

After delivery, fresh runners must be kept cool and moist (but not wet) and planted out as soon as possible. Cool stored runners should be allowed to thaw slowly and planted out within two days. The soil is removed from the roots and the strawberry runners are washed in an appropriate fungicide and insecticide.

Strawberries which are planted early (before March) tend to continue growing vegetatively and are often slow to come into bearing. Late planted strawberries also give reduced yields because they make little growth before winter or the onset of dormancy.

Grading strawberry plants for size before planting will assist in producing a uniform stand and consistent yields. Strawberries planted with their crown too high will be slow to take and will develop poorly. If planted too low, crown and stem rot may occur.

Planting out should never take place when the days are hot or in conditions of low humidity (hot dry winds). Lack of water at this stage or uneven watering can be responsible for uneven stands of plants. This often happens where a pipe system is used that has an excessive slope. In systems involving intermittent feeding it is preferable to give short, regular feeds.

Ratooning

Ratooning has been practised with some success, particularly in cooler areas. It involves cutting back the plant just above the crown in March and carrying the plant through the dormant season to obtain a second season of production.

Ratooned crops begin bearing earlier than newly planted strawberries but the fruit is generally smaller. Hence growers with an interest in the early market retain a section of their more vigorous plants into the second year. In many cases ratooned plants produce better crops in the second year because they have well developed crowns. They can also produce flushes when there are market shortages.

The ability to retain plants into their second year is largely dependent on the hydroponic system used. Most continuous nutrient flow systems do not lend themselves to retaining their plants for more than one season.

Hydroponic Culture

There are many different systems used for strawberry production. The pipe system using rockwool blocks, the half-pipe using an inert media, and the hanging bags are the most popular methods. However, the NFT system using the 50 cm by 100 cm rectangular pipe (or more recently the rectangular channels with removable lids) is gaining popularity. There are a number of successful growers using each system.

Expertise is required for growing strawberries in each of these systems and there is a lack of understanding on the part of many growers about the plant itself and the system that they are using.

The major consideration in the design of any system is the degree of aeration around the root zone in conjunction with adequate water and nutrients. Plants will grow in water provided that the water or nutrient solution contains high levels of dissolved oxygen. However, many growers pump air into their system needlessly. In all recirculation systems it is important to pump air into the nutrient solution to remove the carbon dioxide given off by the root system and replace the oxygen used by the roots or lost from solution. However, in non-recirculating systems, with or without a growing medium, the dissolved oxygen comes from allowing the medium to dry out slightly, hence pumping air into the nutrient is largely ineffective. High nutrient solution temperatures reduce the dissolved oxygen content dramatically once the temperatures start to exceed 25°C.

The system design must also take into account the ease of harvesting and spraying of the crop. The spacing of the plants is important because if they are too close harvesting and spraying will be more difficult, and overall yields will be reduced as the plants compete for light and aerated nutrient. The benching used is also important in these operations. While benches prevent the need for bending over, picking and spraying can be difficult because one has to lean over the bench to pick from underneath the plant or spray under the leaves. In practice, if space is not limited single row plantings, such as individual pipes supported on posts, has given the best results for ease of picking and spraying.

The use of channels or pipes supported on an A frame also separates the plants and gives better visibility of the fruit and improved ability to spray under the leaves when required.

The system design must also allow for the development of a healthy root system. If the plants are planted too close together, the roots will intertwine and interfere with the uptake of nutrients and the availability of oxygen to the plants' roots.

Hanging bags

The typical hanging bag system consists of black irrigation fluming suspended from a strong trellis. It is operated as a run to waste system, with the nutrient being fed through one or more drippers placed at the top, and sometimes another dripper half way down the bag. The plants are fed on a regular intermittent cycle, possibly four times per day for short periods, depending on the growing medium used.

It is one of the cheapest systems to set up but it probably accounts for the highest failure rates in growing hydroponic strawberries because many growers fail to understand the technique.

The hanging bag system involves the use of a polythene sock, about 900 mm to 1200 mm long and 150 mm diameter, filled with growing medium and suspended from an overhead wire (e.g. barbed wire) strung between posts. The strawberry plants are inserted into holes in the side of the sock and the nutrient solution is drip fed into the top of the sock. Some growers insert another dripper into the middle of the bag.

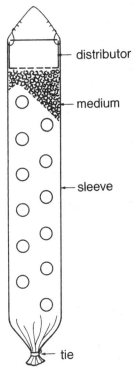

Hanging bag system. This system is widely used for growing strawberries in hydroponics.

The end posts used to support the overhead wires must be reinforced and braced to take the weight of the bags and the medium. Wet weather can cause the foundations of the posts and the bracing to give way and the system to crumble into a heap.

The choice of growing medium is critical and governs the feeding or watering technique used. Peat moss and broken polystyrene pieces are the most commonly used media. This gives a light-weight bag with good waterholding capacity and drainage. A lightweight potting type mix can also be used.

Trials conducted on granulated rockwool have proved it to be an exceptionally good growing medium when mixed with a water repellent rock-wool. Enviropeat, made from crushed coconut shells, is also giving good results.

The bags must be packed down firmly to prevent air pockets forming. If the medium is loosely packed, after a short period the medium will compact and the upper strawberries will be left hanging in the bag without any growing medium around their roots. Air pockets will also cause channelling of the nutrient, which means that some plants will be watered and fed while others die because they have dried out.

The length of the bag depends on the grower's preference, however the normal length is about 1.2 metres. Some growers prefer the shorter bags because they claim that they achieve more even moisture levels in the bag. My preference is for the longer bags with a drainage channel in the middle. The longer bags can rest on the ground, hence taking most of the weight of the bag. The choice of media is important because it controls the final wet weight of the hanging bag. Most new growers are astonished at the final weight of the bag once the growing media has been wetted. Hence the support system for the bags or socks must be very strong. I have seen a number of these systems collapse under the weight of the bags.

Some growers also prefer short bags because they are easier to fill and handle. Although it looks easy, filling the bags is a very time consuming procedure.

A major advantage of the hanging bag system is that it can give rise to very high density of plants in any given area, hence it is usually associated with the use of a polyhouse or igloo. Also the establishment costs are generally about half that compared to the PVC channelling, although long term costs (over ten years) tend to be comparable.

Some of the problems encountered in this system include uneven growth caused by:

a) uneven lighting when the bags are placed too close together.
b) dry patches in the bags due to uneven watering and channelling of the solution through the bags.
c) uneven moisture in the bag due to drainage problems (dry at the top of the bag and wet or soggy at the bottom).
d) inconsistent planting depth of the young plants.

The bags or socks are fed with drippers once or twice a day, using very slow drippers to replace the water and nutrients used by the plants, plus a slight excess which is allowed to go to waste. The feeding cycle is dependent on the growing medium used. For example, a medium based on 80% polystyrene and 20% perlite or peat moss requires feeding about five to six

times per day for short periods (depending on the temperature and the humidity). This medium drains freely and overcomes the problem of variations in moisture content through the bag. It is a very lightweight medium which can be dried out by the plants quickly. Hence short regular feeds are important. However, it is an awkward medium to plant into.

A medium containing 34% perlite, 33% peat moss and 33% polystyrene is easier to plant in and requires fewer feeding cycles but tends to have a greater variation in moisture content through the bag (i.e. moist at the bottom and dry at the top). It also tends to pack down with time.

A potting mix medium requires fewer feeding cycles, is heavier, holds moisture better, and is easier to plant into. However, it is more prone to an uneven moisture content, and is more likely to cause salt buildup at the crown of the plant.

Most books recommend a regular water flush instead of feeding or as part of the feed cycle to remove salt buildup. If it is part of the feed cycle it does not make sense, because the same effect is obtained by using a more dilute nutrient feed every time. In experimental work, it was found that exceptional results were obtained by making up the nutrient solution regularly and in the meantime allowing the nutrient tank level to be maintained by the addition of fresh water. This system is based on providing the plants with a fixed amount of nutrient per week, such as 1 gram per plant per week (or demand feeding). This eliminated the buildup of salts around the crown of the plant. Commonsense tells you that the water flush will go though the medium without removing the salts from the crown of the plants. What is needed is to work from the outside; hence spraying the plants with water (especially around the crown) on a regular basis, such as once a month, will wash the salts off the crown of the plant and send it back into the media. In addition spraying will help control red spider mites. If the bags are outside the rain will carry out this function for you, but beware of the long dry periods because you will have to do it yourself.

The quantity of nutrient solution that is allowed to go to waste depends on the water quality used. The major problem encountered with the use of the bag system is unevenness of nutrient solution held at different sections of the bags, e.g. the top dries out quickly while the bottom tends to remain wet. This is overcome to some extent by using an inner pipe for drainage.

Recently a technique has been developed which gives a more consistent moisture content through the bags. This involves the use of a container with small holes drilled into the base and placed at the top of the bags. The container holds the nutrient and gradually allows it to drip evenly onto the media between feedings. This is equivalent to a continuous very slow feed system.

Pipes and Rockwool

This system involves the use of a full PVC pipe (110 mm, 125 mm or 150 mm diameter) in which large holes have been cut out to hold a block of rockwool in which the strawberry plant is inserted. The system is basically a flood and drain technique in which the pipe is slowly flooded and the solution is allowed to drain away. This procedure may be repeated once, twice, or even three times per day depending on the demands of the plant and the ambient temperature and humidity.

Each plant is grown in its own block of rockwool, which is typically $75 \times 75 \times 125$ mm high. The system uses a PVC pipe with a minimum diameter of 110 mm, and holes 75 mm diameter are drilled into the top of the pipe at the preferred spacing (150 mm to 200 mm) apart. The pipe is supported on a post and held by a bracket at shoulder height. The slope of the pipe is not critical, but most are almost level. This allows the grower to flood the pipe with water, if needed, to flush out salts. The length of each run may be up to 24 m, although 18 m is common.

The nutrient solution is pumped from a holding tank into the top end of the pipe and the outflow is returned to the tank. The nutrient solution is pumped for about 15 to 20 minutes to flood the pipe to about half full. With small plants and in cool weather the solution may be pumped once or twice a day. As the plants get larger or with the onset of warmer weather the frequency may be increased up to five or more times per day.

Some growers have been operating these systems for a number of years and all the systems are still operating successfully.

Technique

A standard rockwool slab is cut up into blocks measuring about 75 mm square. The height of the block should be about 1 cm above the top of the pipe. The block of rockwool is opened up and the strawberry plant inserted. The block is then inserted into the hole in the pipe. The length of each row may be two, three or even four pipe lengths, with a very slight slope or fall.

The separation or spacing of the plants depends on the grower, however it is normally about 150 mm. With a pipe size of 100 mm the distance between the plants is about 175 mm–200 mm. With the 90 mm pipe, the distance between plants should be increased to 200 mm–250 mm. With the 120 mm pipe or the 150 mm pipe the distance between plants is about 150 mm although some growers plant at spacings of 100 mm. Obviously the closer the spacing, the larger the number of plants that can be put into the system. However, if the spacing is too close then the plants will become leggy as they reach for light, and yields and fruit size are usually reduced. It is generally preferable to space the plants as far as possible apart. The spacing required for the smaller diameter pipes is usually further apart than for the larger diameter pipes.

The pipes are usually supported on metal posts or pipes with a support bracket on top. These posts are usually about 1.5 m above the ground and form a single row. It has been found that two rows close together causes problems when spraying and harvesting. The spacing of the rows is important for ease of spraying and harvesting especially when these activities are carried out in the morning and the plants are covered in dew.

The amount of rockwool used per plant is important because the root system grows within the rockwool and into the nutrient solution at the bottom of the pipe. As the roots of the strawberries strike the sides of the rockwool block they tend to be air pruned. If the rockwool block is too small, the root system is restricted. The height of the rockwool block is important because of its drainage and aeration characteristics. The taller the block then the better is the root aeration. If the rockwool extends too high above the pipe, salt buildup tends to occur around the crown of the plant and the plant can suffer from excess salt accumulation, resulting in burning of the crown and subsequent loss of the crop.

The system is flushed with fresh water or nutrient solution at low concentrations every few weeks, particularly if the weather has been hot and dry. Since rockwool is very prone to develop salt buildup on top of the rockwool and around the crown of the plant it is preferable to spray the plants and the rockwool with water.

The washing procedure has one other major advantage in that it can help control the pH of the rockwool. Some growers have found that the nutrient squeezed from the rockwool can have a very different pH (usually higher pH) than the nutrient solution. When they find that this is happening they frequently reduce the pH of the nutrient solution to about pH 5.0 to correct the pH of the rockwool block. Hence if you use this system it is wise to not only test the pH of the nutrient solution but also the nutrient solution in the rockwool block.

Plants in the pipe and rockwool system are normally replaced every two years and the system is maintained during the dormancy of the plant using very low strength nutrient solutions, hence operating costs are low during this period.

Pipes and Pots

This system is very similar to the use of the rockwool in that the 100 mm holes are cut into a pipe such as the 110 mm PVC pipe. Instead of inserting rockwool, a nursery pot is filled with a growing medium such as gravel or a similar support medium, and the pot is inserted into the pipe.

The major problem with this system is that the vigorous root system of the strawberry tends to fill the pot and the plant becomes root bound just when it is producing fruit. The selection of the pot is therefore critical to the success of the system. There are some new pots on the market which have slits cut out of the sides. This allows the root system to grow out of the pot and hence improves root aeration and feeding.

Although this system is very similar to the pipe and rockwool system, the growers leave the nutrient solution in the pipes at all times (although they usually have techniques for controlling the height or amount that remains in the pipe).

Three or five pipes are placed across the bench. Some growers have tiered the pipes for ease of picking and spraying. The length of the system may be up to 18 m or three pipes long. The standard pipes used are the 100 mm and the 90 mm pipes.

The gravel used for these systems is very coarse (5–10 mm diameter). The spacing of these plants in the pipes is similar to those using rockwool, i.e. the plants are 200 mm apart in the 100 mm or 90 mm pipes. Some growers are trialing spacings of 150 mm.

Some growers also use this system for growing lettuce in the off season when the strawberries have finished fruiting.

Half-pipe and media

This system is similar to that used for lettuce. The system uses 100 mm pipes cut in half and filled with a medium-sized gravel (8–10 mm diameter). Nutrient solution is pumped into the top end of the pipe. The flow is stopped after 10 or 15 minutes to drain, and the flow is then started up again. The slope of the channels is critical.

The system works well when the plants are small, but as the root system increases the drainage becomes slower. In hot weather the plants usually suffer severely. Another problem with the use of the half pipe is that the stalk of the plant can be cut or damaged by the sharp edges of the pipe, especially the fruit stalks loaded with fruit. The damage to the stalk may cut off the food supply to the leaf or to the fruit. Also fungal diseases are caused by the leaves and fruit touching the moist growing medium.

I have seen a number of these systems in operation but there are very few successful growers using the system. The system does work under certain conditions. One of the major problems is the use of gravel as the growing medium. The growing medium used is frequently coarse gravel. Gravel tends to become very hot and can burn the roots of the plant, giving rise to leaf tipburn, reduced yields, and increased root diseases. Scoria or volcanic rock is a good growing medium that holds water, gives good drainage, but remains cooler on hot days.

While the half pipe sounds as though it would be cheaper than using a full pipe it does not usually work out this way because the plants need to be spaced much further apart and more framework is required to grow the same number of plants. This system is designed for replanting runners each season and it is difficult to continue growing for more than one season.

In the past, some very large ventures used wrapped rockwool slabs as the growing medium. The ventures were not very successful because of a number of problems such as poor air movement in the polyhouses, poor root aeration, and insufficient expertise in operating the system. One of the problems was the basic nutrient used was not designed correctly.

NFT System

Some growers have experimented with the nutrient flow technique using the 100 mm x 50 mm PVC downpipe. The roots of the plant are inserted into a hole on the topside of the pipe, and the nutrient solution flows through the pipe on a continuous basis. Some growers have used controllers to control the pH and conductivity but most have opted for manual control and adjustment on a daily basis.

This system is currently in vogue in certain areas. However, the design of the system leaves a lot to be desired. The major problem is that the downpipe channels are placed across a bench, thus causing problems when spraying the plant with insecticides or fungicides, and even more importantly, when picking the strawberries. While the bench or tables at first sight seem good they are not very practical. The other problem is that it is difficult to support the plant properly so that wind does not blow the plant out of the channel, or so that the crown does not fall into the channel.

To overcome this problem, many growers tape the plants into the hole; however, the use of Gromesh—an open weave polyester material— has been found to be easier and less laborious. The material is wrapped around the roots up to the crown of the plant. The plant is then inserted into the hole (45 mm diameter) in the pipe. Some growers prefer to use the material in conjuction with NFT cups: the plant is wrapped in Gromesh and is then inserted into an NFT cup prior to clipping the cup into the pipe. This ensures that the plants are held firmly in place and at the correct planting depth.

A major shortcoming of the use of channels on benches is that the system is very expensive and the payback period tends to be very long. As with any nutrient flow system without the use of a medium, the pump must be operated all day resulting in large electrical bills. The loss of plants from crown rot seems to be much higher than for most of the other systems. Currently the cost of the rectangular channels is almost twice the price of the conventional round pipes. Joining pipes is also more difficult (they are more prone to leakages).

Inclined vertical pipes

This system consists of a series of pipes inclined vertically on an A frame and held between two horizontal pipes. The inclined pipes are usually 100 mm in diameter and have about six smaller pipes (of 50 mm diameter) inserted vertically into them to hold the plant. The plant is planted into a piece of rockwool or Gromesh, which is inserted into the smaller pipe. The nutrient solution is trickle fed from the top horizontal pipe, the solution flows down the inside of the vertical pipe, and is collected and returned to the nutrient tank by the bottom horizontal pipe. The system is recirculating and must be operated continuously; hence electricity usage is high.

Every pipe has a small feeder tube at the top. The feeder tubes are prone to blockages and a good in-line filter is essential.

After the strawberry plant has been inserted into the rockwool and then into its pipe, the rockwool must be wet out thoroughly and must never be allowed to dry out since it is difficult to rewet effectively with such a small nutrient flow.

This is a very compact but expensive system. It is usually set up in a polyhouse for protection against the elements and to provide some environmental control.

Horizontal A frame

This system consists of four horizontal pipes on each side of a galvanised angle iron A frame. The length of the pipes may be 18 or even 24 m long. The pipes have very little slope and the nutrient solution is pumped through the system intermittently (30 minutes on and 30 minutes off). The strawberry plants are inserted into a column of rockwool about 3 to 4 cm in diameter, which then fit into a small plastic tube which is inserted into the 100 mm round pipe.

The nutrient flow rate is fairly high, e.g. 5 litres per minute. The level of nutrient in the pipe is about 2.5 cm. Because of its design the growool is designed to drain freely, preventing excessive wetting of the growool blocks.

This is a very compact system which can be readily enclosed in a polyhouse or similar structure. The system allows the harvester to pick very quickly because the fruit hangs freely to the front. Spraying is also simplified in that it is easy to spray the underside of the leaves from behind.

Nutrients

The nutrient required by strawberry plants is a fine balance between a flowering and fruiting nutrient and a foliage development nutrient. If the nutrient is incorrectly formulated the plants can be forced into dormancy.

Many growers fall into the trap of believing that the plant must be big and healthy with a lot of foliage growth. A plant with a large amount of foliage will produce large fruit, but this is nearly always at the expense of yields. Vegetative (leafy) strawberry plants tend to produce fewer flowers and hence the plant's energy goes into a few fruit, which tend to be soft and easily damaged.

The strawberry plant is selective about the type and amount of nutrients it absorbs through the roots. The uptake of nutrients from the solution is not determined by the concentration alone but is closely controlled by the specific requirements as the plant grows.

While the strawberry plants will grow over a wide range of nutrient mixes, the best nutrient is one which does not get out of balance easily. An inferior nutrient formulation can result in lower yields, poor growth or excessively heavy foliage growth, and excessive nutrient wastage.

Many growers, both new and old, believe that it is cheaper to make up their own nutrient. If you look only at the components this is sometimes the case. However, if you take into account the technology of the blending and evaluating different nutrient combinations, the time wasted in weighing and the possibility of errors with

some ad hoc formulation, then the additional cost of a reputable commercial nutrient is minimal. Most reputable suppliers also provide a backup service in case the grower has any problems. Experience has shown that growers who experiment with nutrition pay a heavy price for any improvements and that greater rewards can be obtained by attending to other factors such as production and marketing.

Nutrient concentration

Strawberries have a reasonably heavy demand for nutrients and under cooler conditions concentrations may be of the order of 3000 ppm of dissolved solids. Most growers tend to run their systems at about 1800 ppm. This may be increased when conditions are cooler and more stable or reduced when temperatures are higher and humidity is lower. Under hot dry conditions the nutrient strength should be reduced to about 1500 ppm to avoid tip burn and dry fruit.

Very low nutrient concentrations, i.e. 600 ppm, are fed to dormant plants and plants which are held over from one season to the next. Under these conditions the plants do not grow but remain viable.

The most important test is nutrient concentration or conductivity. On hot and windy days plants will use more water than nutrients and the conductivity will increase, hence it is wise to operate at a lower conductivity level. On cooler days, plants tend to use more nutrient than water hence the conductivity falls, and growers operate at a higher conductivity level.

pH range

With a good nutrient the pH remains relatively constant. In many cases, growers tend to ignore pH almost entirely, because constant pH adjustments create more problems than they cure. Strawberries can tolerate a range of pH levels, but when the nutrient solution becomes acidic (below 5.0) leaf symptoms indicative of magnesium deficiency may appear. If the pH rises above 6.5 to 7.0, symptoms of iron deficiency may occur.

Harvesting

If you intend going into hydroponic strawberry growing, it is important to remember that marketing and presentation is of major importance. Most new growers forget that while growing the strawberries and harvesting is only a small part of the operation it is a very important part.

Small strawberries take much longer to harvest and pack than the larger strawberries and generally do not bring the higher prices; hence the smaller strawberries are less profitable.

Packing the strawberries is a large part of the overall operation and is very labour intensive, particularly grading the fruit.

Strawberries also present a problem in that they are seasonal and the markets established may not be there the following season. Queensland is the first state to supply the market and its season extends from June to November. New South Wales follows and extends from August to late December, with a small autumn crop from March to May. Victoria, South Australia and Tasmania come onto the market from mid September to late December, with a further small autumn crop from January to the end of April.

Strawberries for the fresh food market should be picked with their stems intact; for factory consignments the stems are removed. Depending on the distance from the market, the berries should be picked when they are showing three-quarters to full colour. Regular picking during the season is necessary, i.e. every 2 days,; in cooler weather this may extend to 3 to 4 days.

Yields

A well-grown crop will produce about 500 g per plant through the season, although some growers obtain higher yields of about 1 kg per plant under good conditions. Hot dry winds can devastate and dry out the fruit, hence wind protection is very important.

Packaging

Wet fruit should be allowed to dry before packing. The fruit should be sorted carefully and graded so that the fruit is consistent in size and quality, and all poorly coloured, deformed, over-ripe and damaged fruit should be discarded.

The most common containers used for packing the fruit are plastic or foil punnets. The large fruit are usually pattern packed, while the smaller fruit are volume filled. The punnets are normally 100 mm × 100 mm at the top, 85 mm × 85 mm at the base and 45 mm deep. They will normally hold about 250 g of strawberries.

Perforated cellophane is wrapped over the top of the punnet and secured with a heat seal or clear tape. Twenty punnets are then packed into a standard single layer fibreboard carton for market. Both the individual punnet and the carton should be labelled with the grower's name and address.

Storage

During summer fruit may need to be stored in a coolroom. At a temperature of 25°C the fruit will age five to six times faster than the same fruit stored at 7°C.

Cultural Problems

While there are a large number of hydroponic strawberry growers there are only a few that could be classified as top growers. Apart from their expertise in marketing and sales, the other important feature shared by these growers is that they have a genuine feel for the plants. Also typical of these growers is their attention to sanitation and cleanliness, especially in the removal of weeds from under and around the site.

Strawberries are prone to a number of diseases and pests, including fruit fly. Fruit fly present a problem not only because of the damage that they can do but because they are difficult to control once the fruit is on the plant. It is important to be able to spray under the leaves, hence system design is very important and is a major problem with bench type setups and in soil-grown plants.

Other pests which affect strawberries are nematodes (bud and root knot nematodes), spider mites, two-spotted mites, aphids, thrips, cluster caterpillars, looper caterpillars and leaf rollers. The caterpillars will attack strawberries at most times of the year, but are less troublesome in the cooler months, when they develop more slowly.

Fungal diseases tend to be more prevalent during damp and overcast conditions or in poorly ventilated polyhouses with high humidity.

Grey mould, ripe fruit rot and powdery mildew can attack the fruit. These diseases can be reduced or eliminated by constant cleaning up and removing the ripe fruit and old leaves, and by keeping the plant open and allowing good air movement around the plant.

Leak rot is a common problem late in the season, especially with overripe and harvested fruit. Other diseases which affect strawberries are eye spot, Alternaria leaf spot, leaf blight, leaf scorch, Fusarium wilt, Verticillium wilt and crown rot.

Root rot is favoured by high temperatures and poor root aeration in the root zone. Other factors which may contribute to root rot include inadequate drainage around the roots (possibly caused by the roots clogging the pipe), the pH is too high or low, spikes in salt or nutrient or pH levels, moisture stress due to irregular irrigation or nutrient feed cycles, or low nutrient flows.

Virus diseases may show up as stunted plants with smaller than normal leaves, the edges of the leaves indistinctly fringed by a pale or yellowish margin, the leaves mottled, crinkled slightly puckered leaves.

Conclusion

Although growing strawberries using a hydroponic system is more expensive than soil growing, it has two major advantages—it reduces the labour required and promotes consistent production. It is a lot easier to hire labour to carry out harvesting and maintenance, and the cost of picking is lower. As one hydroponic grower said, 'It takes the backache out of strawberries'.

Under the control of an effective operator, hydroponics can outproduce any soil-based operation. The degree of control that an effective operator can exercise over his crop is far superior to that of a soil grower. The yields are higher; quality is improved; control over pests and diseases is increased; the growing cycle can be regulated; the plants' nutrient requirements can be controlled; and the labour costs are reduced.

While it is important to grow the best quality fruit, it is nothing unless you have a market that will pay the price for the best. Hence no matter how good you are as a grower, you must have markets for your produce and you have to supply them consistently. Presentation of your strawberries is critical in maintaining your market. Once you have an established market then you can relax a little—but not too much.

Problem solving in strawberries

Part of Plant Affected	Possible Cause
Older leaves	
(a) Yellow pattern on leaves	Overspray
(b) Clusters of grubs on undersurface of leaves or damaged leaves	Cluster caterpillar
(c) Brown/purple irregular spots	Leaf scorch
(d) Flame red colouring in leaves	Nitrogen deficiency
(e) General yellowing	Nitrogen deficiency
(f) Red/purple discolouration	N, P, K deficiencies
(g) Leaf margins burnt; red/purple colour	Potassium deficiency
(h) Purpling of leaves, especially small veins	Phosphorus deficiency
(i) Reddish purple spots between veins	Magnesium deficiency

(j) Large irregular V shaped spots on edges of the leaves — Blight

(k) Harsh appearance of leaves; silvering — Red Spider Mite

(l) Black and silver marks on leaves — Wind burn

(m) Brown/purple spots, grey/white centre — Eye spot

Young leaves
(a) Yellow markings on leaves — Weedicide overspray

(b) Puckering of leaves — Crimp (bud nematode)

(c) Occasional leaves puckered — Spray damage

Whole plant and leaves
(a) Slow wilting of older leaves — Verticilium wilt

(b) Whole plant wilting suddenly — Fusarium wilt

(c) Whole plant is a harsh yellowish colour; small centre; flattened appearance — Lethal yellows

(d) Plant wilts and dies. When crown is cut a brown discolouration shows — Phytophthora crown

(e) Whole of plant dies; creamy brown fungus at base of leaves — Sclerotium crown rot

(f) Interveinal chlorosis — Deficiency of iron

Fruit and flowers affected
(a) Brown to purple spots on fruit stalks — Scorch marks

(b) Black spots on ripe fruit — Black spot

(c) Fruit dry, shrivelled and hard brown — Phytophthora rot

(d) Fruit hard with prominent seeds — Spider mite/thrips

(e) Large light brown soft areas on fruit — Botrytis (grey mould)

(f) Ripe fruit breaking down on bushes — Rhizopus

(g) Fruit puckered and distorted — Rutherglen bug / Poor pollination

14 Tomatoes

Tomatoes are one of the major food crops of the Western world, yet breeders are still trying to improve the fruits' disease resistance, shape, flavour and colour.

The tomato is a member of the Solanaceae family which also includes peppers, capsicums, eggplants, potatoes and tobacco. While many consider the tomato to be a vegetable, it is in fact a berry fruit.

There are many varieties and they are used in many different ways. Some are eaten fresh in salads, others are used in cooking. Some varieties are firm and have a large amount of fibre (i.e. they have a high solids content); others are very juicy (i.e. they have a low solids content). Firm varieties are preferred for salads and sandwiches. Hence selection of the correct variety is important.

When deciding to start growing tomatoes commercially it is very important to find out what your market wants. If you are seeking to establish a new market then you must do some research into the market size. It is also important to produce quality fruit. The tomatoes should have a uniform colour, and fruit showing uneven or blotchy areas should be discarded, as well as bruised, split or misshapen fruit.

The techniques used for hydroponic tomato production are very similar to those used for growing cucumbers (see pages 61–65). The systems used include the NFT system and media-based systems.

Varieties

When a prospective tomato grower contacts me and says that he wants to grow tomatoes for the commercial market, is it correct to assume that he knows what *type* of tomato he should be growing? The new grower's image of the tomato can be very different to what the market requires. Too frequently the grower is thinking about a tomato that he enjoys eating, but it is not necessarily a tomato that he can market. His tasty tomato generally has poor storage properties, is easily damaged during transportation, and has a poor shelf life.

It is very important to establish the market you are intending to sell to and then produce for that market. While the grower may be proud to produce large prize-winning tomatoes, the normal consumer buys tomatoes that are 65 to 75 mm diameter and weigh 120 to 150 grams.

Tomato varieties can be placed in four main categories according to their method of production and market use:
1. Canning tomatoes
2. Greenhouse tomatoes
3. Outdoor tomatoes
4. Specialty tomatoes

Within these broad categories, there are two types of tomatoes:
1. Bush tomatoes (determinate flowers)
2. Single-stemmed tomatoes (indeterminate flowers)

The determinate varieties are bushy plants in which the stem terminates in a blossom cluster and no further elongation takes place. Blossoms are produced freely at each node.

The determinate varieties are generally short-term crops which produce heavily during the season and then must be replanted to obtain the next crop. The laterals are not removed and they involve much less pruning and training than the indeterminate types.

The bush varieties are generally grown outdoors, with minimum support and do not require pruning. The common varieties are Floradade, Sunny, Pirate, Duke, Red Mountain and Comanche.

With the indeterminate types, stem elongation continues throughout the growing season. A truss (spray of blossoms) is formed at every third node after the first truss, which is between the seventh and ninth node. The plants are usually trained by removing the laterals as they develop. They tend to produce over an extended period and are generally grown in polyhouses or more protected environments than the determinate types. The most common varieties include Grosse Lisse, Indian Liver and Strobelle.

Some of the more common commercial varieties bear heavy crops of medium-sized bland fruit. Other varieties mature early, produce for a short period and the cropping is light. Some produce a small number of large fruit which are frequently yellowish in appearance. The F1 hybrids generally are heavier yielding and have a high degree of disease resistance, but the seeds are expensive. Some are more tolerant of cooler conditions. Hence selection of the most appropriate variety is very important, depending on the growing conditions and the market sought.

In the drier tropical areas of Queensland the determinate types with large fruit are grown (particularly during winter), giving firm fruit with concentrated setting times and good foliage cover. These fruit are also resistant to the various strains of Fusarium diseases. In recent times several hybrids have become popular because of their ability to produce high yields of large fruit during winter. These new varieties generally have slightly softer fruit.

The following varieties are often grown commercially in hydroponics using polyhouses to protect the fruit from rain damage in summer and to provide a more protected environment in winter, particularly in southern Queensland and northern NSW. Tomatoes grown outside suffer severely from pests, diseases, fruit cracking, splitting, blemishes, and damage to the bushes in prolonged wet periods. While year round production is carried out in these areas, high returns are obtained during the tropical off periods.

Floradade

Floradade has a reputation for producing poor quality 'tasteless' fruit, but if the fruit is allowed to mature before harvesting the taste is very acceptable. The fruit is firm and has a long shelf life, making it a popular selection with greengrocers. The fruit tends to be smaller in winter.

Sunny

Sunny is a highly determinate, jointed hybrid variety. It produces larger fruit and higher yields than Floradade, especially in the winter period in tropical areas. It has been found to produce exceptionally well in the temperate climate of NSW in summer. While the fruit is slightly softer it rates more highly on taste. The seed is currently fairly expensive.

Duke

This variety is also a highly determinate, jointless hybrid. In trials it has not produced the yields obtained with Sunny, however it is reasonably popular and is preferred by some growers. The fruit has a good size but tends to be a little softer than Floradade in warmer weather.

Delta Contender

This is a more recent addition to the range of determinate tomato varieties. It is a jointless tomato that tends to bear larger fruit in winter than Floradade. It also has the advantage that the fruit matures over a fairly concentrated short period and with similar or better yields.

Plant Development

While many growers succeed in growing tomatoes frequently they do not understand why sometimes they are successful yet at other times their yields are low. An understanding of the plant not only increases yields but also allows the grower to maintain consistent production.

There are two stages in the production of hydroponic tomatoes: the seedling and vegetative stage, followed by growing the plant in the system.

While the seeds are quick to germinate (about seven days), they usually take another four weeks before they are ready to transplant into the system. Watering, feeding, temperature, wind control and hardening off are critical factors at this stage of growth and will affect future growth and cropping.

The vegetative stage starts at the time of transplanting and continues until the first flowers start to form two to four weeks later.

Flowers begin to form three to four weeks before the first flower buds are actually visible. For the first cluster this is within a ten day to three week period following the unfolding of the seed leaves. It is at this stage that the plant is most sensitive to temperature, moisture content of the medium, light intensity and duration, carbon dioxide and nutrient supply.

Root activity varies at different stages of the plant's growth:
1. Rapid increase in root length at first truss.
2. Rapid decline until first harvest.
3. Rapid increase in root length after harvest.
Hence watering and feeding is critical between first truss and first harvest.

Temperature

Tomatoes are sensitive to frosts. In sheltered areas it is possible to plant outdoors in June, but most seedlings are set out from September to December.

A mean temperature of 24-27°C is optimum for plant growth and fruit quality under conditions of high light. Under lower light conditions optimum growth takes place at 14-17°C. Night temperatures below 15°C and day temperatures above 38°C may cause barrenness (lack of fruit set). Fruit set appears best when night temperatures range from 15°C to 20°C and day temperatures do not exceed 32°C.

Seedlings should be given a cold treatment to promote development and flowering, e.g. 10-21 days at 11-12°C (ten days in bright sunny weather; longer treatment is required when overcast conditions prevail). Cold treatment gives rise to large cotyledons (seed leaves), thicker stems, fewer leaves being formed before the first flower cluster, and increased flowering. In many cases, up to double the number of flowers may be developed in the first flower cluster and subsequent clusters. Cold treatment of the seedling tops determines the number of leaves; bottom cooling increases the number of flowers in the first cluster. The effectiveness of cold treatment depends on the variety.

Greenhouse culture

It is possible to grow tomatoes all year round in a heated polyhouse or greenhouse. A double layer greenhouse conserves heat much more efficiently than a single layer covering and, in some cases, the need for artificial heating can be halved. However, the extra layer will reduce light penetration—for each percent of light reduction there is a comparable loss in yield.

Heat loss from a normal greenhouse doubles as the wind speed increases from 0 to 32 kph. When the shed is protected from prevailing winds, fuel savings between 3% and 6% can be achieved; up to 10% fuel savings can be achieved by all round protection. The shelters should be as high as the ridge of the house, with 50% permeability, and located at a distance of 10 times the height of the house.

It is important to note that the incidence of diseases increases considerably with enclosure. Temperature control, air movement, increased humidity and depletion of carbon dioxide also present problems in closed greenhouses.

Light

Tomatoes are a short day plant. During short days (9 hours of daylight) the tomato plant will flower and fruit earlier compared to long days (12–18 hours of daylight). High light intensity also results in increased flowering and fruit set while high night temperatures hasten the maturation of the fruit.

Greenhouse orientation is an important influence on light quality. East–west orientation favours light exposure in mid winter, whereas north–south orientation favours light exposure in spring and summer.

Carbon dioxide enrichment

Carbon dioxide enrichment has been shown to increase yields, improve fruit quality and accelerate maturity, particularly in high light conditions. Young plants are particularly responsive: growth rates in young plants can be increased by 50% and flowering and fruiting hastened by seven to ten days.

The optimum range for carbon dioxide levels in the greenhouse is between 1000 and 1500 ppm (the normal level is 300 ppm). The specific effects of elevated carbon dioxide levels include promotion of side shoots, longer and thicker internodes, heavier root growth, more intense pigmentation of the leaves, and earlier senescence of the older leaves. It can be particularly useful for compensating poor growth caused by low light conditions, e.g cloudy days.

All varieties respond to carbon dioxide enrichment, although there are differences in varietal responses.

Air movement

It is essential to have good air circulation and exchange in the greenhouse. Very little difference has been found between plants which have under-gone carbon dioxide enrichment and those in which fresh air is constantly blown across the leaves by the use of fans. In addition, circulating air improves heating and cooling efficiency, and is the best means of controlling fungal diseases which affect the aerial parts of the plant.

In a closed house it is impossible to achieve efficient cooling using the fan and pad arrangement (where the fan at one end draws air through the shed to the moist pad at the other end). It is better to use top-opening greenhouses or igloos which give good air movement and cooling in summer and during the day in winter. The greenhouse can be closed at night to retain the warmth of the day. Thermal screens may also be used to retain warmth in the shed or igloo.

In winter, fresh warm air can be introduced from outside and distributed using plenum ducting. Fresh air should also be taken in regularly during the night.

Fans and air turbulators assist in maintaining uniform temperature and air movement around the leaves. Even in mild weather heating from below or at floor level helps to reduce the humidity levels within the foliage.

Ground level circulation is best achieved by removing the bottom leaves up to the ripening fruit cluster. However, removing too many bottom leaves can stress the plant and create symptoms similar to wilt virus.

Propagation

Seed raising

The aim is to develop strong individual seedlings. Hence it is better to select individual seeds and place them in their own cube of rockwool or into individual cells in the seedling tray. This may be done by hand seeding or with an automated vacuum seeder. However, the problem with automated seeding is that the seeds are flat and tend to be difficult to sow evenly. Pelletised seeds, while a little more expensive, will cut down on time and improve accuracy.

If the seeds are sown thinly in seedboxes they tend to come up in clusters, giving rise to uneven growth and spindly seedlings. Clustering also increases the likelihood of transplant shock due to root damage when the seedlings are separated.

Seeding media

Our experimental work has shown that the seeding medium has a marked effect on the development of seedlings. While a range of media can be used—including rockwool, perlite, sand, vermiculite, and potting mixes containing peat moss—to a large extent, the hydroponic system will govern the selection of the medium.

Rockwool has a major advantage in that the seedlings can be planted out without suffering transplant shock. It is also ideal for growing seedlings which are to be planted into a NFT system (where no medium is used to support the plant). However rockwool is unpredictable in its moisture-holding capacity and the seeds may rot or dampen off easily. Our best results were obtained by placing the seeds in the dry rockwool and then using regular misting to slowly wet the rockwool.

Loose friable media, such as sand, vermiculite, perlite and potting mixes, tend to fall away from the roots easily, leaving them bare and consequently subject to the possibility of transplant shock.

Air pruning of the roots by propagating the seeds in trays placed on top of wire mesh helps to stimulate the development of fibrous roots in the seedling pockets. The seedlings can then be planted in a media system using trays, troughs, nutrient flow systems (with media), etc.

The seeds can also be germinated on inert matting. This technique is used to propagate seedlings which are to be transplanted into an NFT system.

Germination

The optimum temperature for germination is 25°C during the day and 18°C at night. Bottom heating is advisable, particularly during winter, as seeds take about 25 days to germinate at 13°C; 16 days at 14°C; and 6 days at 26°C. As the temperature increases above 26°C, the time taken for germination is not reduced and the number of seeds failing to germinate increases rapidly.

Chilling the seeds before planting increases the number of fruit in the first harvest without changing the date of flowering.

The seeds should be misted with water on a cycle of four seconds every six minutes. If the moisture supply is restricted during germination, the leaf area and fruit size are reduced at first harvest. Once the seeds have germinated it is a good practice to use a nutrient solution to develop the plant before hardening off.

The seedlings have a high light requirement—a minimum of 1000 foot candles is needed for 14 hours each day.

Cold treatment of the seedlings (13°C for 10 days) gives rise to thicker stems, fewer leaves before first flower cluster, and increased flowering.

To avoid seedbed diseases it is advisable to use a fungicide designed to prevent damping off, such as Previcur R, during seedling development.

Transplanting

The young seedlings are very tender and should be hardened off prior to transplanting. This may be done with a special nutrient solution or by allowing the seedlings to slowly become attuned to the ambient growing conditions.

Overwatering and an incorrect nutrient balance at the time of transplanting can result in tomato plants failing to change from vegetative growth to the flowering and fruiting stage. For this reason, it is often advisable to stress the young seedlings prior to transplanting. This can be done by withholding water for short periods, pruning the roots when the seedlings are being transplanting, or pinching out the terminal bud in the early stages of growth.

Recent research has shown that mechanical brushing of the young seedlings produces shorter spacings between the stem nodes and encourages more robust plant growth.

The seedlings are normally transplanted when they are about 15 cm tall. The seedlings should be planted into a moist bed with the medium adhering to the roots of the plant. It is advisable to moisten the growing bed with the nutrient solution.

Long spindly seedlings can be planted on an angle so that no more than 8 cm of the medium covers the roots or stems. The upper stem of the plant will soon grow upright and new roots will develop from the buried stem.

Spacing

Plants should not be crowded. Close planting tends to favour leaf diseases and development of smaller fruit. At the same time there must be room to work along the rows and the plants open enough to allow light to penetrate and air to move through the plants.

The optimum space per plant is between three and four plants per square metre of growing area, and if rows are 30 cm wide then the spacing per plant is 45 cm or 23,000 plants per hectare with aisle widths of 900 mm in the greenhouse. The density of planting may be increased in spring to give 30,000 plants per hectare of shed.

Watering and Feeding

Nutrient Concentration

The initial nutrient concentration is generally maintained at a low level and is increased as the plants grow. Prior to transplanting, nutrient rates of 2 to 4 grams per litre are used, depending on frequency of watering and plant size. High nitrogen and phosphorus levels during the early seedling stage will promote flower and fruit formation and development.

Many growers use a general tomato nutrient for both the initial vegetative stage and the flowering stage. Some growers, however, use a specific nutrient tomato mix for the vegetative stage and then follow this with a special flowering tomato nutrient. The special tomato nutrient shortens the internodes which tends to make the plant shorter and stockier, and improves yields.

While there is no fixed optimum nutrient concentration that suits all situations, it is generally accepted that the concentration should be about 1500 ppm or about 1800 uS. This figure varies, however, according to microclimate conditions. If the plants are grown outside in the open, it is usually advisable to use reasonably low nutrient concentrations, e.g. 1000 ppm or 1300 uS. When the plants are grown in an enclosed or protected environment then the nutrient strength can be increased up to 2000 ppm or about 2600 uS. It is up to the individual grower to determine the concentration that the plants respond to without wilting, or showing signs of deficiencies, etc.

It is important to note that rapid changes in the nutrient concentrations supplied to the plants may induce splitting of the fruit.

Nutrient Solution

The solution composition needs to be finely balanced to correspond with the demands of the plant because the plant must survive for long periods of time (especially the indeterminate varieties) without regular dumping of the nutrient solution. Also, tomatoes demand a finer balance of the nutrient composition because the nutrient must not only stimulate good foliage growth but also stimulate and assist flower and fruit development. All too frequently, growers who make up their own nutrient fall into the trap of producing lush foliage growth at the expense of fruit, or they produce plants with curled leaves and severe tipburn and leaf edge burn, and the bush and fruit are small compact and stunted.

Watering

The plant must be fed on a regular basis to maintain the roots in a moist but not wet condition. Irregular watering and feeding will cause blossom end rot, splitting of the fruit, and poor growth.

In the early stages young plants should be watered regularly. Once the plants are established the medium should be maintained at a barely moist level and heavy watering of the nutrient solution should be avoided. The surface of the medium should remain reasonably dry.

Tomatoes can tolerate reasonably high levels of impurities in the water supply. However it is always advisable to have the water supply analysed before it is used, and to carry out a preliminary trial on a few tomato plants.

Recent research has shown that the use of slightly saline water tends to put taste back into the tomato. It also tends to increase the total dissolved solids of the fruit. However, the use of saline water before fruit set can reduce yields. The higher salinity of the nutrient solution after fruit set is believed to make it more difficult for the plant to extract water from the nutrient solution. The plant compensates by producing more sugars and acids in the leaves and fruit, resulting in higher solids, improved flavour and heavier fruit. (Other research has indicated that increased solids and improved flavour are obtained under higher light conditions, and is dependent on leaf area and size. Root pruning, while it may reduce yields, is also said to improve fruit flavour because it alleviated competition for the available sugars. A modest truss thinning early in the season can also improve the size and sugar content of the remaining fruit, as well as increasing yields.)

Low levels of nutrient in the feed supply should be used occasionally to help reduce salt buildup on the growing medium. The higher the natural salt level in the water supply, the more important it is to use regular flushes with low nutrient concentrations to flush the beds or the growing medium.

While many books claim that the purity of the water supply is critical, for most growers this is of minor importance provided that the water supply is of reasonable quality. Very few growers have a pure water supply. The nutrient solution is the basic determiner of the final pH and the nutrient salts. There are water supplies that may have a high pH, others may have a very low pH, but when the nutrient is added the pH usually settles down to between pH 5.5 and 6.5, particularly if the nutrient is pH stabilised. If on addition of the nutrients the pH is above pH 6.5 then it may be necessary to adjust pH of the fresh water to make it closer to neutral before using it. A lower pH is usually not as critical in hydroponics.

In cases where the water supply has a high concentration of dissolved salts it is advisable to use a flow-through or non-recirculating system. The use of NFT systems or recirculating systems in such cases is potentially disastrous, unless the nutrient is dumped regularly or some nutrient solution bled from the system on a regular basis such as being used on another crop and allowed to go to waste (or not recirculated).

Plant supports

When the bush type or determinate tomato varieties are grown in hydroponics, they are frequently supported within a wire framework on the sides to hold the bushes.

The indeterminate tomato varieties require support or staking. The usual method of supporting the plants are vertical strings tied to wires above the plants. The string is loosely tied to the main stem of the plant or to a peg, and as the plant grows the plant is wrapped around the string or tied to it at intervals of 30 cm, just below a leaf stalk or flower bunch. The stem is twisted slightly so that the flowers face outwards.

Pruning

Indeterminate plants are usually trained to a single stem or possibly a double stem. The laterals (side shoots) which appear where the leaf stalk joins the main stem should be pinched out when they are about 2 cm long, without damaging the leaf stalk.

When the plants are about 1.2 m tall the bottom leaves below the first truss should be removed to improve air circulation. Also any yellow leaves that develop below the first truss should be removed as the season progresses, but don't overdo the deleafing process. Use a clean, sterilised sharp knife or secateurs which have been sterilised, to remove unwanted foliage.

When the plant reaches the top of the string the growing tip is pruned and the side shoots are allowed to grow to extend the crop. At least two to three leaves are left above the top clusters that are in bloom. Topping or removal of the terminal bud is used to restrict fruiting potential to five to six trusses per stem which ensures commercial fruit size on the later hands.

It is important to remember that the flower trusses grow along the main stem so care must be taken to ensure the flowers are not injured when pruning or tying up the main stem. If the larger fruited varieties are grown then the load on the stem may be reduced by allowing one of the terminal buds to develop and form a second stem.

Flowering and Fruit Set

Flowers and fruit clusters are developed on the main stem axis and or lateral branches. The number of clusters varies from 4 to 100 depending on variety and type.

High yields can only be obtained if the flowers set fruit. It is important to shake the plant regularly or use a vibrator daily to assist pollen dispersal and fruit set.

Temperature is important in the shedding of pollen. Temperatures below 20°C tend to delay pollen shedding; the best results occur at 21°C. Temperatures above 32°C result in poor fruit set, in which case shading or misting may be used to lower the temperature.

Poor fruit set on healthy plants is usually a result of adverse climatic conditions prior to and at the time of pollination. Low light intensities, short photoperiods, high night temperatures, and high or low humidity are all limiting factors. Failure of fruit set can also be attributed to a number of causes including sudden temperature changes when the plant are in bloom, hot dry weather or winds, injury by thrips, lack of moisture, or extensive vine growth. Fruit set is abundant only when night temperatures are between 15°C and 21°C.

Good air movement around the plant is also critical for good pollination and the health of the plant. A tunnel house with top ventilation is ideal.

Fruit Development

Fruit colour development is also temperature sensitive; the best red colour forms when the average daily temperatures are 18°C to 24°C. Yellowness increases as temperatures rise above 26°C to 29°C. If the temperature rises above 40°C, the mechanism for producing the red pigment is destroyed. The affected areas on these fruit are yellow or sunburnt.

When the fruit is maturing it is best to reduce the amount of watering to minimise leaf spot damage, as well as fruit damage such as star cracks. Restricting watering also helps to improve the fruits' keeping qualities.

Chemical treatments

Chemical treatments such as N-m tolyphthalmic acid (Duraset 20W) applied to young seedlings during the sensitive period (10–14 days following cotyledon expansion) may increase flower numbers sevenfold. Auxins generally increase flower numbers and may induce plants to flower earlier. CCC accelerates flowering by reducing the time to the first open flower; fewer leaves are formed before the first flower cluster. Gibberellins decrease flower numbers. Maleic hydrazide and phosphon also delay flowering.

The use of ethephon enhances tomato yields by triggering the release of ethylene, a naturally-produced chemical which accelerates fruit ripening and colouration. The chemical is sprayed on the crop two weeks prior to harvest or when 5 percent of the tomatoes are in the breaker stage at the rate of 1000 ppm. Fruit treated in this way tend to bear less consistent sized fruit but the quality is usually very good. Growers also use ethephon towards the end of the harvest period in order to be able to pick all the fruit at the semi-ripe stage.

No relation has been found between growth promoters or inhibition in the tomato plant and flowering. However, anyone who is considering using these compounds should check with the government departments for approval to use them and to see if they are registed for use in your state.

Harvesting

All produce should be suitably mature when harvested. Maturity must not be confused with ripeness. Maturation can only take place on the vine, whereas ripening (fruit softening and colour development) can continue on or off the vine. During vine ripening, sugars, acids and other flavours move into the fruit and the texture is improved.

Tomatoes are ready for harvesting about three months after they are transplanted. Optimal colour development for tomatoes occurs between 15°C and 21°C. Harvesting of the crop is generally spread over two months for the determinate varieties.

Tomatoes are harvested for the local market at the 'breaker' stage which is when the blossom end shows a pink colouring. If you are supplying distant markets the fruit should be green but mature, i.e. the seeds will be fully developed and surrounded by jelly-like flesh that has just started to colour, and the fruit surface is a light green colour.

In warmer weather fruit will need to be picked about two to three times per week; under cooler conditions fruit may be picked less frequently. The stems should be trimmed flush with the top of the fruit to prevent bruising during storage and transit.

Yields

Each plant normally yields 7–10 kg per plant under reasonable growing conditions. Hydroponic tomato yields have reached 400 tons per hectare based on two crops per year.

Post Harvest Handling

The practices involved in post harvest handling are very important. It must be remembered that once the fruit is removed from the vine it is cut off from its supply of water and nutrients, yet it continues to live and consume oxygen and give off carbon dioxide, water vapour and heat. Under these conditions, the fruit is very susceptible to a range of fungal diseases.

The loss of quality in fresh vegetables is very dependent on temperature. The faster the temperature of the fruit can be reduced, the better its storage qualities will be. Hence, early morning picking is preferable to picking later in the day.

A small amount of fruit is picked at a time and conveyed directly to the packing shed for grading and packing. It is very important to avoid damage such as bruising, splitting, etc. The best time for picking is early morning when the fruit is still cool and has developed its maximum fullness overnight. The best temperature for long-term storage of mature green fruit is 11–12°C.

Grading and Packing

The time spent on size and colour grading will pay off through higher prices being obtained for a well presented, uniform product.

The following terms are used to describe harvested fruit:

Firm—the fruit is not soft, shrivelled or water-soaked.

Mature—the fruit has reached a stage of development which ensures the completion of the ripening process; the contents of two or more seed cavities have developed a jelly-like consistency; and the seeds are well developed.

Size—the fruit falls into one of the following sizes:

Cocktail: Fruit are less than 45 mm diameter.

Small: Fruit are more than 45 mm but less than 60 mm in diameter.

Medium: Fruit are more than 60 mm but less than 80 mm diameter.

Large: Fruit are larger than 80 mm in diameter.

Grading tomatoes is very important. Top grade tomatoes consist of sound, clean, firm, well-formed and mature but not overripe fruit. Superficial blemishes, if not affecting the soundness of the fruit, are permitted on fruit 45 mm or greater in diameter provided that the total number of tomatoes so blemished in any package does not exceed 10% by number, and provided that the total surface area covered by such blemishes on any tomato does not exceed 5 mm

diameter on 'Medium' fruit or 10 mm on 'Large' fruit.

Second grade tomatoes should be firm, clean and mature but not overripe and show pink or red colour in the skin at the blossom end. Superficial blemishes, malformations, sunscald and healed growth cracks may be permitted provided they do not affect the soundness of the fruit.

Tomatoes packed for sale should be packed so that only tomatoes of one size are contained in a package.

Only certain sized packages and containers can be used for marketing tomatoes. Growers should check with the appropriate government department for their current rulings and requirements.

Cultural Problems

Tomatoes are prone to a number of problems and the plants should be treated as soon as symptoms appear. Most fungus diseases and insects are found under the leaves, which means that it is essential to spray up into the foliage rather than simply on top of the foliage. Protective clothing, gloves and goggles should be worn when handling insecticides or fungicides.

A daily inspection of a random selection of plants and the use of a magnifying lens to inspect under and on top of the leaves will give an early indication of potential problems. Often the sprays used can do more damage than the problems that they are supposed to correct.

Sanitation

Smokers should remember that tomatoes are susceptible to mosaic virus. It is particularly important for smokers to wash their hands before tying, pruning or picking the fruit.

Many pests and diseases can be spread mechanically. In order to minimise the spread of these pests and diseases a number of steps can be taken:

1. Use only knives, secateurs, and items that have been sterilised with liquid chlorine solution or an antiseptic solution such as Dettol, and dip the instruments into the solution regularly while working with the crop.

2. If handling plants that are diseased or infected with mites, thrips, aphids or insect problems, wash your hands regularly to avoid spreading these problems to other plants.

3. Remove leaves and plants that are affected by viral or bacterial diseases, insect pests and fungal problems. Any crop residues should be destroyed.

4. Prohibit persons smoking while handling the crop or fruit.

5. Use rubber gloves while picking or working with the crop.

6. When harvesting is completed, remove the crop and destroy plant residues, particularly any fruit that may have fallen to the ground. Clean up the area.

7. After harvesting and before replanting seedlings, sterilise the trays, beds, or channels, with either a formalin solution or a solution of liquid chlorine, as well as strings, stakes or supports.

8. Sterilise seedling trays before reusing for a new batch of seedlings by using a strong chlorine solution or even a formalin solution.

9. It is advisable to spray polycovers, walls, etc to avoid cross-contamination between crops.

The diseases which may affect tomatoes include damping off at the seedling stage, grey mould, blossom end rot, target spot, late blight, Septoria leaf spot and tomato wilt virus.

The most common pests are aphids, thrips, tomato russet mites, fruit fly, Heliothus caterpillar and white flies.

Tomato Problems

Yellowing of the lower leaves

A common problem with older plants is that the lower leaves may start to go yellow. This can be one of the first signs that the growing medium is too wet (or the medium is deficient in dissolved oxygen). On close inspection, the base of the stem may be found to be brownish and narrow, and a canker (swelling) may be visible at the base of the stem. The root system may be reasonably healthy.

The plant may recover if the growing medium is allowed to dry out, otherwise the plant will show signs of wilting when stressed and the leaves will become pale and yellow and finally die. The disease can spread rapidly to other plants in the system. The bottom leaves should be removed to allow air to penetrate and a fungicide applied. In severe cases the plant should be removed and destroyed, and the growing medium sterilised.

Very low levels in the nutrient solution may also be responsible for the lower leaves turning yellow. In this case, the yellowing leaves may also develop areas of purple pigmentation before dying prematurely. The younger leaves may turn a pale green colour, and the new leaves tend to be thinner and longer.

Yellowing of the tips of the older leaves can also be caused by low levels of boron or insoluble boron compounds in the nutrient solution. The leaves tend to become very brittle. Corky areas may develop on the fruit near the calyx or on the shoulders of the fruit.

Purpling of young leaves

The older leaves may start to die prematurely, and the veins on the underside of the young leaves may turn a purplish colour. This is normally associated with a deficiency of phosphorus in the nutrient solution or problems with the plant's ability to absorb phosphorus. In more serious cases, the leaves develop small brown areas between the veins, particularly on the lower leaves.

In some varieties of tomatoes the purpling of the petioles and leaves is normal. Purpling may also occur when the night temperatures are low.

Distorted leaves

Rolled leaves do not necessarily indicate the presence of a disease. In fact it is regarded as a good sign in young leaves, provided they are dark green.

The rolling of older leaves is usually associated with excessive defoliation of the plant. It can also be caused by wide variations between day and night temperatures and may also be a response to high levels of moisture in the growing medium. However, leaf rolling is not usually a serious problem, provided that pests and diseases are absent.

There are a number of virus diseases which cause leaf distortion. Virus disease can be transmitted by sucking and gnawing insect pests such as aphids, thrips and mites. They may also be introduced by the use of contaminated seed. Some of the symptoms of virus diseases include mottled, distorted and curled leaves. The stems may have dark vertical streaks; foliage may be thin and distorted (crinkly); growth may be stunted; and the fruit may be mottled and bronzed. There is no cure for virus infection and the plants should be destroyed.

The margins of the mature leaves may tend to curl upwards and inwards when the nutrient solution is very low in copper. The younger leaves often become dark green and the leaf margin may become scorched. These are similar symptoms to those shown when plants are grown in very high nutrient concentrations.

When the young leaves curl downwards and inwards the nutrient solution may contain low levels of zinc. In this case, the main leaf veins will remain green while the leaf tissue between the veins turns yellow. When excessive levels of zinc have been used in the nutrient solution, growth tends to become very spindly.

Yellow leaf margins

The upper leaves of the plant show a distinct yellowing at the margins. This may later turn brown and look scorched, particularly in hot weather. The fruit tends to ripen unevenly, resulting in areas of green and yellow on an otherwise red fruit. These symptoms are characteristic of low levels of potassium in the nutrient solution, and restricted uptake of potassium caused by low temperatures or interference from other nutrient components.

Yellowing at the edges of the leaves may also be caused by prolonged periods of very humid weather.

Plants wilting

The most common cause of plants wilting in warmer weather is water stress caused by the media being too dry, and is easily cured by modifying the watering and feeding cycle. If the nutrient concentration has been increased rapidly, plants may wilt because they cannot take up water. When the plants are subject to warm or hot, dry and windy conditions the plants may start to wilt, particularly if grown in a low nutrient concentration solution. Increasing the humidity

by misting, providing wind protection, increasing the nutrient concentration, or changing the nutrient formula will all help overcome this problem.

If the plants wilt on hot days, and the medium appears moist, check the temperature of the medium or the nutrient solution. If the temperature of the medium (or nutrient solution) is above 30°C, the plants may be suffering from a lack of oxygen around their roots. This will not be corrected by pumping air into the nutrient or the media because the solubility of oxygen at these temperatures is exceptionally low.

If the growing medium is very wet, the plant may be suffering from a form of root rot, in which case the roots will be brown, corky or spongy.

If the plants recover at night from wilting and the bottom leaves are turning yellow, the plant may be suffering from Verticillium wilt. This can be identified by cutting the lower stem and seeing if there are brown streaks in the stem tissue. The plants should be sprayed with a fungicide and the lower part of the stem can be covered with the growing medium to encourage the development of new roots. It may be also be advisable to remove the plants and sterilise the growing medium.

Grey furry patches on stems

These generally indicate the presence of the grey mould fungus. The fungus usually starts on a damaged area of the stem. Other parts of the plant may become infected, e.g. flower stalks, causing fruit drop. Grey mould is usually associated with high humidity, overcrowding of the plants, and poor hygiene (i.e. non removal of decaying leaves and fruit). Spraying with a fungicide can reduce the problem.

Yellowing between the veins

Yellowing between the veins can be symptomatic of a magnesium deficiency. The lower leaves tend to discolour first. The leaf tissue between the veins turns yellow, although the leaf margins may remain green. The discolouration gradually moves up through the plant. The symptoms may be confused with root rot diseases.

Provided that the nutrient solution is balanced, a magnesium deficiency is mostly likely to occur when the pH is unstable and constantly becomes alkaline. Magnesium sulphate or epsom salts may be added to the nutrient solution to overcome the problem, but it is usually safer to dump the solution. Home formulated nutrients frequently have this problem because even though magnesium sulphate has been added to the nutrient, other salts in the solution may interfere with its availability.

Yellowing of the veins

If the younger leaves are yellowish and the veins of the older leaves start to show yellowing and finally chlorosis, the problem could be an iron deficiency. The addition of iron chelate or iron sulphate will help overcome the problem, but it will keep recurring if the pH of the nutrient solution is above 6.5 or is unstable. This problem occurs most frequently when a two-part nutrient mix is used.

In cases where the water supply is alkaline or the pH of the nutrient solution tends to drift upwards into the alkaline region, the iron chelate chosen should be appropriate, e.g. FeHI. When the pH of the water supply is acid then the FeLo should be used to correct the iron deficiency.

This problem is also more pronounced with NFT systems than the flow-through systems, because with time, oxygenation of the nutrient solution, and the exposure of the solution to light all make the iron oxidise and drop out of solution.

Silvery leaves

Silvery leaves can be a result of a tomato mite infestation. They tend to affect the lower leaves first. The leaves are silvery and dry on top and bronze on the underside. Small red dots and webbing may be observed on close inspection. The stems may become corky and the fruit small, corky and rough. With the aid of a magnifying lens it is possible to make out myriads of small red dots on the underside of the leaves.

The mites are most common during hot dry spells and in summer. They can be controlled by increasing the humidity of the air, or by spraying with a miticide or systemic insecticide, but watch the withholding period carefully if the tomatoes are ripening. The predator mite can also help. There are miticides which are specific to adults and some that are specific to the egg stage. However, this pest can develop immunity very quickly.

Blossom end rot

Blossom end rot appears as a leathery dark patch at the bottom of the fruit. While this problem was previously associated with a calcium deficiency, this is no longer thought to be the case because its occurrence is too erratic. The relationship between low levels of calcium in the plant and blossom end rot is thought to relate more to the plant's ability to take in calcium rather than a deficiency of the element in the nutrient solution.

It is probable that the problem originates at the time of pollination and early fruit formation because the other tomatoes on the bush are often not affected. It usually occurs when the medium is allowed to dry out while the fruit is developing, and occurs most frequently when the medium used is sand or gravel. Hence, it is important to maintain a consistent moisture supply at all times. Blossom end rot is also associated with hot dry winds which can cause rapid moisture loss from the leaves affected.

Blossom drop

The flowers may wither and drop off at the knuckle or the fruit may stop growing when they reach the size of a match head. These problems are caused by a number of factors including poor pollination, low or high humidity, inconsistent moisture content of the medium, poor air move-ment, large differences between night and day temperatures, very low potassium or calcium levels, and high nitrogen levels in the nutrient solution.

Flowers infested with thrips or mites may cause the flowers to drop prematurely or develop into stunted corky looking fruit.

Small fruit

This is closely related to the composition of the nutrient solution, as well as low temperatures, low light levels, etc. It can also be related to the number of fruit that the plant is carrying and the plant's ability to supply suffcent food for the development of the fruit. Increased size may be achieved by removing some of the developing fruit or flowers from the plant.

Leaf spots

Leaf spots are usually caused by fungus diseases, and are most prevalent in wet and humid conditions. If left untreated, all types of fungal leaf spots can seriously damage the leaves and affect the yield of tomatoes.

Target spot appears on the leaves as brown spots with target-like markings. Late blight develops when very wet conditions continue for an extended period. The symptoms are dark water-soaked areas forming along the leaf margin. These enlarge rapidly and affect the whole leaf. Septaria leaf spots are smaller leaf spots with light coloured centres.

If glistening bronze spots develop on the leaves and the spots eventually turn black and shrivel, the fruit develops circular blotches, and the plant starts to wilt, this may be tomato wilt virus. This virus is transmitted by thrips, and the infected plant should be destroyed.

Edges of the leaves chewed

Caterpillars usually start eating the edges of the leaves, while snails and slugs tend to eat holes in the leaves. Caterpillars come in a variety of sizes and colours. Quite often they are difficult to see, but can be found fairly easily by looking for their droppings. They are controlled with an insecticide.

Holes in the fruit

The larvae of the Heliothus grub eat the blossoms and bore into the fruit and stems. They have been a serious pest in past seasons, and are particularly prevalent from midsummer onwards.

NFT strawberry system with overhead sprayers and wind protection

Strawberries in hanging bags prior to pruning plants

Lebanese cucumber sheds

Above: Tomatoes growing in perlite beds

Left: Cucumbers growing in gravel media

Below: Cucumbers growing hydroponically using channels

Tomatoes in an NFT system

Tomatoes growing in bags filled with sand

Tomatoes and capsicums in bags filled with scoria

Corn growing in a hydroponic green feed unit

Trays filled with grain seed

Above and below: Fodder production in a controlled environment

15 Green Feed

Many farmers wait until they are short of fodder to look for alternative feed supplies for their animals. This may be in times of drought, in severe winters, or when their paddocks have been burnt out. Hydroponic green feed, in which the whole plant, roots and all, is fed to the animals is a feasible and commercially viable alternative to buying or growing fodder outdoors. Hydroponic green feed simply involves using hydroponic principles to improve the rate of germination and growth of grain seedlings, with the additional benefit of increasing the nutritive value of the feed.

The cost of setting up a hydroponic green feed unit capable of supplying green feed within a matter of days need not be expensive. In times of drought the amount of water required is minimal and is not wasted since most of it is fed to the animals.

The green feed takes about eight days from germination to grow to 25 to 30 cm tall; at this stage it is ready for harvest. Each kilogram of seed can produce eight to ten kilograms (including the roots) of highly palatable and nutritious fodder. The same fodder grown in a paddock under irrigation would take up to 12 weeks from the time of germination until it was ready to be fed to stock. Furthermore, a large proportion of the seeds in the field would be wasted because of poor germination.

The first commercial fodder shed was the result of many years of research and developmental work. The 15 × 5 m shed is capable of producing 500 kg of green feed per day. The major operating cost is the cost of the seeds. The total labour requirement is about one hour per day, which involves harvesting the fodder, sterilising the trays with chlorine, and reseeding the trays.

Applications

While green feed units are especially suitable for increasing the carrying capacity of small farms, they also have a number of other applications. For example, the feed can be used to provide substantial increases in the milk yields of dairy cows; to fatten beef cattle prior to sale; to improve the vigour and performance of race horses and brood mares; and to help sick animals to recover quickly and put on condition. In dry and drought-stricken areas, or when winter conditions reduce the available natural feed, or at any time there is little or no grazing fodder for livestock, the green feed production systems are highly recommended. Another benefit is that the use of hydroponic green feed systems allows the pastures to recover quickly.

Choice of Grains

One of the major factors in the successful operation of a green feed unit is the selection of seeds that are of high quality and free of pesticides and fungicides which may affect the animals. The seed should be fresh and not contaminated with broken seeds, and it should have a high germination rate.

While just about any type of grain can be used, the most popular are oats, wheat, barley, corn, lucerne, peas and sorghum. These seeds may be mixed to give a specific nutrient balance of proteins, carbohydrates and vitamins.

Oats are the most popular grain. Oats generally have a higher protein level than wheat, especially when grown in a green feed unit. The protein level of hydroponically-grown green feed can be as high as 11%, compared to about 5% in grain which is grown under normal conditions. However, the biggest difference between green feed and fodder grown outdoors is the vitamin content, which may be up to 300% higher in green feed.

It is important to note that different varieties will give different results, i.e. some varieties will give higher yields in the green feed system than other varieties.

Temperature

The optimum temperature for production of green feed is between 18°C and 25°C. At lower temperatures germination and growth rates are slow, particularly if the temperatures fall to 10°C or lower. If the temperature exceeds 35°C many seeds will fail to germinate.

Light

While some light is necessary, the grains do not require full sunlight. Natural light from a window is generally sufficient for growth. If the plants lean towards the light source, this indicates they are receiving insufficient light. The use of metal halide lights or fluorescent tubes operated throughout the day will increase the rate of growth.

The Growing Shed

A number of commercial systems have been set up and are in operation. These systems use controllers for temperature (heating and cooling), humidity, misting, feeding, and air movement. Grow lights or fluorescent tubes are used to increase daylength and growth and carbon dioxide injection is used to enhance growth.

However, it is possible to have a reasonably inexpensive setup. Since the grains do not require high levels of light, a section of a machinery shed may be enclosed and clear panels (such as Alsynite) placed in the roof. Alternatively a greenhouse or polyhouse may be set up. If you have made a room in your shed, the ceiling and walls can be lined with thin polystryene foam to insulate the room against extreme temperatures and to allow light in. Fluorescent lighting may be installed in the walls and ceiling (protected from the moisture in the room) to provide additional light if required.

The floor should be made of concrete or, if this is too expensive, the ground can be covered with a layer of sand and gravel to a depth of about 100 mm and covered with weedmesh. The shed should be made vermin-proof by placing bird wire around the bottom of the shed.

While the trays may be placed on the floor, shelving is preferred because it will increase the carrying capacity of the shed. The shelves or racks need to be spaced about 50 to 55 cm apart, and three to four layers high. The shelves should be wide enough to fit two trays and should have a slight slope for drainage. The aisle space needs to be wide enough to allow the grower to work from both sides of the shelves. A nominal size of the trays is 46 cm × 41 cm wide and 3.5 cm deep—this will take about 1 kg of grain and produce 8 kg of green feed.

Imported green feed units usually come complete with controllers, reverse cycle air conditioners, lighting and nutrient recirculation. They are normally packaged as units capable of producing 10 kg of feed per day consistently. The cost of these units is about $6000. Larger units are available, however the price rises steeply.

Operating the Unit

While sophisticated control equipment can be used, the grower may not necessarily desire the consistent output of green feed and may opt for less refined controllers. Temperature control and nutrient feed control are the two most important requirements.

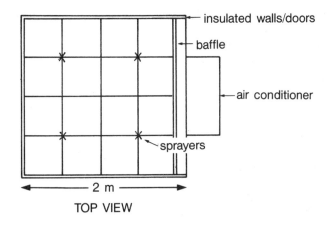

TOP VIEW

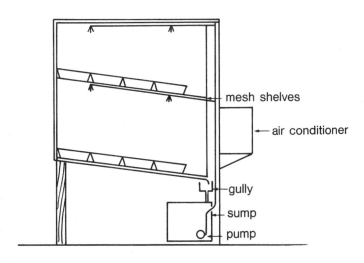

SIDE VIEW

Fodder unit. This is a simple setup for producing about 300 kilograms of green feed for animals during drought or when there is insufficient green feed available.

In commercial sheds, the growing conditions are regulated by a microcomputer designed to control humidity and temperature with the use of air circulation and extraction fans, and a cooling and heating system. The unit can be preset to maintain the optimum growing conditions of 22°C to 25°C and 80% relative humidity. However, if you decide to use less expensive heating and cooling equipment, an evaporative cooling system is ideal for reducing high temperatures in drier conditions, and a good household fan heater with a thermostatic control can be used to warm the shed during cooler days and nights, provided the shed is reasonably well insulated.

The misters are a critical part of the setup and require careful selection. They should give a very fine mist, almost a fog. The misting cycle is also very important and is controlled by a separate controller. The misters are normally operated two to three times per day for short periods.

The water used for misting must be sterilised and enriched with nutrients designed for the growth of the young seedlings. The water is sterilised with calcium hypochlorite or sodium hypochlorite at the rate of about 4 parts per million available chlorine or 5 grams in 1000 litres of water. This means that a storage tank is required in which the water is treated and the nutrient is added. A unit producing about 500 kilos per day will require about 500 litres of nutrient-rich sterilised water per day, hence a good tank size is about 5000 litres.

Operation

1. Set half the trays up on a level bench with the drainage holes to one end.
2. Obtain good quality fresh seed such as barley, oats, corn, etc. and soak the seeds overnight in diluted nutrient solution using 5 ml of concentrated nutrient to 1 litre of water. Each tray will hold about 1 kilogram of seed.
3. Drain the excess nutrient solution and then spread the seed evenly over the tray.
4. Cover the seeded tray with an empty tray or some shadecloth or light cotton fabric. This will maintain the humidity while the seeds are germinating.
5. Mist the seeds with the diluted nutrient solution using a pump sprayer or a household spray bottle until some solution starts to drain from the tray. Misting should be carried out at least once or twice each day. The seeds should not be allowed to dry out.
6. When the seeds have sprouted and reached the top of the tray, remove the covering tray or preferably raise it a few inches above the seeded tray.
7. The sprouted grain will require misting on a regular basis (about two to three times a day or more) in order to keep them moist (but not saturated). Misting is advisable until the sprouted grain is about 100 mm high which should be about three to four days.
8. Once the sprouted grain has reached 100 mm it is advisable to add about 50 to 100 ml of nutrient solution to the end of the tray without holes and allow the excess to drain away. This should be done at least once or twice each day.

What Can Go Wrong?

1. Seeds are slow to germinate
• The seeds chosen may be old or contain insect pests such as weevils. Use only fresh seeds which are free of pests.

• The temperature may be low or too high. The best temperature for germination is normally 18 to 25°C.
• There may be too much light. Some seeds do not like light—covering them with newspaper may assist germination.
• The seeds may be too dry. If the seeds dry out, they may not germinate or they may germinate in patches. Soak the seeds for a longer period, e.g. 24 hours, or mist more regularly during the initial germination period.

2. Seeds go mouldy
• There may be a large number of broken seeds or the seeds may be of poor quality. Wash the tray or trays with diluted chlorine solution, e.g. 1–2 drops of liquid chlorine per litre of water, and take a new batch of seeds and soak them in the diluted nutrient solution (5 ml per litre of water) with 1–2 drops of liquid chlorine (e.g. Zixo bleach) per litre of water. Spread the seeds out on the tray and spray them with fresh diluted nutrient solution (with some liquid chlorine added).
• The seeds may be too wet. If the seeds are sitting in pools of water, raise the tray on a slight slope so that they drain freely and the excess solution will drain away. It is important that the seeds should be kept moist but not sitting in pools of solution.

Feeding to Animals

Since the hydroponic green feed is very rich and digestible, it is normally fed in conjunction with roughage, in the ratio of about 40% roughage to 60% green feed. The amount of roughage can be reduced once the animals have become accustomed to the green feed. The amount of roughage required can also be reduced by supplying the green feed at an earlier stage of growth.

It is not necessary to be precise about the stage of growth that the green feed is supplied to the animals. However if the green feed is kept in the trays for too long the possibility of mould increases.

In some cases the stock may not take to the green feed immediately. If this happens, it may be necessary to add some molasses to get the animals accustomed to the feed.

16 Pest and Disease Management

As our understanding of pests and diseases increases, natural control techniques, such as pheromones (natural scents) and biological control, are playing an increasingly important role in commercial crop production. Within the next decade many of the major pesticide companies will be releasing these more natural forms of pest control. We are entering a new era of pest control.

Integrated Pest Management

Integrated pest management is a schedule for the control of pests and diseases. It involves the minimum use of insecticides and fungicides and favours the use of natural predators.

Most of the time insects, bacteria and fungi live in harmony. Occasionally, however, some of the more nasty diseases and pests get out of control and action is required. When this happens, most growers respond in one of two ways: they either practise preventative maintenance whereby pests and diseases are prevented from attacking the crop, or they destroy them once they appear. Neither technique is satisfactory. The preventative maintenance technique not only keeps predators at bay but also destroys the good guys which provide natural control of pests and diseases and in many cases are also responsible for pollinating the flowers.

Preventative maintenance is a circular argument in that the grower can never stop doing it because the grower has eliminated the natural controlling agents. However, the technique of controlling the pests and diseases once they appear does not work either because the quality of the produce is affected and damaged produce is considered inferior.

There are alternative ways of controlling pests and diseases. In recent years, large sums of money have been spent on researching and implementing biological control. Some of the better known biological control agents are predator mites, bacteria for controlling caterpillars, and bee attractants. However, there are many other natural predators. The common ladybird beetle is a natural predator of aphids, thrips, mites and scale insects. Preying mantis also feed on aphids and mites. Green lacewing larvae attack and eat a vast range of small insect pests. Hover flies are attracted to aphid infested plants; they also feed on the nectar of flowers. Wasps can help control caterpillars. Braconids help to control cabbage white butterflies by depositing their eggs in the caterpillar. Next time you start spraying give some thought to your friends.

Recognising Pests

Aphids
These tiny sap-sucking insects range in colour from green to pink, yellow, black or grey. They attack a wide range of plants, causing new shoots and flowers to become distorted and twisted as they grow. They are often associated with a black

sooty mould which grows on their honeydew excreta. They transmit virus diseases.

Aphids are capable of giving birth to live young and large populations can build up quickly. In milder climates they may be found on plants throughout the year, although heavy rain can decrease aphid numbers and they do not thrive in very hot, dry or cold conditions.

If left undisturbed aphids are often controlled by natural predators such as wasps, ladybirds, hoverflies and lacewings. The honeydew attracts ants which will attack these predators, hence the ants may also need to be controlled.

Heavier infestations will need to be controlled using an insecticide which enters the plant and moves through the sap, e.g. Dimethoate or demeton-S-methyl at the rate of 1 ml/litre of water. However the witholding period must be taken into account (see Appendix 1).

Budworm (Heliothus caterpillar)

These moth larvae are known by a number of names including corn earworm, tomato caterpillar and Heliothus caterpillar. The adult moths can lay up to 1000 eggs overnight. After hatching the small caterpillars feed on young soft foliage and then move on to attack the blossoms, the developing fruit and seed. The older caterpillars are yellow-green in colour with darker markings or stripes along the body and about 40 mm long. They leave the plant and pupate in the growing media.

The crops attacked include tomatoes, capsicums, sweet corn, peas, beans, strawberries, carnations, roses, lettuces and cabbages.

The larvac should be controlled before they enter the flower bud or fruit, otherwise control will be difficult. Carbaryl at the rate of 1.25 g/l every 7–10 days may be used.

Cabbage White Butterfly

This is a serious pest of lettuces, cabbages and related plants. The larvae, which grow to about 30 mm, are green with a faint yellow line along the top of the body and on the sides. Young caterpillars feed on the underside of leaves, but later they may be found on both sides. They generally feed at night. Most damage occurs on the outer leaves.

Cluster Caterpillar

The eggs of these pests are laid in large clusters—up to several hundred eggs in each group—which are covered with a brown fur. The small larvae usually feed in a group under the leaves and remove the epidermis (outer leaf layer) and skeletonise the leaves. As they mature they spread out and feed separately. They may also attack flowers and fruit.

The mature larvae are about 45 mm long, green to brown coloured with two rows of black triangles along the back. They most commonly attack lettuce and strawberries.

Cutworms

Cutworms are usually smooth-bodied and pinkish-brown to grey or black coloured. The older larvae chew through the stems of the plant near ground level; the younger larvae attack the lower leaves of young plants. Seedlings and soft plants are preferred; soft fruit such as strawberries are also attacked. They tend to feed mainly at night and hide under leaves during the day.

In media-based systems they can be controlled by covering the media with newspaper or rags—the larvae will accumulate under the covering; they can then be removed and destroyed.

Earth mite

Earth mites are about 1 mm long, with pink or red legs and black bodies. Both young and adult mites feed on leaves, producing a mottled effect which often begins near the main vein and moves outwards. In severe cases the leaf tips turn brown and die. They also may attack young flower buds.

Damage is most severe in autumn but the mites can be a problem at other times of the year. A broad range of plants may be attacked.

Earworm

Earworms show considerable colour variations and attack a wide range of crops including tomatoes, beans and strawberries. The caterpillars feed on fruit and flowers.

Green Looper

These slim green caterpillars feed mainly at night and hide during the day. They move with a looping action, that is, they move by arching their backs to form a U-shape or loop. They grow to about 40 mm long and are difficult to detect when young. The adult moth can lay up to 1000 eggs which are deposited singly on the undersurface of lower leaves. The caterpillars attack a wide range of vegetables and leafy flowers, including lettuce and strawberries.

Green Peach Aphid
This aphid is extremely common and is a serious pest of vegetables because it can transmit virus diseases. The aphids attack young buds and new shoots, causing the leaves to become twisted and distorted and buds to open prematurely or unevenly. They can be difficult to detect because of their colour.

Green Vegetable Bug
This pest is green in colour, about 13 mm long and 8 mm wide, with half-protected wings and black spots on the top of the thorax (chest). The eggs are laid in groups of about 60. The nymphs or young bugs range in colour from yellow, red and orange to green and black. They are sap-suckers and favour new shoots. Tomato fruit may develop mottled areas.

Harlequin Bug
This bug ranges in colour from reddish-orange and black to red and black. It is about 11 mm long and 3 mm wide. The bugs swarm from native bushes to the vegetables and cause serious damage by sucking the juices out of the plants, resulting in contorted leaves, wilting, stem death and disfigured fruit. They are difficult to control because their occurrence is transitory.

Leafminers
A number of different adult insects are called leafminers, including beetles, wasps, sawflies, moths and flies. A common adult leafminer is a small black fly which inserts its eggs into the underside of the leaf. When the larvae hatch out they tunnel into the leaf and their presence can be identified by squiggly lines on the leaf surface.

The larvae are difficult to control because they are protected inside the leaves. The best control is a systemic insecticide but the witholding period must be watched and the chemical must be registered for this use. Lettuce, cabbages, silver beet, etc. can be attacked.

Nematode
Nematodes attack a number of plants; in particular strawberry plants can be affected by these small worm-like pests.

Bud nematodes are tiny worms which live above-ground in the crown of the plant, causing crimping of the leaves or dwarfing of the plant. The crimping can be seen early in the growing season, and then disappears, and reappears when new runners are produced. Diseased plants tend to be very compact. Leaves are darker green, deformed and strap-like near the crown. Flowering can be delayed, and the fruit may be misshapen on short stalks. The life cycle takes only eight days in warm conditions.

The presence of root knot nematodes is detected by the presence of galls or small knots on the roots. They can severely affect plants which are subjected to moisture stress.

Queensland Fruit Fly
Fruit flies attack a range of fruit, including tomatoes and capsicums. The adult fly has a 6–8 mm long reddish-brown body with yellow markings. The eggs are laid in small groups just below the skin of the fruit. As the larvae hatch they penetrate deeper into the fruit.

The population tends to build up to a maximum in summer and they overwinter in the soil before emerging in spring as mature flies.

Fruit flies are difficult to control. In non-builtup areas baits can be used to attract adult flies. A suitable bait consists of 7 ml of maldison (50%) and 50 g of sugar dissolved in 1 litre of water. The mixture should be splashed onto non-absorbent surfaces and applied every 7 days when the fruit is ripening. However, it will not affect the larvae already in the fruit.

Red mite
Red mites are smaller than other mites and have a brownish body with white spots. They cause mottling of the leaves: affected leaves become pale and then bronze and finally brown prior to the leaves dropping. These mites do not produce webbing on the leaves. They are particularly troublesome on roses.

Rose scale
This scale is most common on roses. Affected plants are spindly, stunted and covered with white flaky crusts of scales on the bark. The young scales or crawlers are pale red. Each female can lay about 40 eggs and possibly a second batch. Their life span is about one year and several generations may be found on the

one bush. They are treated by spraying with white oil at the rate of 25 ml plus 2 ml of maldison per litre of water. Badly affected stems should be pruned and burnt.

Rutherglen Bug

These silvery-grey bugs are approximately 5 mm long and cause considerable damage by sucking sap from the leaves. In hot weather they generally move in swarms from grasses and woodlands to the cultivated crop when the unwatered plants have dried off; hence it is a good reason to mist-spray lettuce in hot weather. They are a serious problem in lettuce and strawberry crops.

Spider Mite

Spider mites usually congregate inside leaves and flower buds. Petals may discolour or become speckled with dark spots. The leaves tend to twist and curl up and lose their vigour. Control is difficult because the insects are protected by the foliage and petals.

The mites attack a wide range of plants; in particular, they are a major pest of strawberries. The adults breed on a wide variety of host plants, so it is very important to keep the area clean of weeds and to prevent the transfer of this pest when handling strawberry plants. The major outbreaks normally occur from July through to November.

Thrips

Plague thrips attack a wide range of plants including carnations, lettuces, tomatoes, peas, beans, cucumbers, roses and strawberries. They are very small, thin insects, about 1 mm long, with a yellowish-grey to brownish-grey body. They are frequently found in large numbers when picking strawberries. The fruit is frequently dull and flat. The insects can also attack the flowers, causing malformed fruit and poor pollination. They feed on the surface of the leaves with a gnawing action, giving the plant a dull appearance and exposing the tissue to further attack from diseases—especially spotted wilt on tomatoes and cucurbits. Damaged foliage is blotched with silver, grey, or white. Roses can be seriously affected with the petals turning brown and falling early.

Spraying is normally done at the end of the day when the bees have stopped working.

Tomato Russet Mite

This extremely small mite attacks tomatoes, capsicums, eggplants and related Solanaeceous species. The lower leaves and the stems develop a papery, brown and corky appearance. As the mites increase in number, they gradually move up the plant and may cause blossom and fruit drop. Infected fruit turns purplish-brown in colour and develops a rough, corky appearance.

Two-spotted mite

Two-spotted mites are commonly referred to as red spider mites because of the very fine webbing that they create. They generally can be found on the underside of the leaves and they are just visible with the naked eye; generally appearing as small red dots (the females) in the cooler months. In spring the mites change back to a green colour with dark spots.

They are most damaging in hot dry weather and their numbers are decreased in rainy weather. They cause a faint mottling of the leaves initially until the leaves become silvery, thin, and papery.

The mites are a particular problem on roses, strawberries, cucumbers, tomatoes, capsicums, beans and cut flower crops. They have many natural enemies including the predator mites. The two spotted mite has developed a resistance to many of the current insecticides.

White Flies

White flies congregate on the underside of tomato and cucumber leaves and suck on the sap of the plant, causing leaves to become mottled in appearance. The underside of the leaves often show signs of a black mould which develops on the honeydew excreted by the flies. The fruit can also be damaged.

The flies are difficult to control and the crop may need spraying two to three times at regular intervals. They are a particular problem in greenhouse crops.

Recognising Diseases

Alternaria Leaf Spot

Carnations and strawberries are affected by this disease which initially appears as circular spots, 3 to 6 mm in diameter, with a reddish margin and brown centre. The spots are usually numerous and eventually join together, causing the rapid death of the leaves. Severely affected plants deteriorate quickly and often die. The disease is favoured by extended wet weather, particularly in late spring and early summer. Affected plants should be sprayed with Zineb.

Angular Leaf Spot
A bacterial disease which attacks cucurbits; Lebanese cucumbers are particularly susceptible. It first starts as watersoaked spots on the leaves which grow to about 3 mm in diameter. They are angular in shape and appear brown on the upper surface and white underneath. The centre of the spots may dry out, crack and fall away. Spots may also occur on the leaf stalks, stems and fruit. Affected fruit may develop a brown rot under the spot.

Anthracnose
Anthracnose attacks a wide range of crops including capsicums, cucurbits, lettuce, roses and tomatoes. The disease appears on the leaves of capsicums and cucurbits as black or reddish circular spots with a watersoaked edge. Sunken and elongated spots may also appear on the stems. The disease can spread quickly through the crop and harvested fruit may develop symptoms during transit and storage.

In lettuce tiny spots appear on the leaves and enlarge and change colour from yellow to brown with a reddish margin. The centre of the spot may dry and fall out. Severely affected plants may be stunted.

In roses the edge of the spot goes purplish and the centre may fall out to give a shot hole appearance.

Tomato fruit are particularly susceptible to the disease. Small, round, watersoaked and slightly depressed spots appear on the fruit. The spots can develop into depressions about 1 cm in diameter with concentric rings and cause the fruit to rot.

Bacterial Canker
The first sign is wilting of the lower leaves and wilting progresses up the plant. Affected plants are stunted and develop brown streaks on the stems and leaf stalks. The disease may come from infected seeds or plant debris.

Bacterial Leaf Spot
The bacteria causes spots on the leaves that enlarge and may grow together to form large dead areas. It can also affect the fruit. This disease occurs in lettuce, capsicums and cucumbers and is spread by water. It favours tissue that has been damaged, mechanically injured, frost, fungal attack, aphids and thrips. The bacteria do not usually attack healthy leaves. There are no control measures except to control the causes of the damage.

Bacterial Soft Rot
The rot is usually soft, slimy and foul-smelling. This disease affects the more fleshy parts of plants especially lettuce, celery and capsicums. It often occurs after the plant has suffered a fungal attack such as Pythium in lettuce.

Black Spot—roses
A fungal disease which causes black spots on the leaves which can be up to 10 mm across with irregular or fringed edges. Leaves frequently turn yellow and fall off. Young stems may also be affected, causing stem dieback. The problem occurs mainly in cool humid weather.

Black spot—strawberries
This is a fungal disease that affects the fruit, foliage and flowers of strawberries. It is favoured by warm humid conditions. It shows up on the fruit as firm, circular dark brown, sunken spots up to 20 mm in diameter. The spots then become covered with pink to green spores. Dark, elongated spots may also form along the stalks. It is important to remove dead leaves and diseased berries from which the spores can originate. The spores can be spread by rain splash, overhead watering or on the hands of pickers.

Blossom End Rot
Blossom end rot occurs most frequently on tomatoes and capsicums. The blossom end of the tomato becomes sunken, brown and tough. The problem is usually noticed when the fruit is enlarging.

While the problem has been attributed to calcium deficiency this does not seem to be correct because only some plants in a crop will be affected even though they are all grown in the same nutrient solution. It is generally more prevalent with irregular watering or when a plant is under stress.

Collar Rot
This fungus can cause stem rot, collar rot, root rot and crown rot. It can attack many different plants and usually does so in the early stages of growth. This disease is most prevalent in warm weather of late spring and autumn. It is often referred to as Rhizoctonia.

Crown Rot
Crown rot attacks strawberry plants. It is favoured by warm wet conditions. The outer leaves and then the inner leaves wilt, turn brown and die and the roots become black and rotted. The wilt is most severe in water-stressed plants and it is easily spread by recirculating the nutrient solution. The plants should be removed from the system and in severe cases the system flushed with chlorine or fungicide solution.

Damping Off
Damping off is caused by a number of bacterial or fungal diseases and most frequently attacks seedlings. A rot develops at the base of the stem and the seedling falls over. The most common fungi which cause this problem are Pythium and Phytophthora. It occurs most frequently when the seedlings are overwatered, sown too thickly or grown in contaminated seedling trays. Lettuce seedlings are particularly susceptible to Pythium.

Downy Mildew
Downy mildew refers to a group of fungi which produce similar symptoms. Patches or spots appear on the upper surface of the leaves while the undersides develop a furry or downy growth.

The spores are wind or water borne and the fungi are most likely to occur in humid moist conditions. A wide range of crops is affected, particularly cucurbits in which the spots are angular and infected area may turn brown and fall out. Lettuce are also affected and subsequently become infected with bacterial soft rot.

Eye Spot
This fungal disease attacks strawberry foliage in particular and appears as small reddish to purple spots, about 4–5 mm diameter, on the upper side of the leaves. The fungus is most prevalent during cool conditions and high humidity, or in situations where the leaves and the plant are shaded.

Fusarium Wilt
This disease affects a wide variety of plants, including tomatoes, cucurbits, carnations and strawberries. When the stem of the plant is cut it shows a brown discolouration of the water conducting tissues.

Carnations are very prone to this disease at all stages of their development. In older plants the leaves take on a bluish-white or bleached appearance which gradually changes to a white or yellowish colour. At this stage the plant wilts and dies.

Most infections start near the surface of the media and the disease follows the path of water flow in the beds. The disease spreads rapidly to nearby plants and is spread by water, by cutting implements, or contact with infected plants.

The first sign of the disease in tomatoes is usually rapid wilting on hot days or when they are under stress. The lower leaves turn yellow and wilt, and the disease gradually spreads up the plant. Infected plants usually die. The disease spreads most rapidly in warm weather. Remove infected plants and in severe cases, the entire system should be treated with a strong chlorine solution.

Grey Mould (Botrytis)
This fungal disease affects a number of plants including carnations, lettuce, cucurbits and strawberries. It occurs most frequently in cool and moist conditions. A soft brown rot develops at the crown or on the lower leaf stalks. The stem becomes completely rotted and the plant dies.

The fruit of tomatoes, cucumbers and strawberries may develop a grey furry growth on the surface. Infected carnation flowers develop a tan to light brown decay and then become covered with a fluffy growth.

This fungus grows on dead or decaying vegetable matter; removing old fruit and leaves, keeping the plant open and allowing good air movement around the plant will help to control the disease.

Gummy Stem Blight

This fungal disease most commonly occurs on cucurbits. It may affect the stems, leaves and fruit. The stem is attacked at ground level. A watersoaked canker develops and may become light brown or whitish and sunken. The canker may split open and exude a reddish gum. If the canker encircles the stem the vine may wilt and die.

The disease is most prevalent in tropical and sub tropical areas, and in greenhouse conditions with poor ventilation or air movement. Cucumbers grown in greenhouses may develop this disease as a postharvest storage rot.

Leaf Blight

This disease is most common on strawberries and attacks the fruit stalks and the leaves. The spots are 6–25 mm in diameter and begin as reddish-purple colour. Later they darken in the centre, and develop a reddish margin. The spots are irregular in shape and often V-shaped at the leaf edge. The spots may joint up, giving the leaf a reddish-brown appearence. It is most prevalent in damp shady areas.

Leak or Rhizopus Rot

This is a common problem late in the season and is favoured by hot wet weather, especially with overripe and harvested fruit. This fungus produces a soft watery rot on ripe fruit, and is associated with injuries to the skin caused by insects or handling while harvesting.

Lettuce Big Vein

Large transparent bands develop along the veins of infected plants. This viral infection is most prevalent in winter. The virus can be transmitted by thrips, aphids and sucking insects.

Mosaic Virus

Mosaic, caused by the potato virus, is a serious disease of capsicums, particularly in southern Queensland. The leaves on affected plants are mottled and narrow with discontinuous bands of dark green tissue developing along the main veins and yellow-green tissue between the veins. The leaves may also be puckered. Plants affected early in their growth are stunted and yields are reduced. The virus can also cause mottling of the fruit.

The disease is spread by migrating aphids which may colonise the plants. Other hosts include weeds, tomato and tobacco plants. The best control measure is sanitation. Remove infected capsicums and tomatoes and keep the area free from weeds. Some cultivars are known to be resistant to strains of this virus.

Necrotic Yellow

A common lettuce virus causing yellowing and stunted growth, particularly in autumn and winter. It also shows up as lopsided development of the lettuce and fine crinkling of the leaves. In severe cases plants collapse and die. Control is mainly by destroying the insect pests which carry the disease, e.g. aphids, and removal of weeds, particularly milk thistle.

Phytophthora Root Rot

Phytophthora affects a wide range of plants including lettuce, strawberries, carnations, tomatoes, cucumbers, roses and many vegetable crops. This fungal disease attacks the root hairs and fine roots. This restricts nutrient uptake and the leaves start to yellow and die. The root system becomes black and brittle instead of a healthy white colour. It can be confused with copper toxicity, especially in hydroponic systems where the plants have been sprayed with a copper fungicide.

Good root aeration or aeration of the nutrient solution will help the plant to stay healthy. With NFT systems it is advisable to stop the pump on a regular basis and allow the solution to drain away from the roots. This hardens the plant and makes it more resistant to this disease. The disease can also be controlled by the use of low levels of chlorine added to the nutrient solution on a regular basis, such as once a week.

Powdery Mildew

This disease is generally noticed as a slight dull colour on the leaves in the early stages, which on closer inspection appears as a white powdery blemish. Stems, leaves and fruit may be infected. These fungi require cool weather and high humidity to grow and spread. It is very common on strawberries, capsicums, cucumbers, roses, and many other vegetable and cut flower crops.

Pseudomonas

This disease appears as dark green watersoaked

spots on the leaves which rapidly turn brown. The leaves take on a bleached appearance and start to die. It can also affect stems and flower buds. It can be transferred from other plants such as statice or clovers.

Ring Spot
Whitish-tan spots, up to 6 mm diameter, form on the leaf tips, stems and calyx of carnations. The spots are surrounded by a narrow reddish purple margin. The disease is spread by wind, water and infected plant debris.

Rust
Rust affects a wide range of plants, including roses and carnations. It is especially common on carnations that are grown out in the open. Small yellow patches or spots appear on the upper surface of leaves or stems. Within a few days small blisters develop and burst open, exposing a mass of reddish-brown dust (spores). Each rust has a limited host range.

Sclerotinia Rot
This fungal disease is characterised by a soft brown rapidly spreading rot which develops a white fluffy growth on the surface. It is normally found at the bottom of the stem, just above the level of the media. The rot may be up to 10 mm across and may also be formed within the stem of infected plants. It affects a wide range of vegetable and cut flower crops, including lettuce and carnations.

Septoria (Late Blight)
This fungal disease causes small brown spots, 0.5–2 mm diameter, on the lower leaves. The spots may run together causing the whole leaf to wither and die. It most commonly occurs on celery and is also a problem in field-grown carnations, especially in northern New South Wales and Queensland.

Spotted Wilt
This virus affects tomatoes in particular. It starts

as small brown spots on the smaller leaves. Brown coloured spots appear between the veins on older leaves and the stems become streaked with brown. The fruit tends to ripen unevenly and are marked with circular blotches. The virus is spread by aphids, thrips, and mites.

Target Spot
A fungal disease which attacks tomatoes. Sunken black areas develop on the top of the tomato or near the fruit stalk. Dark brown or black spots with a series of concentric rings develop on the leaves (hence the name target spot). The stems of the tomatoes may develop elongated marks or lines. The disease is favoured by warm moist weather.

Verticillium Wilt
This fungus attacks the plant through the root hairs and invades the water conducting tissues. The stem may appear normal on the outside but if split open reveals a dark brown discolouration. With tomatoes the lower leaves start to wilt and dry out first, and the whole plant may die.

It is usually detected by the sudden wilting of the plant on hot days during late spring or early summer, or during periods of stress. Some plants recover but the older leaves turn yellow, develop marginal and interveinal scorching, and die. This fungal disease occurs frequently with the half-pipe and gravel system in areas subject to very high temperatures. The fruit does not develop and remains hard and small.

Xanthamonas
A bacterial disease which affects lettuce. On larger plants the disease commonly starts on the edges of the leaves, forming yellowish brown areas which increase in size as the plant grows. These edges become thin and papery and tear easily. The disease may also appear as small greasy-looking spots on the leaves. These spots enlarge and the leaves become tattered as the area dries out. It is spread by splashing rain, water, insects, etc., and is often confused with tip burn.

Chemical Sprays

Product	Type	Problem	Rate of Application	Withholding Period
Afugan (pyrazophos)	fungicide	powdery mildew	0.5 ml/L	1 day
Allisan (dichloran)	fungicide	botrytis, sclerotinia	1 gm/L	
Alphacord 100EC (alfacypermethrin)	insecticide	helicoverpa, plague thrip, cluster caterpillar, cutworm	refer label	1–3 days
Ambush (permethrin)	insecticide	heliothus, cutworm, caterpillars, thrip	10–50 ml/100L	1–3 days
Ampol D-C-tron NR (petroleum oil)	insecticide	aphids, mites, scales, leaf spot, fungi	refer label	1 day
Antracol (Propineb)	fungicide	target spot, late blight, grey leaf spot, downy mildew, septoria leaf spot, anthracnose, gummy stem blight	refer label	3 days
Apron 350 SD (metalaxyl)	fungicide	treat seeds for phytophthora stem rot, pythium, downy mildew	refer label	do not feed to stock
Azodrin 400 (monocrotophos)	insecticide	(systemic)	refer label	
Barmac Carbene (carbaryl)	insecticide	insect pests	refer label	3 days
Barmac Chloroturf (quintozene)	fungicide	soil-borne diseases	refer label	28 days
Copper oxychloride	fungicide	fungal and bacterial diseases	1.8-5 g/L	1 day
Gomite (dimethoate)	insecticide	aphids, mites, thrips, lace bug, leaf hoppers, mealy bug	refer label	7 days
Mancozeb	fungicide	fungal diseases	1.5-2 g/L	7-14 days
Thiram	fungicide	fungal diseases	1.5 g/L	7 days
Wettable Sulphur	fungicide & insecticide	mites, fungal diseases	2-5 gm/L	do not mix with oil
Zineb	fungicide & insecticide		1.2-1.7 g/L	7 days
Bavistin FL (carbendazim)	fungicide	(broad spectrum systemic)	0.2-2 gm/L	2 days

Product	Type	Problem	Rate of Application	Withholding Period
Bayfidan 250 EC (triadimenol)	fungicide	systemic, powdery mildew	refer label	1 day
Bayleton 50WP (triadimefon)	fungicide	systemic, powdery mildew	refer label	1 day
Benlate (benomyl)	fungicide		refer label	5 days
Bravo 500 (Clorothalonil)	fungicide		refer label	1-3 days
Bugmaster 800 (carbaryl)	insecticide		1-1.3 g/L	3 days
Cabbage Dust (carbaryl & rotenone)	insecticide	thrips, aphids, grubs, caterpillars	dust every 5-7 days	3 days
Chlorfos (Chlorpyrifos)	insecticide		0.5-5 ml/L	3 days
Copidul (cuprous oxide)	fungicide		1.3-4 g/L	1 day
Copper Curit (copper oxychloride, zineb)	fungicide		2-4 g/L	7-14 days
Cronofos 400 (mono crotophos)	insecticide		label	7 days
Curamil (pyrazophos)	fungicide	powdery mildew	0.5 ml/L first signs 10-14 days	1 day
Diazinon 800 (diazinon)	insecticide			14 days
Dithane M 45 (mancozeb)	fungicide		1.5-2 g/L	7 days
Endosulfan 350 EC (endosulfan)	insecticide	heliothus, thrips, aphids, green vegetable bug	3 gm/L	7 days
Lannate (methomyl)	insecticide	caterpillars, thrips, aphids, broad range		
Methyl Parathion 500 (Methyl parathion)	insecticide	aphids, green vegetable bug, cluster caterpillar	0.65 ml/L	14 days
CK Saboteur (dimethoate)	insecticide			7 days
Cucumber Dust (endosulfan, dicofol, dino cap)	insecticide & fungicide	two-spotted mite, aphids, thrips, powdery mildew	dust plants	21 days
Cuprox (copper oxychloride)	fungicide		1-5 gm/L	1 day
Curit (zineb)	fungicide	mites and fungal diseases	1-2 gm/L	7 days
Cymbush 250 (cypermethrin)	insecticide	heliothus, cutworm, caterpillars, thrip	0.15-0.4 ml/L	1 day
Decis 25 EC (deltamethrin)	insecticide	heliothus	0.4 ml/L	3 days
Dek (maneb, zineb)	fungicide		1.5 g/L	14 days
Derris Dust (rotenone)	insecticide		dust	1 day
Dipel (bacillus)	insecticide		when seen	nil
Dipterex 500SL (trichlorfon)	insecticide	rutherglen bug, armyworm, cutworm, green vegetable bug, fruit fly, leaf miner		2 days

Product	Type	Problem	Rate of Application	Withholding Period
Disyston 50 granular (disulfoton)	insecticide	aphids, thrips, two spotted mite		70 days
Dithane Df (mancozeb)	fungicide		1-2 gm/L	14 days
Dominex 100 EC (alpha methrin)	insecticide		0.2-1 ml/L	3 days
Ekatin systemic (thiometon)	insecticide	aphids, thrips	.75-1 ml/L	21 days
Endosan EC (endosulfan)	insecticide	aphids, thrips, budworms	1.5-2.5 ml/L	1-14 days
Endosulfan	insecticide	aphids, thrips, budworm, heliothus	1.5-2.5 ml/L	1 day
Previcur	fungicide	control damping off	1.5 ml/L	
Folidol M500 (methyl parathion)	insecticide	aphids, mites, scales, caterpillars		14 days
Folimat 800 (omethoate)	insecticide	aphids, loopers, heliothus, mealybug, green vegetable bug, cutworm		7 days
Fulasin (ziram)	fungicide		1-2 g/L	7 days
Galben M (benelaxyl, mancozeb)	fungicide	downy mildew, anthracnose, gummy stem blight, alternaria leaf spot, septoria spot	2.5 g/L	7 days
Malathion (maldison)	insecticide	aphids, thrips	3-6 g/L	3 days
Rogor 100 (dimethoate)	insecticide	chewing and sucking insects	0.6 ml/L	7 days
Gesapon 800 (diazinon)	insecticide	aphids, caterpillars, thrips	0.3-1.4 ml/L	
Gusathion (methyl azinphos)	insecticide	mites, thrips, leaf miner		14 days
Hallmark 50 EC (esfenvalerate)	insecticide			14 days
Helothion EC (sulprofos)	insecticide	tomato grub, leaf miner, heliothus		3-14 days
Hymal (maldison)	insecticide	chewing and sucking insects	0.5-0.9 ml/L	3 days
Karate 50 (lambdacyhalothrin)	insecticide	heliothus, budworm		7 days
Karathane LC (dinocap)	fungicide	powdery mildew	.5 ml/L	21 days
Kelthane EC (dicofol)	insecticide	two-spotted mite	2 ml/L	7 days
Kilval (vamidothion)	insecticide	aphids, mites, thrips	1 ml/L	28 days
Kipsin (methomyl)	insecticide	caterpillars, thrips, aphids, broad range		
Kocide (copper hydroxide)	fungicide		2 gm/L	1 day
Kumulus DF (sulphur)	fungicide & insecticide	mites and fungus	2-3 g/L	
Lansul (sulphur)	fungicide & insecticide	powdery mildew, mites	2-4 gm/L	
Larvin 375 (thiodicarb)	insecticide	heliothus	0.5 ml/L	1 day
Lebaycid (fenthion)	insecticide	fruit fly, thrips, army worm		7 days
Le-mat (omethoate)	insecticide	mite		
Lepidex 500 (trichlorfron)	insecticide	wide range	0.8 ml/L	2 days

Product	Type	Problem	Rate of Application	Withholding Period
Le-sulf (sulphur)	fungicide	powdery mildew, rust, mites		1 day
Lime Sulphur (polysulphide sulphur)	insect & fungicide	mites and fungus, not cucurbits	10 ml/L	
Lorsban 250 W (chlorpyrifos)	insecticide	cutworm		
Maldison 500	insecticide		0.3-1.6 ml/L	3 days
Manzate DF (mancozeb)	fungicide	diseases		7-14 days
Marlin (methomyl)	insecticide	caterpillars, thrips, aphids		
Masta Mite (dicofol, tetradifon)	insecticide	all stages of mites	2 gm/L	7 days
Mavrik (fluvalinate)	insecticide	heliothus, cabbage moth and white butterfly, aphids, two spotted mite	0.4 ml/L	2 days
Metasystox 1 systemic (demeton-S-methyl)	insecticide	aphids, mites, sucking insects		21 days
Milcurb (dimethirimol)	fungicide	powdery mildew on cucurbits		1 day
Monitor 500 (methamidophos)	insecticide	heliothus, leaf miner, aphids	0.5 ml/L	4-14 days
Morestan (oxythioquinox)	fungicide	mites and powdery mildew on cucurbits		7 days
Nitofol (methamidophos)	insecticide	tomato grub, leafminer, potato moth, aphids		4-7 days
Rover 500 nufarm (chlorothalonil)	fungicide	(residual fungicide)	3.2 ml/L	1 day
Nuvacron (monocrotophos)	insecticide	broad range including aphids, caterpillars, heliothus		4 days
Octave WP (prochloraz)	fungicide	anthracnose, damping off	0.3 g/L	
Omite 300W (propargite)	insecticide	mites—first sign	1-2 g/L	7 days
Orthene 750 SP (acephatc)	insecticide			3 days
Oxydul (copper oxychloride)	fungicide		2 gm/L	1 day
Parathion 500 E (ethyl parathion)	insecticide	aphids, thrips	0.2 ml/L	14 days
Perfekthion EC 400 (dimethoate)	insecticide			7 days
Phosdrin (mevinphos)	insecticide			2 days
Pirimor (pirimicarb)	insecticide	aphids		2 days
Plantvax 750 W (oxycarboxin)	fungicide	rust in cut flowers	1.3 g/L use fortnightly	
Polyram DF (metiram)	fungicide		1.5-2 g/L	2-7 days
Prefect (methamidophos)	insecticide		1 ml/L	4-14 days
Purasoil (quintozine)	fungicide	soil-borne fungus		28 days

Product	Type	Problem	Rate of Application	Withholding Period
Pyrethrum (pyrethrum & piperonyl butoxide)	insecticide	aphids, caterpillars, thrips	0.06 ml/L	1 day
Recoil (mancozeb & oxadixyl)	fungicide	downy mildew, anthracnose, gummy stem blight	2.5 g/L	7 days
Ridomil 250 EC (metalaxyl)	fungicide	phytophthora, downy mildew, septoria leaf spot, anthracnose (systemic)	1-2 g/L	7-14 days
Ronilan 500 FL (vinclozolin)	fungicide	grey mould (botrytis), sclerotinia, blossom blight, brown rot	1 gm/L	1 day
Rovral (iprodione)	fungicide	applied at transplanting	1 gm/L	7 days
Rubigan 120 EC (fenaimol)	fungicide	powdery mildew in cucurbits	0.2 ml/L	3 days
Sevin 500 (carbaryl)	insecticide			3 days
Spectrum (copper as hydroxide)	fungicide	(broad spectrum)	2 gm/L	1 day
Spin (carbendazim)	fungicide	(broad spectrum systemic)	0.2-0.5 ml/L	2 days
Sulfine (sulphur)	fungicide & insecticide	powdery mildew, black spot, mites	2 gm/L	
Sumicidin 75 (fenvalerate)	insecticide			
Sumisclex (procymidone)	fungicide		1-2 ml/L	2 days
Supracide 400 (methidathion)	insecticide	aphids, thrips, caterpillars, mites, scales, mealy bugs, plant bugs, leafhoppers	0.5-1 ml/L	7 days
Tedion Ec (tetradifon)	insecticide	two-spotted mite, bryobia mite	2.5 ml/L	3 days
Terrachlor (quintozene)	fungicide	rhizoctonia, sclerotium soil diseases	3 gm/L	28 days
Thimet 100G (phorate)	insecticide	aphids, thrips, two-spotted mites		
Thiodan EC (endosulfan)	insecticide	heliothus, thrips, aphids, green vegetable bug		7 days
Thiram 800	fungicide		1.5-2 gm/L	7 days
Thuricide (baccilus)	insecticide	certain caterpillars	0.5 g/L	nil
Tokuthion (prothiophos)	insecticide	cabbage moth, white butterfly, heliothus, cluster caterpillar		7 days
Wettable Sulphur	insecticide & fungicide			
Topsin M (thiophanate methyl)	fungicide	powdery mildew, black spot	0.8 g/L	
Ziram	fungicide	black spot	1.5 g/L	7 days

Note: These are general recommendations. Growers should check before using the products that they are registered by the appropriate authorities for use on the crop.

APPENDIX 2
Rose Propagators

Victoria
Brundrett & Sons Pty Ltd,
Brundrett Rd,
Narre Warren VIC 3805
Ph: (03) 796 8305.

John Neil,
Lot 1 Ferndale Rd,
Silvan VIC 3795
Ph: (03) 737 9226.

New South Wales
F D Catt Wholesale Nursery,
10 Blacks Rd,
Arcadia NSW 2159
Ph: (02) 652 2425.

Coxs Rose Nursery,
RMB 216 Oaks Rd,
Thirlmere NSW 2572
Ph: (046) 818 560.

Engalls Nursery,
999 Old Northern Rd,
Dural NSW 2158
Ph: (02) 862 177

Keenes Roses,
11 Hezlett Rd,
Kellyville NSW 2153
Ph: (02) 629 1666

Langton Roses,
P.O. Box 19,
Mudgee NSW 2570
Ph: (046) 512 347

Oz Plants,
Box 274,
Cowra NSW 2794
(063) 422 010

Premier Nurseries Pty Ltd,
P.O. Box 400,
Griffith NSW 2680
Ph: (069) 622 537

Roy Rumsey Pty Ltd,
P.O. Box 1,
Dural NSW 2158
Ph: (02) 652 1137.

Swanes Nursery,
2821 Mitchell Highway,
Narramine NSW 2821
Ph: (068) 891 545

Queensland
Runcorn Nurseries,
150 Nursery Ave,
Runcorn QLD 4113
Ph: (07) 345 3322.

Suppliers of Certified Strawberry Runners

New South Wales
Camilleri Strawberry Nursery,
22 Koala Way
Horsley Park NSW 2164
Ph: (02) 620 1511

Speets Strawberries,
80 Old Pitt Town Rd
Oakville NSW 2765
Ph: (02) 627 2864

Victoria
Toolangi Certified Strawberry Runner Growers
Assn,
Main Rd
Toolangi VIC 3777
Ph: (059) 629 220

Vic Certified Strawberry Runner Grower Coop
Ltd,
Myers Creek Rd & Chum Creek Rd
Toolangi VIC 3777
Ph: (059) 629 429

Queensland
Qld Strawberry Runner Approved Scheme,
C/- COD Brisbane Markets QLD 4106
Ph: (07) 379 0317

Summit Strawberries,
P.O. Box 36
The Summit QLD 4377
Ph: (076) 813 267

Tasmania
Tasmanian Berry Gardens Pty Ltd,
329 Clarke Ave
Battery Point TAS 7000
Ph: (002) 231 494

Hydroponic Growing Media

Media	Characteristics	Use
River gravel This is a white silicaeous pebble. It is washed and graded. The particle size used depends on application.	It is non-absorbent and free draining. The moisture is held on the surface only. Acts as a heat sink—heating up and cooling down slowly. Inert and easily sterilised. Comes away from the roots easily. It is relatively inexpensive.	The 8–11 mm diameter is used for lettuce in recirculating systems. The finer material 2–4 mm is used in bag systems for tomatoes, etc.
Road base gravel Similar to river gravels but usually mined. Tends to be darker in colour.	Similar properties to river gravel. The darker colour tends to cause it to heat up a lot more. Frequently contains soluble salts.	Use is similar to river gravel. It is relatively inexpensive.
Scoria or volcanic rock This material is very uneven in shape with numerous holes or pores. It is found in areas in which volcanic action has occurred. The colour varies depending on the source. Also used for decorative driveways.	Water is held on the surface and also within the particles. Tends to cling to the roots of the plant. It is inert but difficult to sterilise. It heats up and cools down more slowly than gravels.	Used widely for non-recirculating systems, e.g. tomatoes, capsicums. May be used in recirculating systems.
Expanded clay (leca) A lightweight expanded clay pebble. A manmade material from clay which has been fired and pelletised.	It has consistent particle size, is lightweight, holds moisture, and heats up and cools down slowly. It is inert and sterile. An ideal media for hydroponics.	Widely used for hydroculture or indoor plant growing. It is very expensive compared to other media.

Media	Characteristics	Use
Perlite This material is mined and fired. When heated the material exfoliates (i.e. it expands like popcorn). It is a white to greyish material.	It has a good waterholding capacity as well as good aeration depending on the particle size. It is inert and sterile. It heats up and cools down slowly (used for insulation).	Widely used in non-recirculating systems including carnations, flowers, and simple home systems. Not recommended for recirculating systems.
Vermiculite A form of mica which has been exfoliated or heated to a very high temperature and expands like popcorn.	It has a very high waterholding capacity, is inert, sterile and has good insulating properties—maintains constant temperature. Generally mixed with other media such as perlite.	Used in non-recirculating systems in conjunction with other media such as perlite and in propagation.
Sawdust, seed hulls, bagasse These are obtained as natural byproducts from timber, seed dehulling, sugar cane, etc.	They usually have good water and nutrient holding capacity. They tend to undergo decomposition over a period which increases their water-holding capacity. The possibility of root diseases is increased.	These materials are used in non-recirculating systems for crops such as strawberries, tomatoes, cucumbers, etc.
Rockwool This material is made from rocks which have been fired and made into a wool-type matting. It has a good waterholding capacity.	It is inert and sterile. It should be washed with fresh water to remove any soluble salts and excess wetting agents. It is an insulating material which maintains a relatively stable temperature. It has good water-holding and drainage characteristics.	Is widely used for propagation of cuttings and for non-recirculating systems such as carnations, roses, tomatoes, etc.

Glossary

Topic	Description
Acid	Any material that has a pH below 7.0. These include acetic acid (vinegar), nitric acid, hydrochloric acid, phosphoric acid and sulphuric acid.
Aeration	A process whereby air or more importantly oxygen is incorporated or dissolved in the nutrient solution.
Aeroponics	A hydroponic system in which the roots of the plant are suspended in air and sprayed or misted on a regular basis with nutrient solution.
Air movement	The steady movement or passage of air across the plant at slow speed such as the use of fans.
Air velocity	The speed of the air as it moves past the plant.
Alkali	Any material with a pH above pH 7. This includes caustic soda (sodium hydroxide), caustic potash (potassium hydroxide), soda ash (sodium carbonate) and lime (calcium hydroxide).
Automatic dosing	The technique of automatically regulating the addition of concentrated nutrients with the use of controllers that test for conductivity and pH.
Bag system	The use of polythene bags, containers, or buckets filled with a growing medium. The nutrient solution may or may not be recirculated.

Topic	Description
Balanced nutrient	The supply of a combination of mineral salts in the correct proportions required by the plant for vigorous growth.
Birdnetting	An open weave mesh material used to protect the crop from birds.
Bottom heating	The technique of conserving energy by means of root warming to stimulate plant growth. This may be by electric cables, hot water tubes, or similar techniques.
Carbon dioxide	A naturally occurring gas in the atmosphere which is essential for the process of photosynthesis. It is the gas formed in respiration by plants and animals as a result of the release of energy to do work.
Channels	Narrow beds which may contain media or hold nutrient solution for growing plants.
Chlorination	The technique used for sterilisation of the nutrient solution by adding an active chlorine material such as pool chlorine as sodium or calcium hypochlorite.
Chlorophyl	The green constituent of plants which is used to trap light and store it for processing by the plant.
Cloning	An American term used to describe propagation. It refers mainly to propagation using plant cuttings and rooting hormones.
Complete nutrient	The supply of all the essential mineral salts required by the plant

Topic	Description	Topic	Description
	for growth and in a form that the plant can assimilate. These include all the major elements as well as the minor (trace) elements.		material in which clay particles are fused together to give a porous structure.
Condensation	The droplets of water or moisture formed when very humid air is cooled.	Expanded earth	A diatomite material which has been heated to give a porous structure. It is inert and is very absorbent.
Conduction of heat	The transfer of heat or cold across a solid as a result of proximity. Energy passes from one body to another body in contact with it.	Filtration	The process by which solid particles are removed from the nutrient solution.
Conductivity	A measure of the amount of total dissolved salts in the nutrient solution. It does not identify the specific salts present in the nutrient solution. It measures the flow of ions between two electrodes.	Float valve	A cistern-type valve that regulates the flow of water or nutrient solution into a nutrient tank or bed. It is used to control the level of water or nutrient solution.
Convection of heat	The transfer of heat or cold as a result of movements within the gas or liquid as a result of changes in the density of gases or liquids. Hot air rises while cold air (which is more dense) falls.	Flood and drain systems	Hydroponic systems in which the roots of the plant are submerged in a nutrient solution and then the solution drained away from the roots on an intermittent cycle.
Cooling	Any technique by which the temperature around the plant or its parts is reduced.	Flushing	The process of adding water or diluted nutrient solution to remove the buildup of excess salts in a growing medium.
Dissolved solids	The quantity of nutrient salts that are available to the plant in soluble form.	Fogging	The technique by which a liquid is introduced into the air as very small particles or droplets which stay suspended in the air and settle very slowly.
Drip feed	The technique of feeding the plants by using emitters or drippers along a pipe or tube so that the nutrient solution is applied as drips.	Foliar feeding	The technique of feeding the plants through the leaves or stems by spraying the plant with a nutrient solution or with a solution containing trace elements in order to supplement the nutrients that the plant cannot obtain through the root system.
Environment	The conditions in which the plant exists and over which it has very little control.		
Environmental factors	The conditions in which the plant is subject to and includes light, temperature, air movement, humidity and gases.	Free draining	The term used to describe growing media which allow the free passage of water through them as opposed to medias with a high waterholding capacity.
Enzymes	Chemical compounds produced in the plant which act as triggers for many complicated processes within the plant. They are present in very minute amounts. They frequently work or are used in conjunction with some of the minor elements.	Genetics	The inbuilt determiners of plant characteristics, behaviour and responses to environmental factors, diseases, etc.
		Glasshouse	A building designed for growing plants and covered with glass panels.
Evaporative cooling	A technique for reducing the temperature by evaporating water such as passing air across a wet surface or by misting or fogging.	Go to waste systems	These are also called static systems or non recirculated systems in which only a small amount of nutrient goes to waste and most of the nutrient solution is taken up by the plant.
Expanded clay	A manmade lightweight pebble		

Topic	Description
Gravel	Naturally occurring rock which is mined, crushed, and washed. It may also be found as small pebbles in rivers.
Greenhouse	A building designed for growing plants which is covered with shade cloth.
Hanging bags	Bags or tubes filled with a growing medium which are hung or suspended from above and the plants or seedlings are inserted into the side of the bag.
Heat pumps	Systems utilising the expansion and contraction of a liquid to generate heat such as employed in reverse cycle air conditioning.
Heat sink	The storage of energy (usually heat) by a material which absorbs the heat and can release it slowly at a later stage.
Heating	Any technique by which the temperature around the plant or its parts is increased.
Hormones	Chemical compounds produced by the plant in very small quantities to activate specific growth functions such as flowering, root development, etc.
Humidity	The amount of moisture contained in the air. The humidity of the air increases as the temperature of the air is reduced such as at night time.
Hydroponics	The technique by which plants can be grown whereby the grower provides the plants with their basic needs such as root aeration, nutrients, water, support, etc.
Intermittent flow	The practice of cutting off the nutrient flow for short periods to allow the nutrient solution to drain away from the roots of the plant and to improve root aeration.
Ion exchange capacity	The ability of a material to absorb ions from a solution and replace them with other ions.
Ion exchange resins	The use of materials which preferentially absorb specific ions from a solution and replace them with other ions such as replacing sodium ions with potassium ions or ammonium ions.
Ions	The basic charged components into

Topic	Description
	which nutrient salts dissociate or separate in water.
Latent heat	The energy which is absorbed when liquids, gases, or solids change state or transfer to another form such as a gas into a liquid.
Light frequency	A particular band of colour received by the plant, such as red, blue, yellow, etc. Technically it is the wavelength of the light.
Light intensity	A measure of the amount of light which the plant receives at any time, particularly specific wavelengths which the plant needs.
Limiting factors	Factors which have an overriding effect on the plant's growth because they are not available to the plant in sufficient quantities. These may include warmth, moisture, a particular nutrient, oxygen and carbon dioxide.
Macro elements	These must be present as mineral salts and are required by the plant in reasonably large amounts. They include nitrates, ammonium ions, phosphates, and potassium ions. Sulphates, and magnesium, calcium, and ferric ions are often included.
Media	Material used in hydroponic systems which the roots use to support the plant. They may also have other beneficial characteristics such as waterholding capacity, assisting in root aeration, etc.
Micro elements	Must be present as mineral salts but are required in much smaller amounts. These include boron, manganese, copper, zinc, molybdenum, silica as ions.
Moisture holding capacity	Relates to the amount of moisture or water held by the growing media or by the roots.
Moisture meters	Instruments used to measure the moisture content of the growing media.
NFT	Stands for nutrient film technique in which an aerated nutrient solution flows as a thin film across the roots of the plants.
Non recirculating systems	Any hydroponic system in which the nutrient solution is used only once. Most of it is used by the plant and

Topic	Description	Topic	Description
	the remaining small percentage may go to waste.	Panda film	A plastic which is white on one side and black on the other side.
NPK	A simplified method of expressing the combination of salts in a nutrient in terms of nitrogen, phosphorous and potassium. It has very little meaning unless the other important nutrients are available in sufficient quantities.	Particle size	Relates to the average particle size of the growing media which has a mixture of individual particles.
Nursery systems	The technique used by some growers to take seedlings and transfer them into small channels in order to grow them on before transferring them into the main system; the purpose being to increase the turnaround in the main system.	Perlite	A volcanic rock which has been heated at a high temperature causing it to exfoliate (or go like popcorn). It is a lightweight media.
		pH	A measure of the acidity or alkalinity of the nutrient solution. A pH of 7 is neutral, pH below 7 is acidic, pH above 7 is alkaline. In hydroponics most plants grow best at a pH between pH 5.5 and pH 6.5.
Nutrient concentration	A measure of the total dissolved salts present in a nutrient solution expressed as parts per million or as a conductivity reading in terms of CF (conductivity factor), milli or micro seimens.	Phase change materials	Solids, liquids or gases which undergo a change of state from liquid to a gas, a solid to a liquid or vice versa.
Nutrient deficiency	Occurs when a particular mineral salt is not present in the nutrient solution, not available to the plant, or the plant lacks the ability to adsorb for any number of reasons.	Photosynthesis	The process which occurs only in plants by which water and carbon dioxide are combined to give the basic organic building blocks and storage of energy.
Nutrients	The basic chemical salts required by plants for their growth and include the ions such as nitrates, sulphates, phosphates, ammonium, potassium, calcium, magnesium, and the minor mineral elements as ions.	Pillow system	The use of a flat container in the shape of a pillow which is filled with growing media such as perlite, scoria, sawdust, etc for growing plants.
		Plant spacing	This relates to the distance between plants when planting out.
Organic	Any material which is based on carbon, and generally includes oxygen and hydrogen such as insecticides, fungicides, sugars, cellulose, petroleum, starches, fats, etc.	Plant stress	This occurs when the plant is undergoing trauma caused by any number of factors such as heat, shortage of water, disease, insect attack, insufficient light, low humidity, winds, etc.
ORP	Oxidation-reduction potential which is applied to nutrient solutions and is used to 'zap' or 'burn up' organic particles and bacteria, virus, and fungi in the nutrient solution.	Polyhouse	A building designed for growing plants and covered with a plastic material such as polythene.
ORP generator[*]	A device used for the generation of ORP. It may be placed in line or suspended in the nutrient tank. [*]A registered product of R&D AQUAPONICS.	Polystyrene foam	A growing media consisting of crushed or broken polystyrene which is usually mixed with other growing media to reduce the weight or improve drainage.
		Preferential nutrient uptake	The selective uptake of specific nutrient ions by the plant.
Osmotic pressure	The pressure required to move water and mineral salts across the root membrane.	Propagation	The technique for producing plantlets. This may involve germination of seeds, producing plants from cuttings or buds, tissue culturing or cloning.

Topic	Description	Topic	Description
Protected environment	The implementation of techniques that will improve the growing conditions for the plants such as air movement, temperature, humidity, covering, etc.		other materials resembling soil without the addition of nutrients.
Pumice	A naturally occurring porous volcanic rock which is lightweight.	Solubility	The amount of mineral salt that can be dissolved in a given amount of water. Some salts are very soluble and others dissolve with difficulty.
PVC	A plastic made from poly vinyl chloride in the form of channels, sheeting, etc.	Sprayers	The use of emitters which force the nutrient out of a pipe as discrete particles thereby covering a given area.
Radiation of heat	The transfer of heat across a gap such as occurs with infra red heaters.	Static systems	Hydroponic systems where the nutrients are not recirculated and a medium is used by the roots to support the plant and there is a reservoir of nutrient solution which the plants can draw upon.
Recirculated system	A hydroponic system in which the nutrient solution is continuously reused and usually adjusted for dissolved solids concentration and pH.	T tape drippers	A manufactured tape or pipe with drip holes set at intervals to distribute nutrient solution along its length.
Respiration	The process within a plant whereby the cells of the plant uses simple sugars as an energy source to carry on growth, nutrient uptake, and its functions. This process requires oxygen.	Thermal insulation	The ability of a material (or growing medium) to conduct heat. Steel is a good conductor while perlite is a poor conductor.
Reverse osmosis	A technique used to remove salt contaminations from the water supply by equipment for desalination.	Thermal screens	These are screens, usually made of fabric, designed to retain heat energy within an area such as a polyhouse. Some reflect the radiant heat back into the closed area and reduce heat losses.
Rockwool	A manmade wool created from molten rocks at very high temperatures.	Tissue culture	A technique used for propagation whereby plant tissue is provided with moisture, nutrients, and hormone in a gel suspension under aseptic conditions to promote individual cell division and tissue growth.
Root aeration	The process of supplying and replacing dissolved oxygen to the roots of the plant. This may take the form of air dissolved in water or as air pockets between the particles of the growing media.	Transpiration	The process whereby plant breathe by losing water through their leaves and stems. It also assists in the removal of waste products of respiration and is part of the method for translocation or water movement within the plant.
Salt buildup	This occurs when the level of salts in the growing media increases. It can be caused by surface evaporation, the formation of insoluble salts, or absorption by the media.	Troughs	Beds formed to contain media or nutrients for growing plants.
Sand	Silicaceous rocks with small particle size between 0.5 and 3 mm diameter.	UV steriliser	The application of ultraviolet light for sterilising nutrient solutions.
Scoria	A volcanic rock which is mined and crushed. It has a porous honeycombed structure. It is widely used in hydroponic systems as a growing medium.	Venturi	A device in which a liquid goes from a high pressure to a reduced pressure causing an increase in volume and thereby drawing air into the liquid,
Silicaceous	A rock or gravel composed predominately of silica.		
Soilless mixtures	Growing media composed of sand, composted bark, peat moss and		

Topic	Description	Topic	Description
	or it may be used to suck concentrated nutrient into a water supply.		holding capacity.
		Weedmat	A close weave fabric which restricts weed growth but allows the movement of moisture through it.
Vermiculite	A mica which has been heated to a high temperature causing it to exfoliate (or go like popcorn). It is lightweight and has very high water-	Windbreaks	Natural or artificial restrictions on the movement of air, particularly at high velocity, across the plants.

Index